The Road to Sustained Growth in Jamaica

THE WORLD BANK
Washington, D.C.

 printed on recycled paper

1 2 3 4 06 05 04

ISBN: 0-8213-5826-X
eISBN: 0-8213-5827-8
ISSN: 0253-2123

Cover Art by Jamaican painter Milton Messam, 2003.

Library of Congress Cataloging-in-Publication Data

The road to sustained growth in Jamaica.
     p. cm. — (A World Bank country study)
   Includes bibliographical references.
   ISBN 0-8213-5826-X
    1. Jamaica—Economic conditions. 2. Jamaica—Economic policy. I. World Bank. II. Series.

HC 154.R62 2004
330.97292—dc22

2004045519

TABLE OF CONTENTS

TABLES

ANNEX TABLES

BOXES

FIGURES

ACKNOWLEDGMENTS

This Country Economic Memorandum (CEM) was prepared by a core team consisting of Sanjay Kathuria (Task Leader), Errol Graham, James Hanson and Rina H. Oberai. From the core team, the principal responsibilities for different parts of the report were: Chapters 1, 3 (Errol Graham); Chapters 2, 4 (James Hanson); Chapter 6 (Rina H. Oberai); Chapters 5, 7 and Part I (Sanjay Kathuria). In addition, Rina H. Oberai provided analytical support for the full report.

Kin Bing Wu prepared the first draft of Chapter 5. Michael Corlett, Kevin Tomlinson, and Phaedra Chrousos provided research support. Ayesha Aparakka-Hemantha did the desktop publishing, helped by Margarita Chavez-De Silva and Fernanda Brito. Homa-Zahra Fotouhi helped to secure Dutch trust funds. The Country Director is Caroline Anstey, the Lead Economist and Sector Leader is Antonella Bassani, the Sector Manager is Mauricio Carrizosa, and the Sector Director is Ernesto May.

The report draws on the work of an interdisciplinary team from within and outside the World Bank. Several background papers were prepared for the report. From the University of the West Indies in Kingston, a team consisting of Alfred Francis, Anthony Harriott, Claremont Kirton, and Godfrey Gibbison prepared a paper on crime and violence, and also conducted a business victimization survey of 400 firms across the island. Warren Benfield prepared a paper on poverty. From outside Jamaica, a team from the Netherlands Economic Institute prepared papers on trade and competitiveness (Huib Poot), productivity (Eric Bartelsman), and National accounts (Ivo Havinga). Other papers prepared were on infrastructure (David Erhardt, Basil Sutherland and Winston Hay, Castalia Advisory Group), and poverty (Carolina Sanchez-Paramo and Diana Steele, World Bank). The report also drew on the World Bank's cross-country growth analysis done by Norman Loayza, Pablo Fajnzylber and Cesar Calderon.

The team benefited from interaction with Pablo Fajnzylber, Indermit Gill, Orsalia Kalantzopoulos, Ali Khadr, Daniel Lederman, Norman Loayza, Humberto Lopez, and Arvind Subramanian. Comments were received from Caroline Anstey, Antonella Bassani, Mauricio Carrizosa, Wendy Cunningham, Toby Linden, Yira Mascaro, Ernesto May, Guillermo Perry, Claudia Sepulveda, Roberto Zagha, and country counterparts from the IMF and IDB. The peer reviewers were Nancy Birdsall, Shahrokh Fardoust, and Damien King.

The World Bank is very grateful for the support of the authorities in the preparation of this report. The team has benefited from interaction with the Finance Minister (including in defining the scope of the work), Bank of Jamaica, the Ministry of Finance, the Planning Institute of Jamaica, the Statistical Institute of Jamaica, the Ministry of Education, Youth and Culture, the Department of Economics at the University of the West Indies, the Private Sector Organization of Jamaica, and development partners. The report was discussed with the authorities at a workshop on October 30, 2003, and written comments were provided subsequently.

The World Bank is grateful for the support provided by Dutch trust funds that enabled key background papers to be prepared by the Netherlands Economic Institute.

ABBREVIATIONS

ACP	African, Caribbean, and Pacific
AG	Auditor-General
ASD	Additional Stamp Duties
CAD	Current Account Deficit
CARIBCAN	Caribbean Canada Trade Agreement
CARICOM	Caribbean Community
CBI	Caribbean Basin Initiative
CBTPA	Caribbean Basin Trade Partnership Act
CCI	Current Competitiveness Index
CET	Common External Tariff
CFAA	Country Financial Accountability Assessment
CGCED	Caribbean Group for Cooperation in Economic Development
CMT	Cut make and trim
CPI	Consumer Price Index
CRI	Crime Rate Index
CXC	Caribbean Examination Council
DBJ	Development Bank of Jamaica
ECE	Early Childhood Education
ER	Exchange Rate
ESSJ	Economic and Social Survey of Jamaica
EU	European Union
FAA	Financial Administration and Audit Act
FDI	Foreign Direct Investment
FINSAC	Financial Sector Adjustment Company
FTAA	Free Trade Area of the Americas
GCI	Growth Competitiveness Index
GCT	General Consumption Tax
GNFS	Goods and Non-factor Services
IDB	Inter-American Development Bank
IFS	International Financial Statistics
IMF	International Monetary Fund
JDIC	Jamaica Deposit Insurance Corporation
JHSCE	Junior High School Certificate Examination
JLP	Jamaica Labor Party
JPSCo	Jamaica Public Service Company
JSLC	Jamaica Survey of Living Conditions
KMA	Kingston Metropolitan Area
LAC	Latin America and the Caribbean
LRS	Local registered stock
MFA	Multifibre Agreement
MOEYC	Ministry of Education, Youth and Culture
MOFP	Ministry of Finance and Planning
MOU	Memorandum of Understanding
NAFTA	North American Free Trade Area
NHT	National Housing Trust
NPL	Non-performing loan
NWC	National Water Commission
P&JH	Primary and Junior High Schools

PAC	Public Accountants Committee
PAYE	Pay-as-you-earn
PIOJ	Planning Institute of Jamaica
PNP	People's National Party
PSIP	Public Sector Investment Program
QRs	Quantitive Restrictions
REER	Real Effective Exchange Rate
SCJ	Sugar Company of Jamaica
SCT	Special Consumption Tax
SESP	Social, and Economic Support Program
SLC	Survey of Living Conditions
SME	Small and Medium Size Enterprises
SP&CMP	Strategic Planning & Community Mobilization Project
STATIN	Statistical Institute of Jamaica
TFP	Total Factor Productivity
TRN	Taxpayer Registration Number
UN	United Nations
UNDP	United Nations Development Program
UNICEF	United Nations Children's Fund
UNODC	United Nations Office on Drugs and Crime
UWI	University of West Indies
VAT	Value Added Tax
WDI	World Development Indicators
WTO	World Trade Organization

CURRENCY EQUIVALENTS
Currency Unit: Jamaican Dollar (J$)
US$1.0 = J$ 60.50 (as of December 1, 2003)

FISCAL YEAR
April 1 to March 31

EXECUTIVE SUMMARY

Jamaica's economic history is a story of paradoxes and potential. It has an English-speaking and a reasonably well-educated labor force, is close to the world's largest market, the USA, and has an abundance of natural beauty, which has spurred tourism. Many of its social and governance indicators are strong. School enrollment for 6- to 14-year-olds is near universal. Poverty declined significantly in the 1990s, and is below the average of comparable countries.

Nonetheless, measured GDP growth has been disappointing since 1972, and was negligible over the 1990s (although growth in the 1990s may be underestimated) despite high measured rates of investment. Agricultural and manufacturing output fell. Employment has declined since the mid-1990s owing to the large fall in formal private sector employment, and the equivalent of 80 percent of the tertiary graduates during the 1990s are estimated to have emigrated. Crime rates are very high. Government debt reached 150 percent of GDP in 2002/03, one of the highest ratios in the world. The particular confluence of changes that helped reduce poverty in the 1990s is unlikely to continue in the current decade, and may even reverse.

Sustained growth will be fundamental to further declines in poverty and Jamaica's realizing its potential. This paper offers policy options for increasing growth in a sustainable way. In doing this, it attempts to explain the paradoxes of low growth in GDP and employment despite high investment and strong poverty reduction. Achieving sustained growth will involve dealing with the growing debt burden on a very urgent basis, ensuring a sustainable fiscal situation, and improving international competitiveness. Competitiveness is beginning to improve with the recent depreciation of the exchange rate but will also depend on limiting increases in public and private sector real wages, and on improvements in infrastructure. Efforts will also be needed to reduce crime, which is a major cost to business and a major deterrent to the quality of life in Jamaica. Education quality needs to be improved and the subsidy to tertiary education reduced in order to stem its drain on the treasury and improve equality.

Jamaica's poor growth performance has a number of well-known explanations, but they need to be supplemented for the latter half of the 1990s by the loss of competitiveness. The negligible (measured) GDP growth in the 1990s is usually attributed to two factors: an adverse external climate and the financial crisis that arose from bank privatization to poorly capitalized investors, and financial liberalization unaccompanied by appropriate regulatory strengthening. These two factors offset the liberalization in the real economy at the beginning of the decade. In addition, the second part of the decade was characterized by an appreciating real exchange rate induced by the approach to monetary policy, rising real wages, rising costs associated with rising crime, and an increasing burden of government consumption, all of which reduced international competitiveness to the point where the output of agriculture and manufacturing declined, and tourism lost some of its share of the Caribbean market.

The poverty headcount was halved between 1992 and 1998 despite negligible measured GDP growth, which can be largely explained by a conjunction of several factors particular to the period. First, GDP growth could be underestimated by 1–2 percentage points per annum in the second half of the 1990s, judging from the growth in consumption of power and meat and fish, as well as the rapid growth of currency usage. The underestimate may reflect the difficulty of estimating GDP in an increasingly service-dominated economy, particularly one that is highly open, and where the informal sector is large. Second, inflation, which hurts the poor disproportionately, fell sharply. Third, the relative price of food declined, owing largely to trade liberalization and the appreciation in the real exchange rate, which reduced a major element of cost in the budget of the poor. Other factors in the decline in poverty may have been the rise in real wages and remittances, though their role is less clear. However, inflation is already low and the real exchange rate has begun to depreciate, not appreciate as in the past. Hence two important poverty-reducing factors are unlikely to continue to operate in the future, which means that further reduction of poverty is likely to depend on achievement of sustained growth.

The apparent paradox of low measured growth and high measured investment rates can be explained by the underutilization of much of the capital created in the early 1990s, the investment to protect against crime, and the concentration of investment in a few, rapidly growing sectors that may have some tax distortions and whose contribution to GDP is hard to measure. Of course, correcting for possible underestimation of the level and growth of GDP would reduce this apparent paradox.

Whatever growth has occurred has not created much employment, largely because of the loss of competitiveness in the 1990s that hurt tradable goods production and thereby formal private sector employment. Employment rose less than 0.3 percent per year from 1991–2001. Between 1996–2001, only public sector employment rose, while informal sector employment was stable; both rose as a share of total employment. Despite weak employment and productivity growth, real wages rose, suggesting an imperfectly functioning labor market. Poor employment prospects, along with high crime, have encouraged high rates of migration, and the equivalent of 80 percent of tertiary graduates in the 1990s are estimated to have migrated.

Moreover, fiscal and debt dynamics have worsened significantly owing to the resolution of the financial crisis and a rising Government wage bill. Debt is now about 150 percent of GDP and the Government interest bill is about 16 percent of GDP. Simply stabilizing the debt at current ratios will require extremely high primary surpluses, exceeding 10 percent of GDP. This has inevitably led to investor concerns, indicated by increased spreads on Jamaica's international bonds over the last year, sharply increased domestic interest rates and pressure on the exchange rate. Increasing confidence will require not just a stable but a declining debt to GDP ratio, which means that tackling the debt burden will need to be the top current priority of the Government. If the primary surplus were to fall to, say, 6–7 percent of GDP, the ratio of debt to GDP would rise, since a 6–7 percent primary surplus would stabilize the debt to GDP ratio only if debt were lower by some 50 percentage points of GDP.

The question, then, is how can Jamaica restore self-sustaining and job-creating growth? The report argues that this requires improving international competitiveness and productivity, while also tackling short-term exigencies. The policy options are grouped into three categories—those necessary to limit the risk of a crisis and its effect, with a likely immediate impact; those likely to have an impact in the short-term; and those likely to have an impact in the medium- and long-term, but on which action is nonetheless needed now. This categorization is based on the time period of likely impact. The report suggests that a "bandwagon" approach to reforms may be needed, with policy actions needed on several important fronts in order to improve prospects for sustained growth, including measures that help avoid crises, since crises hurt the poor and damage growth prospects. Such an approach could involve the following actions:

Crisis-proofing actions: Given the current macroeconomic situation, crisis-avoidance measures are necessary. Being vulnerable to a crisis also affects confidence and hence growth, as has occurred in Jamaica. Crisis-proofing would also mean being ready to offer relief to the poor in case a crisis does take place, because it is the poor who will suffer most if a crisis should occur. Actions along these lines could include: generating large primary surpluses by implementing revenue generation measures and expenditure reduction measures quickly; continuing to strengthen social safety nets; and maintaining and improving transparency and speed of communication of economic news to the public.

Actions with short-term impact: These could include:

- ensuring that the recent gains (since 2002) achieved via real exchange rate depreciation are preserved;
- reducing significantly the growth of the public sector wage bill and avoiding policies that will push up the wage rate in US dollars;
- continuing to search for cost-cutting measures in the public sector, for example by expediting the preparation and implementation of the report of the Task Force on expenditure management;
- privatizing the remaining public entities and selling Government shares in private entities expeditiously;
- accounting for and reducing substantially the contingent liabilities taken on by Government, which have often resulted in an increase in national debt;
- equalizing the effective tax rates across different sectors and extending the tax base through presumptive taxation;
- eliminating the stamp duties that are levied on selected imports, which will limit the price increases (especially of food) that accompany depreciation; and increasing cost sharing in tertiary education.

Actions with medium/long-term impact: Such actions would be critical for improving sustainable growth prospects over time, and could include:

- tackling crime with all-out and systematic efforts (through improving information on crime and its incidence, improving clear-up rates for violent crimes, and applying targeted interventions);
- putting more effort and resources in schools where low income students study, gradually reducing wage compression in teacher salaries, and increasing reliance on private schools that strive for quality improvement;
- reducing the cost and providing better coverage of water and sewerage services, improving roads, especially rural roads, and improving the reliability of power supply, and ensuring that all these are fully financed by user charges, i.e., by levying and increasing tolls and user fees on existing and upcoming infrastructure facilities;
- increasing transparency in accounting for contingent liabilities and thereby limiting their growth;
- and improving lending to the private sector, especially small borrowers, by accelerating the starting up of credit registries.

Finally, given that policy choices are likely to be difficult, an approach based on social dialogue and consensus-building is essential to creating ownership for future reforms by all stakeholders, and for maintaining and improving social peace.

POLICY MATRIX

*** Policies necessary for crisis-proofing (reducing vulnerability), immediate impact
** Policies with short-term impact
* Policies with medium and long-term impact
(Note: the above categorization indicates the time period of likely impact. Policy action is needed on all fronts in order to improve sustained growth prospects.)

Key Constraints	Policy Options
1. The debt crisis and fiscal deterioration Debt/GDP has risen from 79 percent in 1996/97 to about 150 percent in 2002/03, and domestic debt from 35 percent to 90 percent. The rise reflects the large costs of the financial crisis but also deterioration in other parts of the fiscal accounts. High debt constrains growth by crowding out private investment as well as productive expenditure in the government budget, and also raises concerns about macroeconomic stability. **Fiscal deterioration:** The central Government primary surplus of 10.5 percent of GDP in 1995/96 has fallen to 7.7 percent in 2002/03, while the fiscal balance deteriorated from a surplus of 1.8 percent of GDP to a deficit of 8 percent. Interest costs have risen from 8.7 percent to 15.7 percent of GDP; the wage bill has increased from 7.7 percent to 13 percent of GDP; other non-interest, non-capital expenditure from 4.7 percent to 6.9 percent of GDP. Capital expenditures have fallen from 5.4 percent to 2 percent and businessmen complain about infrastructure bottlenecks. Explicit and implicit contingent liabilities are growing, created by government on its own behalf or on behalf of other public sector entities or even entities that have been privatized.	**Increase primary surplus, control wage bill and contingent liabilities, and increase government investment** *** Increase the primary surplus, the key policy instrument. Primary surpluses of over 10 percent of GDP are needed just to maintain the current, high debt to GDP ratio of about 150 percent. ** Limit growth of wage bill, reduce government employment and non-interest, non-capital expenditure including contingent liabilities (see below). ** Privatize remaining public entities and sell Government shares in private companies. * Increase expenditure on infrastructure to "crowd-in" overall private investment; finance it with user charges. ** Account for and reduce contingent liabilities taken on by Government. * Limit growth of contingent liabilities by increasing transparency—classify full range of direct and contingent liabilities, as well as the associated risk, including contingent liabilities from riots, natural disasters and from public sector and "quasi-public sector" entities. ** Expedite preparation and implementation of report of Task Force on expenditure management.
Revenues are already high, at 29.6 percent of GDP in 2002/03 (tax revenues 26.4 percent of GDP). Tax revenues will need to increase further in order to make the fiscal and debt situation more sustainable. This could be achieved if the informal sector could be better taxed and tax rates across sectors rationalized.	**Extend tax base, rationalize taxes and reduce tertiary education subsidy** ** Reduce the disparity in tax rates across sectors. ** Extend the tax base to include more of the informal sector by a system of presumptive taxes based on consumption indicators. * Levy and increase tolls on upcoming and existing infrastructure facilities. ** Reduce subsidy on tertiary education (see 3.) * Build social consensus and buy-in for difficult, but necessary, economic policy choices.
2. Pervasive and high crime and violence Jamaica has very high rates of violent crime, including the third highest homicide rate in the world. Crime imposes major costs on society and business, which limit growth (see below). The empirical foundation for action on crime is weak.	**Identify and measure crime better** * Strengthen official data collection on crime, and conduct frequent victimization surveys. These would be an input for policy-making, improving policing methods, public debate and better accountability.

Crime costs society at least 4 percent of GDP explicitly, including lost production, health expenses, and public and private spending. In addition, exporting firms' security costs can be as high as 5 percent of sales, small firms' losses due to extortion, fraud, robbery and arson can be 9 percent of revenue, with an average of 3–6 percent for firms in manufacturing and distribution.

Crime reduces the efficiency of capital use by limiting multi-shift operations, and of schooling because of closures. It results in major implicit social costs.

The costs of crime limit growth. Some 10–20 percent of firms in the business survey suggested that they may close down in the next three years because of crime.

Improve enforcement, increase social capital, and target high crime areas
* Upgrade investigative capacity of police to improve clear-up rates for violent crime, which would deter such crime.

* Form effective partnerships between police, business and local communities, by setting common goals and sharing information.

* Build social capital such as greater trust and lower tolerance to crime and violence, especially through interventions in the home, school and the workplace.

* Target high crime urban areas, especially the Kingston Metropolitan Area, to reduce the impact of crime on the business community.

Young males are the most likely victims as well as perpetrators of violent crime. Amongst those arrested for major crimes, 53 percent, predominantly male, were from the 16–25 age group. About 32 percent of the 15–16 year olds in the poorest quintile were not enrolled in school in 2001, and even if enrolled, some do not have a positive school experience. This breeds frustration and unemployment, leads to a cycle of anti-social behavior, and reduces the contribution of a potentially productive segment.

Enhance quality of school experience
* Improve the overall quality of the school experience, especially for poor students (see below).

* Enhance school programs to include teaching of social and conflict resolution skills to students (see below).

---

3. Poor education outcomes
Education expanded remarkably, real Government expenditure doubled in the last ten years. By 1989, enrollment was universal for 6–14 year olds. But expansion came at the cost of quality. About 30–40 percent of grade 6 leavers are functionally illiterate. Only 30 percent pass the Caribbean CXC mathematics examination in grade 11. Jamaican-educated workers receive amongst the lowest returns in the US labor market. Poor education outcomes limit general productivity gains and growth—measured TFP growth in Jamaica has been negative in the 1990s.

Increase focus on early learning
* Increase focus on early learning—through teacher training, setting service standards, providing educational material and toys—to improve overall education outcomes, making later education less costly and more effective.

* Raise functional literacy target to 100 percent in grade 6 instead of the current goal of 80 percent, because functionally illiterate are likely to become part of the youth at risk—see below.

The quality of schools is very uneven—Traditional High School students score much higher than Comprehensive and Primary and Junior High students in grade 9 examinations, have better facilities and teachers, and much higher participation and scores in the CXC examinations than former Comprehensive schools.

Improve incentives and facilities for below-average schools, and make school results public
* Allocate funds to schools based on enrollments, not teacher positions approved, thus allowing more flexibility in the use of funding.

* Give special grants to schools with large needs, for example, those with a large proportion of students reading below grade.

* Provide free foundation books to students in All-Age and Primary & Junior High Schools.

* Create incentives for more qualified and educated teachers to teach in schools other than the Traditional High Schools.

* Gradually reduce wage compression in teacher salaries.

* Make school results public so that parents and community can monitor progress.

Poor students get tracked into lower quality schools, have higher absenteeism, face a more difficult home environment, see lower enrollment after age 14 (owing to lack of seats in schools) and higher dropouts, and end up far less educated. All this creates a vicious cycle of youth at risk, especially males, and unemployment and poverty. Tackling these problems would involve a coordinated approach that would address issues of school quality of below-average schools (see above), increase school space after grade 9, and pay special attention to those falling behind and reading below grade level.	**Utilize private schools more intensively and increase parental involvement** * Buy places in private schools that target and achieve quality improvement, rather than construct new schools, to address problem of insufficient school space after grade 9. * Pay private schools to provide compensatory, results-based education to repeaters. * Increase parental involvement through publicity campaigns to inform parents about their role in child learning, such as discouraging absenteeism, providing money for book rental, and creating a more conducive home environment.
4. Inadequate credit access for private sector Jamaica quickly resolved its massive financial crisis, and strengthened financial regulation and supervision but at great cost. Jamaican Government debt is now about 45 percent of bank deposits, about twice the share of private credit. With high and relatively risk-free returns on government debt, banks have become more reluctant to lend to private firms, especially small firms and start-ups, which constrains a potentially vibrant source of GDP and export growth. In fact, with the current returns on government debt, even some current and potential entrepreneurs may become *rentiers*.	**Start credit registries and improve collateral procedures** ** Reduce the demand for resources by government, which means increasing the primary surplus—see above. This will increase availability of credit for the private sector, gradually reduce interest rates, and also improve the incentives for entrepreneurial rather than *rentier* behavior. * Accelerate the startup of credit registries to improve lending quality and quantity. Registries allow financial intermediaries to lend to borrowers more likely to repay and give borrowers an incentive to repay to maintain a good credit record. Credit registries can increase access by including small borrowers and records of loan repayments as well as defaults. * Improve collateral procedures, perhaps by creating debt tribunals separate from the court system, as other countries have done. Lenders and businessmen have complained about the courts' handling of commercial cases.
5. Appreciation of the exchange rate and other factors reducing competitiveness in the 1990s Jamaica's competitiveness has declined significantly in the 1990s, reflected in declining shares of exports in world trade and in Jamaica's GDP and stagnation in export earnings. This adverse performance is closely linked with the appreciation of the CPI-based REER over 1992–98, and an even greater appreciation in the wage-based REER. Besides creating incentives for production of more non-tradables, the appreciated exchange rate also reduces growth, because it is the export and import-competing sectors which usually see the most rapid productivity increases.	**Maintain credible macro policies and continue to encourage exchange rate flexibility** *** Maintain credible macro policies. Because the exchange rate depends so much on market sentiment, credible macro policies, especially reducing the debt overhang and maintaining a high primary surplus will be crucial to prevent an excessive correction in the exchange rate, which could spark high inflation and increase poverty incidence. ** Ensure that policies do not offset the gains in competitiveness achieved via real exchange rate depreciation since 2002, which would also require that public and private sector wages do not increase in US dollar terms.
Survey results show that exports have been hurt by high wage increases in the 1990s, exchange rate appreciation, high and rising crime, difficulties in accessing inputs, and high cost of utilities, adding up to an increasingly high-cost economy. The most successful exports are based on exploitation of natural resources, especially tourism and bauxite, but even tourism has been hurt by the above constraints, and	**Improve enabling environment for exports** * Encourage employers and trade unions to conclude productivity-based wage agreements to prevent future erosion in competitiveness. * Improve quality of infrastructure and extend coverage, especially for water and roads, by levying and increasing tolls and user fees.

the once successful apparel sector is in the doldrums. High wage costs are especially constraining. Besides the direct effect of high wages on private sector costs, the high share of wage costs in the government budget leads to higher deficits and more crowding out of private borrowing and of productive government expenditure (see above). Also, the imposition of additional stamp duties has generated upward pressure on prices for the average Jamaican consumer.

* Improve access to imported inputs by making customs procedures more efficient.
** Eliminate the stamp duties that are levied on selected imports, especially food, which will reduce the price increases that accompany depreciation, and so reduce the potential impact of food price increases on the poor.

PART I

OVERVIEW AND POLICY OPTIONS

This review of Jamaica's poverty and economy by the World Bank comes after a long hiatus. It follows up on the commitment made in the Country Assistance Strategy of November 2000, and is a major milestone in the World Bank's deeper engagement with Jamaica. It is complemented by a Bank study on 'Youth Development in the Caribbean,' first presented at the CGCED meeting in June 2002. It will be followed up by a Public Expenditure Review. Also, Jamaica is a key component of an ongoing report on tertiary education in the Caribbean, as well as of a proposed analysis of the likely impact on Caribbean countries of trade negotiations in the context of the Doha development agenda, the FTAA and the Cotonou agreement with the EU.

In the 1990s, poverty in Jamaica was reduced despite negligible growth in measured Gross Domestic Product (GDP) and a major financial crisis, owing to a conjunction of several factors. However, these factors are unlikely to continue to operate (see section III) and, moreover, there is the additional drag on poverty reduction imposed by the current fiscal crisis. Future sustained reduction in poverty is therefore likely to depend on sustained growth in the Jamaican economy as well as the implementation of policies to ensure that the poor are empowered to take advantages of the opportunities that arise from increased growth.

Accordingly, the report focuses on reducing impediments to sustained growth, paying particular attention to policies that will continue to reduce poverty. It is divided as follows: an Executive Summary and Policy Matrix; Part I, which provides a fuller Overview and Policy Options; and Part II, which comprises the Main Report and provides the analytical backing and details behind the conclusions and policy options.

Part I of the report is organized as follows. The first section highlights the most important policy issues that bear consideration. The second section discusses some of the major successes in the 1990s, as well as the areas where Jamaica fell behind. The third section analyzes the reasons for the trends in poverty, and points to the need for growth in order to reduce poverty in the future. The fourth section provides a discussion of growth and productivity, and shows that growth is probably underestimated, but is nevertheless very low. The fifth section analyzes the grave fiscal challenge that

9

confronts Jamaica, including issues of debt sustainability, crowding out and the decline in public investment. The sixth section discusses the financial sector crisis and its costs, while pointing to the improvement in governance of the financial sector and the functioning of the financial institutions. The seventh section explores the education sector, trends in enrollment and outcomes, and the reasons for less than satisfactory outcomes. The eighth section, on crime and its impact on business, starts by providing a comparative picture on Jamaica's governance indicators, analyzes trends in crime and estimates the economic costs of crime, and discusses firms' coping strategies on the basis of a business victimization survey. The ninth section discusses trends in competitiveness including the exchange rate and the export environment for firms, and provides case studies of tourism and apparels. Each of the sections also provides policy options.

Part II of the report, which provides the analytical backbone for this study, follows an organization similar to Part I, and consists of seven chapters.

A Configuration of "Bandwagon" Reforms Could Make a Difference

What can be done? This report concludes that there is no magic wand to kick-start sustained growth in Jamaica. Raising growth in a sustainable way is likely to be a slow process. This owes to the twin tyrannies of the very large debt overhang and the high level of violent crime, both of which are amongst the highest in the world. These are key underlying reasons for Jamaica being a high cost economy, and for its lack of competitiveness and growth, and have encouraged the departure of human capital (whose development is heavily subsidized by Government) from Jamaica.

With concerted action on several fronts—a "bandwagon" approach—it is possible to make a difference. Simultaneous, coherent and mutually reinforcing action on several fronts can serve not only to increase growth that is self-sustaining and job-creating, but also to improve perceptions, so vital to both domestic and foreign investment. This requires improving international competitiveness and productivity, but of course short-term exigencies need to be tackled. Some of the most important ingredients in a 'bandwagon' approach to reform are outlined below.

Crisis-proofing actions. Given the current macroeconomic situation, crisis-proofing (borrowing from Williamson 2003), which will help reduce the risk of a crisis, is a top priority, especially since it is the poor who will suffer most during a crisis. Moreover, being vulnerable to a crisis also affects confidence and hence growth, as has occurred in Jamaica. Also, in case a crisis does occur, its impact on the poor could be mitigated by pre-crisis strengthening of safety net schemes, which would enable the Government to offer quick and well-targeted relief to the poor. Such policies could include:

- Generating large primary surpluses by implementing revenue generation measures quickly and cutting expenditures where possible.
- Continuing to strengthen social safety nets, an area where Jamaica has been devoting much attention.
- Maintaining and improving transparency and speed of communication of economic news to the public.

Actions with short-term impact. These could include:

- Ensuring that policies do not offset the recent gains in competitiveness achieved via real exchange rate depreciation since 2002.
- Reducing the growth of wage costs in the public sector by reducing public employment and limiting wage growth, and avoiding policies that increase wages in US dollars.
- Continuing to search for cost-cutting measures in the public sector, for example by expediting the preparation and implementation of the report of the Task Force on expenditure management.
- Privatizing the remaining public entities and selling Government shares in private entities expeditiously.

- Accounting for and reducing substantially the contingent liabilities taken on by Government, which have often resulted in an increase in national debt.
- Equalizing the effective tax rates across different sectors and extending the tax base through presumptive taxation.
- Eliminating the stamp duties that are levied on selected imports, which will limit the price increases (especially of food) that accompany depreciation.
- Increasing cost sharing in tertiary education, and moving the student loan scheme in tertiary education away from reliance on public resources to the private sector.

Actions with medium/long-term impact. These actions are necessary since they would be critical for enhancing sustainable growth prospects over time, and could include:

- Tackling crime with all-out and systematic efforts, including better information on crime and its incidence, improving clear-up rates for violent crimes, and applying targeted interventions.
- Putting more effort and resources in schools where low income students study, gradually reducing wage compression in teacher salaries, and increasing reliance on private schools, in order to improve the quality and skills of the labor force.
- Reducing the cost and providing better coverage of water and sewerage services, improving roads, especially rural roads, and improving the reliability of power supply, and ensuring that all these are fully financed by user charges, that is, by levying and increasing tolls and user fees on existing and upcoming infrastructure facilities.
- Increasing transparency in accounting for contingent liabilities and thereby limiting their growth.
- Improving lending to the private sector, especially small borrowers, by accelerating the start-up of credit registries and improving collateral procedures.

The difficult policy measures highlighted above require social consensus. An approach based on social dialogue and consensus-building is essential to creating ownership for future reforms by all stakeholders, and for maintaining and improving social peace. Countries such as Ireland formulated a tripartite social pact in 1987 between unions, employers and government (later widened to include voluntary and community organizations, representatives of the unemployed and women's groups) to help evolve a national consensus to support large macroeconomic adjustments, including the fiscal crisis of the 1980s (McCarthy 2001). In Mauritius, an economy similar to Jamaica in many respects such as size, and dependence on tourism and sugar, social and political consensus was achieved despite inequality and diversity in ethnic composition, and helped in the evolution of strong domestic institutions that played a key role in Mauritius' strong economic performance over the last three decades (Subramanian and Roy 2002).

The Big Picture—Past and Present

Jamaica has not lived up to its early promise. Jamaica has many advantages—proximity to the world's largest market, an English-speaking work force, fairly good initial endowments, and widespread education. Spurred by the development of bauxite mining and tourism, it enjoyed rapid GDP growth of 6.3 percent annually between 1952–72. However, the period since then has been quite difficult—per capita income has been stagnant for the last three decades, and major macroeconomic problems have periodically occurred, including high inflation, large debt accumulation, and, most recently in 1995, a financial crisis. Many of these problems arose from various combinations of economic nationalism, two oil price shocks, declining export prices, and political unrest. To address many of these problems, Jamaica implemented a series of broad-based reforms, especially since the late 1980s.

Jamaica achieved some major successes in the 1990s, particularly in reducing poverty and inflation (Tables 1 and 2), and cleaning up quickly, albeit expensively, the huge financial crisis. In spite of low measured growth, poverty incidence was halved between 1992–2001. Inflation has

TABLE 1: JAMAICA—SELECTED ECONOMIC AND SOCIAL INDICATORS, 1980–2002

	1980	1990	1995	1996	1997	1998	1999	2000	2001	2002	Avg. 1995–2002
Poverty and Social											
Population (million)	2.13	2.41	2.49	2.52	2.54	2.56	2.56	2.63	2.60	2.63	2.6
Labor Force (thousand)	699 (1981)	1059	1150	1143	1134	1129	1119	1105	1105	1125	1126.1
Poverty (headcount index)	—	28.4	27.5	26.1	19.9	15.9	16.9	18.7	16.8	—	20.3
Life Expectancy (years)	70.7	73.2	74.4	—	74.8	—	—	75.3	75.5	75.7	75.1
Infant Mortality (pier 1,000 live births)	—	27.0	—	—	—	—	—	—	24.5	—	—
Gross School Enrollment (% of school-age population)											
Primary	103.1	101.3	101.5	99.6	—	95.3	98.7	99.6	—	—	98.9
Secondary	66.7	65.3	65.7	66.1	—	84.2	83.6	83.3	—	—	76.6
Unemployment (% of total labor force)	27.3	15.7	16.2	16.0	16.5	15.5	15.7	15.5	15.0	15.1	15.7
GDP and Prices											
Gross Domestic Product											
US$ billion, current prices	2.7	4.6	6.6	6.5	7.4	7.7	7.7	7.9	8.1	8.4	7.5
Jamaican $ billion, current prices	4.8	33.0	230.2	241.5	262.9	282.2	300.9	338.7	372.2	407.7	304.5
per capita US$, current prices	1266	1907	2631	2582	2923	3016	3010	3016	3112	3203	2937
per capita, constant J$ (1986 base year)	6460 (1986)	7996	8111	7938	7725	7629	7542	7548	7642	7688	7728
GDP growth, annual % change, constant J$	−5.7	5.5	0.5	−1.3	−2.0	−0.5	−0.4	0.7	1.7	1.0	0.0
Gross Domestic Investment (% of GDP)	15.9	25.9	29.3	29.7	29.8	26.7	25.1	27.6	31.0	34.3	29.2
Gross National Savings (% of GDP)	10.8	16.0	23.3	24.9	23.2	20.6	20.0	21.1	21.9	17.5	21.6
Consumer Prices, annual change (%)	27.3	21.9	19.9	26.4	9.7	8.6	6.0	8.2	7.0	7.1	11.6
Exchange Rate, J$ per US$ (period average)	1.78	7.18	35.14	37.12	35.40	36.55	39.04	42.70	46.00	48.4	40.0
Real Effective Exchange Rate	151.5	100	92.4	109.9	126.9	134.2	133.0	130.6	131.8	131.0	123.7
Interest Rate (treasury bill rate, % per annum, eop)	9.97	26.21	27.7	38.0	21.1	25.7	20.8	18.2	16.7	15.5	23.0

		1990/91	1995/96	1996/97	1997/98	1998/99	1999/00	2000/01	2001/02	2002/03
Structure of the Economy (% of GDP)										
Agriculture	8.2	7.1	9.0	8.4	8.0	7.8	7.3	6.7	6.6	6.0
Industry	38.3	40.5	36.9	34.3	33.1	31.3	31.4	31.5	31.7	31.4
Manufacturing	16.6	18.6	16.1	15.5	14.9	14.0	14.0	13.7	13.8	13.5
Services	53.5	52.4	54.1	57.4	58.9	60.9	61.3	61.8	61.8	62.7
Public Sector (% of GDP) (fiscal year April–March)										
Revenue and Grants (central government)		25.9	28.3	26.4	25.4	26.6	29.8	30	27.6	29.6
Expenditures (central government)		23.7	26.5	32.6	33.0	33.5	34	31	33.3	37.6
Interest payments (central government)		7.9	8.7	11.4	9.4	12.4	13.8	12.8	13.7	15.7
Primary Balance (central government)		10.0	10.5	5.2	1.8	5.5	9.6	11.8	8.0	7.7
Adjusted Central Government Balance[1]		2.2	1.8	−6.3	−8.7	−12.3	−8.3	−5.5	−5.7	−8.0
Public Sector Balance		−1.6	2.0	−5.3	−9.2	−10.9	−7.2	−5.6	−6.8	−9.3
Total Debt		138.3	85.9	79.1	102.3	115.7	132.7	131.9	130.6	148.5
Domestic		38.1	26.4	35.4	59.3	73.1	90.0	83.6	78.2	89.8
External		100.2	59.5	43.7	43	42.6	42.8	48.3	54.2	58.8
External Sector										
Exports of Goods and Non-factor Services (US$ mn)	1421.6	2325	3541	3465	3547	3540	3643	3782	3573	3229
Imports of Goods and Non-factor Services (US$ mn)	1678.3	2928	4246	4231	4504	4502	4507	4989	5248	4829
External current account balance (% of GDP)	−5.1	−6.8	−1.7	−2.2	−4.6	−4.4	−2.9	−5.0	−10.1	−13.3
Net International Reserves, US$ million	−442.8 (1982)	−397.3	428.2	692.6	541.0	582.0	450.2	969.5	1840.7	1597.0
Gross Reserves, US$ million	105.0	168.2	681.3	880.0	682.1	709.5	554.5	1053.7	1900.9	1645.4

1. Includes FINSAC interest payments on a full year basis.

Source: International Financial Statistics, IMF; IMF; World Development Indicators, World Bank; Economic and Social Survey, PIOJ.

TABLE 2: JAMAICA—MILLENNIUM DEVELOPMENT GOALS, ACHIEVEMENTS AND 2015 TARGET

Millennium Development Goal (MDG)	Indicators	1980	1985	1990	1995	2000	2001	MDG Target 2015	Status*
Eradicate Extreme Poverty and Hunger	Poverty headcount, national (% of population)	—	—	28.4	27.5	18.7	16.8	Half of 1990 level	On track
Achieve Universal Primary Education	School enrollment, primary (% net)	96.2	94.2	95.7	96.8	95.4	92.8	100.00Achieved	
Promote Gender Equality and Empower Women	Ratio of girls to boys in primary and secondary education (%)	—	99.4	97.2	100.0	101.0	98.0	Eliminate gender disparity in education	Achieved
	Ratio of young literate females to males (% ages 15–24)	111.0	110.2	109.3	108.3	107.4	107.3		
Reduce Child Mortality	Mortality rate, under-5 (per 1,000 live births)	34.0	27.0	20.0	20.0	20.0	20.0	6.7 (reduce by 2/3 from 1990)	Far behind
	Mortality rate, infant (per 1,000 live births)	28.0	22.5	27.0	24.5	24.5	24.5	—	
Improve Maternal Health	Maternal mortality ratio (modeled estimate, per 100,000 live births)	—	—	—	120	106.2	106.2	30 (reduce by 2/3 from 1990)	Far behind
Combat HIV/AIDS, Malaria and Other Diseases	Prevalence of HIV, female (% ages 15–24)	—	—	—	—	0.40 (1999)	0.9	Halt spread	Lagging
	Incidence of tuberculosis (per 100,000 people)	7.5	5.6	4.6	4.9	4.9	4.7		
Ensure Environmental Sustainability	Improved water source (% of population with access)	—	—	93.0	—	92.0	—	96.5 (half of 1990 proportion without access)	On track

*Using UNDP guidelines for assessment of progress toward each goal. See Human Development Report, UNDP 2002.

Source: World Bank; Economic and Social Survey, various issues, PIOJ; PIOJ

been reduced to single digits since 1997, an unprecedented post-Independence record. The financial sector was cleaned up quickly, although the cost of the financial crisis was one of the largest in the world in terms of GDP. In addition, international reserves reached new highs with major increases in 2000 and 2001. The tax effort has been consistently strong, varying mostly between 25–27 percent of GDP, which is among the higher rates in the developing world. Fiscal management benefits from a relatively strong legal and institutional framework. Enrollment in school in the 1990s continued to expand in early childhood, senior secondary and tertiary education, following near universal primary enrollment of all children between 6 and 14 by 1989. Finally, and importantly, Jamaica comes out well in cross-country comparisons of democratic traditions and institutions, voice, government stability, quality of the bureaucracy, and the regulatory framework.

Millenium Development Goals (MDGs). Jamaica is likely to meet many of these goals (Table 2), including those on poverty and under 5 malnutrition, universal primary education, and access to safe drinking water, though it is unlikely to meet the targets on child and maternal mortality (even thought the proportion of births attended by skilled health personnel remains high at 95 per cent). Also, HIV/AIDS has been spreading, with the youth being particularly vulnerable. On education, while net primary enrollment is very high, the key issue relates to inadequate quality of the education system. Also, while gross completion rates in primary education are high (95 percent in 2000), only 68 percent of those who enrolled completed secondary education (World Bank 2002d).

Unfortunately, the 1990s also left a legacy of debt, crime, and very low growth. The financial crisis increased the public debt sharply, particularly domestic debt. The debt to GDP ratio was reduced from 138.3 percent in 1990/91 to the still high level of 79 percent in 1996/97 but it rose again after the financial crisis and rising fiscal deficits to reach about 150 percent in 2002/03. This debt and its servicing crowds out private borrowing and public capital formation. The crime rate rose in the 1990s (Jamaica has the third highest rate of violent crime in the world), after being quite steady in the 1980s, exacting a major cost on the economy, equivalent to a minimum of 4 percent of GDP every year. Partly owing to these factors, GDP declined each year from 1996 to 1999. The 1990s also saw a loss in Jamaica's competitiveness, with a decline in market share and total factor productivity, as well as an appreciation of the real exchange rate that hurt tradable goods production. Finally, even as education expanded, outcomes continued to be poor, particularly for the underprivileged. And, the lack of opportunities along with crime, contributed to migration equivalent to nearly 80 percent of the well-educated and highly subsidized tertiary graduates.

Growth and Poverty Reduction

Poverty in Jamaica declined substantially in the latter half of the 1990s, paradoxically despite a small decline in measured GDP and a major financial crisis. Poverty declined from an estimated 27.5 percent of the population in 1995 to about 17 percent in 1999 (Figure 1). Consistent

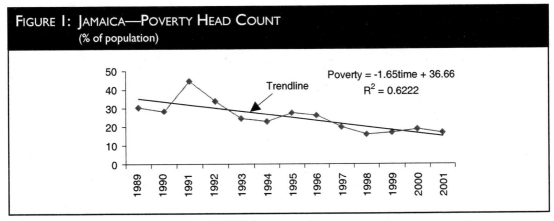

FIGURE 1: JAMAICA—POVERTY HEAD COUNT
(% of population)

Poverty = -1.65time + 36.66
R^2 = 0.6222

Source: Survey of Living Conditions, PIOJ-STATIN, for poverty data.

with the general decline in poverty, vulnerability to poverty appears also to be somewhat less in 2000 than in 1993.

The decline in poverty is likely due to a confluence of factors particular to the period. First, output probably grew somewhat faster than measured GDP (see Chapter 2). The informal sector and the underground economy have continued to provide employment, which may be one of the factors in the underestimate of GDP as well as the decline in poverty. Second, inflation, a "tax" that particularly hurts the poor, has fallen. Inflation hurts the poor because more of their assets are in currency, which depreciates with inflation, and because inflation generates larger relative price movements, to which the poor are vulnerable. Third, the relative price of food has fallen, reflecting lower prices of primary products worldwide and the real appreciation of the exchange rate, as well as reduced trade protection. Food, of course, accounts for a major portion of the budgets of the poor. In addition, rising real wages (partly because of backward indexed wage contracts, and partly because of strong union pressure) and remittances may have helped reduce poverty. However, rising real wages also contributed to the decline in private employment and may have mainly benefited the already better-off workers. Remittances from overseas have grown sharply in dollar terms, but have not increased much as a proportion of GDP, and in fact declined by 2 percentage points of GDP between 1995 and 1998. Their effect on poverty seems to be one of maintaining incomes and keeping people out of poverty, rather than raising people out of poverty.

For the period 1989–2001, a strong statistical relationship exists between poverty and real GDP, inflation, and the relative price of food. This relationship explains relatively well not only the sharp rise in poverty in 1991 but also the observed fall in poverty over the latter half of the 1990s, as can be seen in the low residuals in Figure 2 (see footnote 10 in Chapter 1 for full details). According to that relationship, the elasticity of the poverty head count with respect to GDP (percent change in the headcount divided by the percent change in GDP) is 2.8, a relatively large figure by international standards. This elasticity implies a ten-percent increase in real GDP would reduce the head count by the relatively larger figure of 28 percent—from the 17 percent currently to 12 percent. A ten-percentage point fall in inflation would reduce the poverty head count by 3 percentage points (from 17 percent to 14 percent) and a ten-percentage point reduction in the relative price of food would reduce the poverty head count by almost 4 percentage points (from 17 percent to 13 percent).

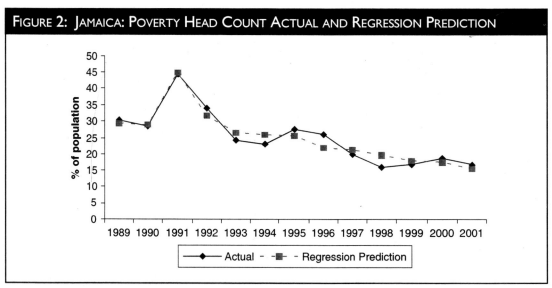

FIGURE 2: JAMAICA: POVERTY HEAD COUNT ACTUAL AND REGRESSION PREDICTION

Note: The predicted equation is based on the following regression (see Chapter 1): Poverty Head Count = 48.1 −0.0036** Real GDP + 0.30** Inflation + 37.8* Rel Price of Food
Source: Survey of Living Conditions, PIOJ-STATIN, for poverty data, and STATIN for other data.

Of course, these estimates reflect both any underestimate of GDP growth and the other forces that were at work during the decade and their correlation with these 3 variables.

Unfortunately, it is unlikely that the macroeconomic factors that contributed to the recent poverty reduction and offset the impact of slow growth on GDP will continue to operate in the next few years. Indeed the slowing impact of these factors may explain why the incidence of poverty has leveled off since 1999. Further gains from falling inflation and lower relative food prices are unlikely—inflation has leveled off and the real exchange rate has begun to depreciate. Only further reductions in protection of agriculture, such as cuts in stamp duties, are likely to limit rises in relative prices of food. Growth of the informal sector has helped maintain employment and contributed to unmeasured GDP growth, but it is unlikely to grow rapidly without faster growth in measured GDP. Whatever the impact of rising real wages has been, it is unlikely that employers will be able to continue to give wage increases in excess of inflation and productivity, given the openness of the economy and associated competitive pressures. Pressures for wage increases not justified by higher productivity are likely to continue to reduce employment and to slow growth, especially since the need for fiscal stringency will reduce the public sector's demand for labor. Remittances may play a greater role in poverty reduction in the future, assuming remittances continue to grow in dollar terms and the real exchange rate depreciates. Finally, it should be noted that in all countries, poverty becomes harder to reduce as the proportion of people in poverty decline. A closely related point, as suggested by international experience, is that the elasticity of poverty with respect to GDP declines as the level of GDP rises.

Future sustained reduction in poverty is therefore likely to depend on sustained growth in the Jamaican economy as well as the implementation of policies to ensure that the poor are empowered to take advantages of the opportunities that arise from increased growth. A recent World Bank study, based on cross-country regressions, suggests that on average the income of the poor rises one-for-one with overall growth (Dollar and Kraay, 2001a).

It will also be important to ensure that Jamaica's growth is pro-poor—that growth raises the income of the poor at least as much as average income growth, if not more. The poor face a number of problems in benefiting from growth alone. This is illustrated by the aforementioned World Bank study, which implied that in half the countries, income of the poor rose less rapidly than overall growth. As in most countries, Jamaica's poor are more likely to be members of larger households, be in female-headed households, have less education, and be employed in the rural sector—agriculture or fishing. In Jamaica, poverty also appears to be strongly correlated with social factors including: teenage pregnancy; single parenting; drug abuse; domestic violence; and child abuse and delinquency, though these associations are often the result of poverty, rather than its cause. As the cross-country evidence demonstrates, policies that promote growth in demand for labor, and access to education, health and social services can help to reduce poverty, reduce the vulnerability of the poor and allow the poor to take advantage of opportunities that are generated when the economy grows. Policies that address structural rigidities in factor markets will also be important to ensure that Jamaica's growth is broad-based.

Rural poverty is also an issue that should be addressed. The incidence of poverty in the rural areas, at 24.1 percent, is more than three times higher than that in Kingston. However, the low correlation between the fortunes of agriculture and the level of rural poverty suggests that rural poverty issues are much broader than agriculture alone and the non-farm productive sector may require attention. There is therefore need for a comprehensive rural strategy that embraces the multidimensional nature of rural development.

Understanding Growth in Jamaica

Growth in GDP and employment was low in the 1990s while, paradoxically, investment was high. Average measured GDP growth actually was negative over the period 1996–2001 (Table 3). A loss of external competitiveness led to a fall in agricultural and manufacturing output, and also led to the exit from Jamaica of some textile (a major source of female employment) and tire manufacturing

TABLE 3: JAMAICA—GDP GROWTH, EMPLOYMENT GROWTH AND INVESTMENT RATES: 1981–2001

	1981–1985	Average 1986–1990	1991–1995	1996–2000	1996	1997	1998	1999	2000	2001	Average 1996–2001
Percent per year											
GDP growth	0.1	4.9	0.9	–0.7	–1.3	–2.0	–0.5	–0.4	0.7	1.7	–0.3
Employment growth	1.7	2.6	1.5	–0.6	–0.4	–1.4	0.7	–1.0	–1.1	0.6	–0.4
Percent of GDP (nominal)											
Gross Cap Formation % GDP	20.4	22.7	27.8	27.8	29.7	29.8	26.7	25.1	27.6	30.1	28.2
Construction % GDP	10.0	10.8	13.1	12.2	12.6	12.2	12.0	12.4	12.0	12.2	12.2
Machinery & Equip. % GDP	7.3	7.8	9.9	10.9	12.8	10.8	10.2	9.1	11.7	13.4	11.3
Transport % GDP	3.1	3.4	4.3	4.5	4.2	6.6	4.3	3.5	3.7	4.3	4.4
Public Investment	8.0	6.9	5.0	3.9	5.6	5.1	2.7	3.1	2.9	—	—
Private Fixed Cap Formation	12.4	15.8	22.8	23.9	24.1	24.7	24.0	22.0	24.7	—	—

Memo:

	Estimated GDP Growth	Est. Contrib. to Growth: Capital Growth	Emp. Growth	Growth of Total Factor Productivity (Residual)
Sources of Growth 1991–2000				
Loayza et al. (WB sources and estimates)	0.3	1.9	1.4	–3.0
Bartelsman (STATIN Sources and estimates)	0.7	1.2	0.3	–0.8

Sources: National Income Product 2001, STATIN; Economic and Social Survey, PIOJ, various issues; WDI/GDF Central database, World Bank; Chapter 2.

companies. Positive growth was seen only in a few sectors including (a) nontradable sectors such as communications (average annual growth of 10.5 percent in 1995–2001), and power (5.5 percent); and (b) location- and natural resource-based activities, such as transport (4.5 percent); mining (2.5 percent), and hotels (2.5 percent). During 1996–2001, employment declined at an annual average rate of 0.4 percent, down from the 1.5 percent annual growth in the first half of the 1990s. Only public sector employment has grown; private sector employment has fallen, with the decline of 30,000 in female employment roughly equal to the total decline. (Employment did rise between 2000 and 2002, but this owed largely to an increase in short-term contractual public employment, and there are also questions of statistical comparability of the data). The labor market also appears to be functioning imperfectly, with real wages rising despite weak GDP growth. The wage demands have probably contributed to the decline in employment and generated some substitution of capital for labor. At the same time, investment has been high, about 28 percent of GDP in the last half of the 1990s and nearly 30 percent in 2001. These figures are similar to the first half of the 1990s and in the top quarter of developing countries. Investment was concentrated in communications, power, hotels, mining, and housing construction.

Given the negative growth in GDP, the marginal increase in employment (over 1991–2000), the continued low education outcomes, and high rate of investment, the standard "sources of growth analysis" suggests that in the aggregate, (total factor) productivity declined over the period (see the summary in Table 3, the discussion in Chapter 2, and Bartelsman, 2002, and Loayza et al., 2002).

Jamaica's recent lack of growth is often explained by the financial crisis, the poor external climate, but also by the appreciation of the real exchange rate and increase in real wages, all of which offset the gains from the liberalization of the early 1990s. The importance of all these factors is borne out statistically in a recent World Bank study (Loayza, et al., 2002). The appreciation of the real exchange rate arose from the post-crisis stabilization, and the rise in real wages hurt tradable goods production in particular. Even tourism, which is largely priced in dollars, suffered from surprisingly slow growth and loss of market share—the appreciated exchange rate and high wage costs meant lower profits and/or a need for higher dollar prices, reducing competitiveness and the potential income from Jamaica's natural beauty.

The costs of crime and the rising government consumption also limited growth. Crime reduced the attractiveness of Jamaica to investors and tourists and required spending on security that did not lead to additional production (see Chapter 6). Crime has raised exporters' costs and made it difficult/costly to run multiple shifts, a staple of the textile and call service industries around the world. Jamaica's high tax collections largely go to pay for government interest costs, and other current expenditures that do not contribute to growth (see Chapter 3).

Some indicators suggest GDP growth may be underestimated but even an adjustment for the possible underestimate would not make growth performance satisfactory. STATIN applies standard techniques to estimate GDP growth, but estimates of the output in the services sector is always difficult, particularly in an open economy where incomes from tourism and services may be booked offshore. Other issues are the imputed income from housing, which appears low, the size of the drug economy, and output from the whole informal sector. Finally, the huge increase in imputed banking services, a large negative in the accounts, may bear some reconsideration. Indicators that GDP may be underestimated are the decline in poverty (Chapter 2), the rapid growth of some indicators of demand (apparent meat and fish consumption, power consumption and automobile registration, see Table 4), and the rapid growth of currency usage—a standard indicator of the growth of the underground and informal economy. Nonetheless, growth, even adjusting for a possible underestimate of 1–2 percentage points per annum, has not been high.

The apparent paradox of high rates of capital growth/investment and slow growth probably reflects the underutilization of much of the capital created in the early 1990s, the costs of crime, and the concentration of investment in a few, rapidly growing sectors that may have some distortions. Much of capital created in the pre-crisis construction boom of the early 1990s and in the development of export zones now lies underutilized as a result of the lack of

TABLE 4: JAMAICA—INDICATORS OF CONSUMPTION
(Average Annual Growth Rates)

	1990–1995	1995–2001
Meat & Fish Apparent Cons.*(tons)	0.7	6.4
Power Sales (kwh)	3.9	6.5
Household Consumers of Power (number)	4.5	4.3
Cars & Trucks Passing the Fitness Test (number)	8.3	8.5

*Apparent Consumption = Production + Imports – Exports.
Source: Economic and Social Survey, PIOJ, TIN, various issues.

demand and lack of external competitiveness discussed above. Investments to offset crime do not yield increases in GDP, and crime may even reduce the productivity of existing capital by making it necessary to stop multiple shift operations. Investment remains high in housing, but its contribution to output is hard to measure. Other recent investment was concentrated in communications, transport, mining, and hotels, but in some cases output in these sectors is hard to measure and in some cases the investment may have reflected not simply profit potential that would lead to higher national output but differential taxation rates (Artana and Najas, 2002).

Whatever growth has occurred has not created much employment, partly because of the loss of competitiveness and the functioning of the labor market. Private sector employment has fallen in the formal sector, obviously hurt by the decline in tradable goods production. Partly the lack of formal employment seems related to large increases in real wages, which has fed back into the loss of external competitiveness.

Many secondary graduates and most tertiary graduates continue to migrate, which in turn raises the issue of the large subsidy to higher education. While the average outcomes in education are poor and limit productivity gains, migration continues to be large, suggesting that tertiary education, in particular, performs relatively well. Canada, US and UK actively recruit Jamaican tertiary graduates like teachers and nurses. The equivalent of about 80 percent of the tertiary graduates in the 1990s appear to have emigrated. High crime rates may be a push factor contributing to migration. High rates of emigration among tertiary graduates, whose education is highly subsidized and who typically do not come from among the poor, raise an important issue of the need to recoup a greater portion of the costs of tertiary education.

Generating higher growth in tradables is the key to growth in Jamaica's open economy but is likely to be difficult because of the country's high costs. Dependence on further growth in the informal sector and further increases in public sector employment is not a viable strategy for improving economic performance. Yet expanding tradables will be difficult without tackling distortions. The impact of exchange rate appreciation (despite recent real depreciation) and high wage increases in the 1990s continues to keep costs high compared to Asia or regional competitors. Capital costs are high because of the debt overhang and government demands for financing the debt and its rising non-interest consumption. Crime and security costs generate high overheads. Inadequate infrastructure, especially in roads and water, as well as unreliability of power supply, also acts as a constraint to exports. As a result, imports have substituted for most manufacturing production, other than that protected by transport costs, and some agro processing. Some exports do occur to the other Caribbean countries but that is a slow growing market. Other exports are to the niche market of Jamaicans overseas but, for instance, exports of Red Stripe beer pale in comparison to the success of Mexico's Corona. Export-oriented textile production shifted to the Dominican Republic, Honduras, Haiti, among others, and to Mexico after the formation of NAFTA (see Chapter 7), a loss in GDP of about 1 percent. Banana and sugar export are possible largely because of quotas. Sugar is largely a public sector operation and the attempt to privatize it collapsed because of the unattractive exchange rate, but some of the private sector firms are said to have substantially lower costs. In the IT-related sector, the attempts to take advantage of the big improvement in telecommunications and English language skills have run into high labor cost and the crime issue (night time workers need to be transported to and from their homes). The bauxite industry is still a major contributor to exports, but the falling productivity of the old mines has reduced their dynamism and require substantial investment. Tourism is competitive because of the climate and beaches and it continues to bring in substantial foreign investment, even with higher wages, partly because much of the competition is elsewhere in the Caribbean, which also has high wages in US dollar terms. However, the benefits that tourism brings are somewhat eroded by the subsidies and tax concessions offered by the government. The crime issue, or the perception that there is a crime issue, also limits tourism growth. Indeed, in the second half of the 1990s, growth of tourism has slowed, and Jamaica has lost out to popular destinations such as the Dominican Republic.

Policies that improve international competitiveness and increase productivity are thus the key to growth in Jamaica's open economy. Improving competitiveness means wage growth much more in line with productivity; a reduction in crime to reduce its associated overhead costs; better customs services, so smaller firms can access imported inputs better; and a reduction in the tax and interest rate burden imposed by the public sector. Allowing a gradual nominal depreciation would also tend to increase competitiveness: the pass through into prices is likely to be limited by the weakness of the economy and low inflation in recent years, according to recent research. The resulting depreciated real exchange rate will reduce the local component of costs in US dollar terms and thereby stimulate output in agriculture, manufacturing and tourism. The events of 2003 have demonstrated that a real depreciation is possible—in the first half of 2003, the nominal exchange rate depreciated about 15 percent, but consumer prices rose about 7 percent, leading to a real depreciation of 11 percent. This real depreciation also demonstrates the enhanced credibility achieved by the central bank in recent times, and that credibility will continue to be key to maintaining the gains in exchange rate competitiveness. It is also important to note that, while depreciation will benefit agriculture by raising prices of imported foodstuffs, it will hurt poor urban consumers and raise the burden of external debt. A one-time, step devaluation alone is unlikely to sustain export growth. Sustained growth in exports will depend on policies that generate a perception that exports will be kept profitable for some time and therefore investment in outward oriented production will pay off. Finally, better infrastructure also is needed. In addition to general infrastructure improvements, infrastructure will be needed to maintain tourism's dynamism and decisions will need to be made: a) whether to improve infrastructure in existing tourist areas or start new ones, and b) how to pay for it. Unless growth picks up, the demand for labor will continue to grow slowly, and migration (labor export) will continue.

Reducing the Fiscal and Debt Burden

In the early 1990s, Jamaica made considerable progress in its fiscal affairs. Tight fiscal policy was part of the overall macroeconomic strategy to stabilize the economy and stimulate economic growth. From 1990/91 to 1995/96, the government ran a fiscal surplus and a significant primary surplus (the difference between revenue and non-interest expenditure), although these surpluses declined over the period. These surpluses, plus Paris Club and bilateral debt restructurings, reduced the total public sector debt from US$5427 million (US$3942 million external) in 1990/91 to US$4435 million (US$3070 million external) in 1995/96; the ratio of debt to GDP declined from 138.3 percent in 1990/91 to 85.9 percent in 1995/96.

The financial crisis of the mid-1990s, together with the rising government wage bill and falling revenue over 1996/97 to 1997/98 (relative to GDP), worsened the fiscal and debt position dramatically. It is possible that the trends in revenue and expenditure would have worsened the debt position even without the financial crisis (Figure 3 and Table 3 in Chapter 3). However, in response to the massive financial crisis, the government replaced all of the financial institutions' weak lending with government debt.

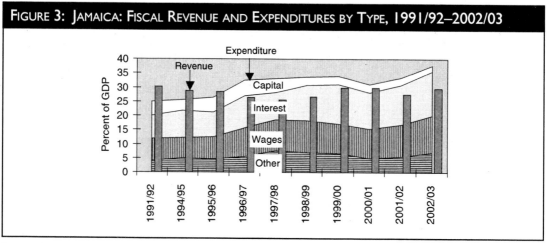

FIGURE 3: JAMAICA: FISCAL REVENUE AND EXPENDITURES BY TYPE, 1991/92–2002/03

Source: IMF.

This policy protected the depositors, but generated a major Government debt increase. The resulting interest costs, together with the deteriorating underlying balance, have reversed the fiscal gains of the first half of the 1990s as well as 1999/00 and 2000/01. The deterioration occurred despite cuts in government investment that would have been desirable for growth. With the crisis, the economic contraction over 1996–1999 and then the recent, significant fiscal slippage of 2001/02 and 2002/03, the ratio of debt to GDP has risen to about 150 percent of GDP (Figure 4). This is one of the highest ratios in the world. All this has meant that short-term risks rose substantially, access to external markets deteriorated and the exchange rate came under pressure in 2003.

Reaching fiscal and debt sustainability are critical to a return to sustained growth, but primary surpluses of more than 10 percent of GDP are needed just to sustain the current, high debt to GDP ratio of 150 percent. This is the case even under optimistic scenarios for growth and interest rates (for example, growth of 2 percent, and real interest of 9 percent). Moreover, the

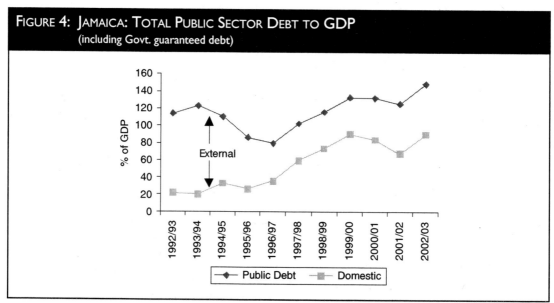

FIGURE 4: JAMAICA: TOTAL PUBLIC SECTOR DEBT TO GDP
(including Govt. guaranteed debt)

Source: IMF; See Table 3-1.

required surplus is extremely sensitive to growth and interest rates, as Table 5 demonstrates. In addition, reducing the debt stock to 123 percent of GDP by the end of 2005/06 through higher surpluses will demand primary surpluses of about 15–17 percent of GDP (assuming 2 percent growth, interest rates of 15–17 percent, and inflation of 8 percent). In this context, it is worth noting that the Government in June 2003 floated 2 and 5 year LRS at about 34 percent (implying a real rate of about 25 percent). Finally, since external debt is now almost 60 percent of GDP, a J$1 depreciation versus the US dollar increases the stock of debt roughly by 1 percent of GDP. To mitigate this, real exchange rate depreciation (which will help improve competitiveness) would need to be accompanied by growth and productivity enhancing measures, and preferably reduction in real interest rates.

Fiscal slippage, to a primary surplus of 6–7 percent of GDP, would lead to a rise in the debt to GDP ratio. A primary surplus of 6–7 percent of GDP, would, under assumptions in the table, only stabilize debt if the debt were lower by some 50 percentage points of GDP. The near-term challenge for the government is to chart and maintain a transparent course to improved fiscal and debt indicators in what is likely to be a less friendly external economic environment.

TABLE 5: PRIMARY SURPLUS/DEFICIT (% OF GDP) REQUIRED TO STABILIZE THE STOCK OF PUBLIC DEBT

	g = 0		g = 1		g = 2		g = 4	
d = 150	f = 8	f = 6	f = 8	f = 6	f = 8	f = 6	f = 8	f = 6
i = 10	2.8	5.7	1.3	4.1	−0.2	2.6	−3.1	−0.3
i = 12	5.6	8.5	4.0	6.9	2.5	5.4	−0.4	2.4
i = 14	8.3	11.3	6.8	9.7	5.2	8.1	2.2	5.1
i = 16	11.1	14.1	9.5	12.5	7.9	10.9	4.9	7.8
i = 18	13.9	17.0	12.3	15.3	10.7	13.7	7.6	10.6
i = 20	16.7	19.8	15.0	18.1	13.4	16.5	10.3	13.3

Note: g: real growth rate; d: debt to GDP ratio; i: nominal interest rate; f: inflation.
Source: World Bank staff estimates.

Not only has the debt mushroomed, but 60 percent of the debt is now domestic as a result of the crisis and more is held by private creditors. The share of domestic debt in total debt has risen from 8.3 percent in March 1992 to 60 percent in March 2002, largely because of the crisis and its ensuing impact on the deficit. The share of external debt has fallen correspondingly, though in US dollar terms, and relative to GDP, external debt has also risen since 1999. Within external debt, the share of concessional debt (bilateral and multilateral) fell from 85.5 percent in fiscal year 1991/92 to 52.6 percent in fiscal year 2001/02. At the same time, the share of private creditors in total external debt grew from 14.5 percent in 1991/92 to 47.4 percent in 2001/02. Apart from this, the Jamaican banking system, which is emerging from the financial crisis of 1995/96, has more than one-third of its assets consisting of Government debt (which, net of government deposits, represented about 45 percent of deposits in June 2003). The rest of the financial system (merchant banks, brokers, building societies) also has a large holding of government debt.

To strengthen the fiscal situation and keep debt sustainable, strong Government action is needed on expenditure and revenue. A key element in reducing Government expenditure is control over wage and salary expenditure, which now accounts for over a third of Government expenditure. Rising real public sector wages are inconsistent with a sustainable debt ratio and a slow growing economy, unless public sector employment is reduced, in percentage terms, by more than the increase in real public sector wages. The proceeds from the sale of shares or privatization of the remaining public sector entities could be used to write down the debt, although the proceeds may not be as large as they were in the past. The Government has made progress on the privatization agenda but the experience has been mixed and the Government still has substantial holding in some entities, including Air Jamaica (in which the Government recently increased its holding to 45 percent, after privatizing it in 1994), mining companies, the power company and the sugar industries, and it also owns many relatively small enterprises in activities like agriculture and tourism. In addition, the transfer of the entities to the private sector could reduce, if not eliminate, the contingent liability risk. Reducing and improving the quality of government expenditure is an area where more detailed analysis is required, and will be taken up in the Bank's forthcoming Public Expenditure Review.

Revenue increases will not be easy, since Jamaica already has a fairly high ratio of taxes (25–26 percent) and other revenues (2–3 percent) to GDP. Areas for improvement include increasing compliance and increasing reliance on user fees. The growth of the informal sector, in part, to avoid taxes, has tended to reduce the tax base. Further simplification of the tax system including the merger of some taxes such as the Education Tax and the National Housing Trust Tax with income tax may reduce transactions cost for tax compliance and encourage more informal sector business to come into the tax net. Another approach to increase informal sector coverage and also to increase revenue from income taxes would be identification of potential taxpayers by a system of indicators (such as auto ownership and overseas trips). Also, significant subsidies exist in the tax system and could be reduced. A particular issue is taxation of the hotel industry, where competition for investment has led to the Government's offering concessions. Finally, fees for tertiary education could be increased to reduce the large subsidy that mainly goes to the better-off, who often migrate.

Jamaica's ability to manage the fiscal situation technically is strong, but contingent liabilities need to be better managed. Jamaica is considered to have a sound legal and institutional framework for fiscal management. A recent assessment of the budgetary process by the World Bank Country Financial Accountability Assessment (CFAA), 2001, confirms the strength of the budgetary process but also points out some adjustments that would improve efficiency and transparency. In addition to issues of prudent management of expenditures, management of direct and contingent liabilities are also important. Since the central government is ultimately responsible for the debt or other liabilities of non-central government accounts such as public enterprises, this increases the difficulty of managing the fiscal balance, especially since the GOJ budget includes only half of these accounts. Also, realized contingent liabilities have in the past created budgetary problems, including large debt write-offs. Most recently, in May 2003, a J$6.3 billion external loan was guaranteed for the sugar industry. In moving towards achieving and maintaining fiscal stability, there is need for the government to establish a budgetary planning framework that identifies and classifies the full range of fiscal liabilities, both direct and contingent as well as the associated risk.

Revitalizing the Financial System

Jamaica's growth, development, and the solvency of the banking system are affected by the debt overhang from the enormous financial crisis of 1995–96. The crisis, one of the largest in the world (in terms of GDP), was resolved relatively quickly and has led to a significant improvement in regulation and supervision of the financial system, but also to a huge increase in an already large public sector debt. This debt burdens the economy, investment, and the public sector, crowding out private sector credit and public investment, as discussed below, and thereby limits Jamaica's growth. Increasing credit to the private sector, particularly small and medium industries that are potential exporters, and home loan mortgages, will depend on a primary surplus that reduces the importance of public sector debt in the financial system, improved credit information systems to help reduce the risk of lending, particularly to smaller borrowers, and better systems of collateral execution to protect creditors' rights and increase the incentives to repay debt promptly. Given the large share of Government debt in the financial system (in banks equal to about 45 percent of deposits), maintenance of Government solvency is critical to maintaining the solvency of the financial system. Without continued public confidence in the Government's ability to service its debt, which backs the majority of deposits, a run could develop on the banks and the currency that would lead to a new crisis.

The seeds of Jamaica's massive financial crisis were sown in the early 1990s, with the privatization of financial institutions to weak investors and the financial liberalization, in the context of weak regulation and supervision. In this environment, and with attempts to tighten monetary policy ineffective, a huge credit boom developed. Credit was allocated poorly by the poorly managed institutions, often highly concentrated and to related parties, according to a study by FIN-SAC (Financial Sector Adjustment Company Ltd., the agency created in 1997 to deal with the institutions). At the macro level, higher investment, much of it in construction, did not produce growth. Then, in the mid-1990s, when the government tightened credit to cut inflation, the weakness of the lending was exposed.

The crisis was among the world's largest (over 40 percent GDP), but its resolution was **quick.** The government guaranteed all liabilities, replaced bad loans with government debt, and took over institutions and collateral on the loans. Within five years of its formation, in 1997, FIN-SAC had liquidated or sold all of the assets that it taken over. The remaining institutions are much stronger.

Regulation and supervision were strengthened substantially but further improvements are needed. Regulation has raised capital requirements to 10 percent of risk weighted assets and strengthened income recognition and provisioning. Bank of Jamaica's independence in supervision has increased and it has strengthened its prompt corrective action procedures. Consolidated supervision has also improved, but further improvement is needed, along with better sharing of information with bank supervisors in other countries. Better harmonization of the many new laws and regulations related to finance also would be desirable.

The crisis left a massive debt overhang. Jamaican public sector debt, already large before the crisis, is now about 150 percent of GDP; domestic debt is about 90 percent of GDP, largely reflecting the replacement of financial institutions' loans by government debt. The resulting 45 percent ratio of government debt to total bank deposits is one of the highest in the world. Government debt also grew sharply in merchant banks and building societies. Correspondingly, banks' private sector credits have fallen to only about 10 percent of GDP, though there was some rise in 2002 (see Figure 5).

The large ratio of public sector debt to GDP raises concerns about Jamaican financial intermediation and growth prospects. Across countries there seems to be a negative relationship

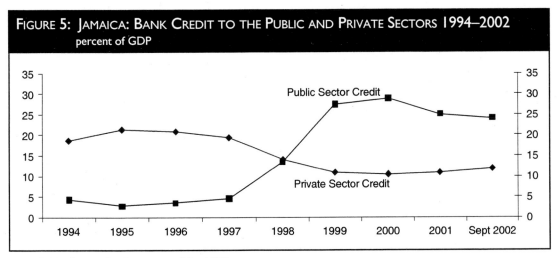

FIGURE 5: JAMAICA: BANK CREDIT TO THE PUBLIC AND PRIVATE SECTORS 1994–2002
percent of GDP

Note: Public Sector Credit estimated for 1998
Source: Bank of Jamaica; IFS, IMF.

between public sector debt and GDP growth (see Figure 6). Three reasons, relevant for Jamaica, probably explain this relationship:

1. The large stock of public sector debt mostly represents claims on future tax receipts and the government's borrowing capacity, not increased productive capital, since the debt replaced loans that were largely unproductive.
2. Higher rates of return on government debt and deposits may turn some potential entrepreneurs into *rentiers,* with a corresponding loss of economic dynamism, a fear expressed by some Jamaican bankers.
3. Traditional crowding out of private investment. Even with Jamaica's often large primary surpluses, public sector debt has grown relative to GDP. Thus, additional deposits from the public have been absorbed by deficit financing related to the large interest costs. This crowding out of private investment may be by higher real interest rates or by credit rationing to risky borrowers. Foreign loans, mostly short term, have provided some respite but only to the best borrowers.

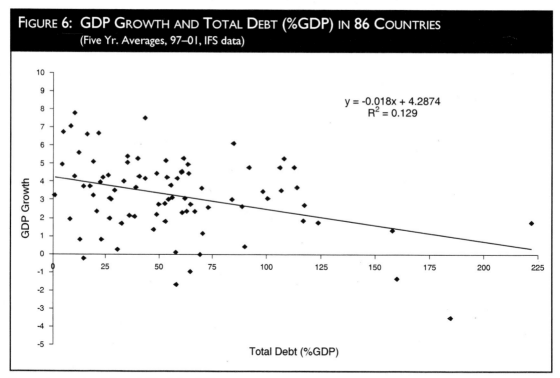

FIGURE 6: GDP GROWTH AND TOTAL DEBT (%GDP) IN 86 COUNTRIES
(Five Yr. Averages, 97–01, IFS data)

Source: International Financial Statistics, IMF.

What can be done to increase credit to the private sector? More private sector credit would be desirable, but credit alone cannot lead to a sustained private sector recovery. It makes little sense to increase loans to companies with poor repayment prospects and in any case Jamaica's openness makes lowering the interest rate difficult.

■ **More credit could be made available to the private sector by reducing the government's demand for financing**—achieving a larger primary surplus as discussed in Chapter 4. The small firms bear much of the burden of the crowding-out by public sector debt because of the segmentation of financial markets. Larger firms still have access and may be able to borrow abroad. Note that the Government's attempts to channel credit—it is now the largest source of housing finance, for example—may add to the future needs for borrowing since in the past the public lending institutions have had poor recoveries and Parliament has questioned the political linkages of the credit programs.

- **Better quality lending, as well as increased access to credit can be encouraged through credit registries.** Credit registries can provide better information to allow financial intermediaries to lend to borrowers who are more likely to repay. Moreover, credit registries give borrowers incentives to repay, to maintain a good credit record. If they cover even small borrowers, they can increase access to credit by allowing the small borrowers to build up the intangible asset of a good credit record. However, since banks are often loathe to share information about their clients, credit registries often have to be started by Government legislation.
- **Improve collateral execution, perhaps by creating special courts for debt disputes and bankruptcy.** Surveys show dissatisfaction with the courts' performance on commercial issues.

From a short run standpoint, the solvency of Jamaica's financial system has become much more dependent on the public sector's solvency, and less on the private sector's servicing of its debt. The full bail-out of the depositors after the crisis, by replacement of all bad private debt with government debt, has left total public sector debt at about 45 percent of deposits, as noted. Hence, Government's capacity to either rollover its debt or service it out of the budget is critical to the banks' capacity to cover the interest costs of their deposits. Moreover, if the Government debt service ratio becomes large, the public may lose confidence in its capacity to service its debt, on which the interest on deposits depends. Such a loss of confidence may not simply make it hard to rollover government debt; it might generate a run on the banks and the currency. Hence the high post-crisis ratio of Jamaican public sector debt to GDP creates a substantial risk for the financial system and the currency, one that can only be reduced by improving the ratio of the Government's primary surplus to its debt service.

Improving Education Outcomes

Jamaica has emphasized education and achieved near universal enrollment and gender parity. By 1989, enrollment was practically universal for children between 6 and 14, and 95 percent for 12 to 14 year olds from the poorest quintile. There is gender parity at all levels before grade 9. Government commitment is also reflected in average spending of about 6 percent of GDP on education, well above the Latin American region average. In addition, education forms about 5.5 percent of total household spending.

   Private and social returns to education are positive. Private returns in 1996 to an additional year of education were 5, 3.3, 1.1 and 8.4 percent for primary, secondary, technical and vocational training, and tertiary education respectively. However, the low private rates of return, particularly at the low and middle levels, may reflect not only Jamaica's slow GDP growth but also poor quality (see Chapter 5). Social benefits of education include the link to reduced fertility—from over 100 live births per 1000 women in the reproductive age group in 1991 to 76 in 2002—leading to a lower school-age population and potentially freeing up resources to improve educational quality. Smaller families also allow parents to devote more resources and attention to their children. Another social benefit comes from positive school experiences, which tend to be associated with much less risky/criminal behavior in survey data. Surveys also suggest that students who perform well scholastically do not want to jeopardize it through risky behavior that may have long-term repercussions. In contrast, the weaker students may feel alienated from school and school achievement, and drop out to a life of anti-social behavior. Even as the overall school enrollment rate has increased and illiteracy has gone down, violent crime has increased over the last fifteen years (Chapter 6). The dropping out and hence inadequate education leads to more unemployment (unemployment of 14–19 year old poor youth was 47 percent in 2001) and may be linked to participation in violence. Poor male children between 14–24 are an especially vulnerable group, prone to be both victims as well as perpetrators of violence. More details on issues and policies relating to youth at risk can be found in the World Bank report on Youth Development in the Caribbean (World Bank, 2002a).

With increasing age, enrollment of the poor and of males declines. Overall, 22 percent of all students enrolled in grade 9, about 11,000 students, still cannot access grades 10 and 11 because of the lack of school places. The lack of places, social and economic pressures, and quality issues (see below) affect the poor students disproportionately. Enrollment ratios of the poorest and richest quintiles diverge sharply after age 14; by the ages of 17 and 18, the respective enrollment ratios are slightly under 30 percent and 80 percent (Figure 7). Also, while males and females start out equally in enrollment in basic education, a disproportionately high number of males drop out after grade 9, so that in tertiary education females account for about 66 percent of enrollment. Not surprisingly, boys formed 61 percent of the 12–18 year olds out of school in 2000.

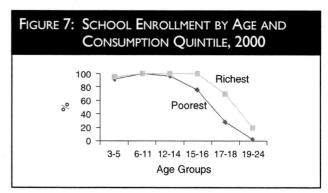

FIGURE 7: SCHOOL ENROLLMENT BY AGE AND CONSUMPTION QUINTILE, 2000

Source: PIOJ-STATIN 2001

Other indicators suggest the quality of education is low. About 30–40 percent of students are functionally illiterate at the end of primary education, and about 30 to 40 percent of Grade 6 leavers read below grade level. Absenteeism is high especially in junior secondary education. Many adolescents are disengaged from educational pursuits, and tend to drop out before completion of the cycle (more pervasive among the poor and boys). The national pass rate of less than 60 percent in Grade 11 CXC (Caribbean Examination Council) English examinations and 30 percent in mathematics is below that of Dominica, St. Kitts, St. Lucia, Belize, Trinidad and Tobago, and St. Vincent and the Grenadines. In a standardized comparison of workers in the U.S. labor market, for workers educated in Jamaica the return to an extra year of school was only 3.5 percent in 1990, worse than 53 of the other 66 sample countries. Some of these quality problems partly reflect inequality and poverty, including the family environment, but also the school system (see below).

The quality of schools is very uneven. At the end of grade 9, students in Primary and Junior High Schools and the former Comprehensive High Schools score much lower in mathematics and English than the Traditional High Schools. Only a small percentage of students in the former Comprehensive High schools participate in the CXC examination, and their pass rate is half or less that of Secondary High students. These differences partly reflect the selection process and curriculum differences. The academically-oriented, Traditional High Schools employ a higher proportion of university-educated teachers. Textbook and ancillary educational equipment also are better in Traditional High Schools. The highest proportion of untrained teachers is concentrated in rural schools.

Poor students get tracked into lower quality schools, and their home environment exacerbates the situation. Richer children receive better quality education. Students from affluent families attend private preparatory primary schools and pay for extra tutoring to prepare for the end of the primary cycle (grade 6) examination. This better preparation allows them to be placed in better schools—in 2000, about 43 percent of students in all-age schools were from the poorest quintile, while over half of the students in the academic, traditional high schools were from the top two quintiles. In tertiary education, 91 percent of students were from the top two quintiles. Also, school attendance is far more irregular for poor students—in 2001, only 60 percent of the poor students had full attendance, compared with 87 in the richest quintile. Poorer students also live in homes with a greater chance of not having a father figure. For boys, the absence of a male role model contributes to lower achievement, lower educational aspirations, absenteeism, and the risks of dropout and delinquent behavior.

The poor thus end up far less educated, which creates a vicious circle of poverty. Facing these handicaps, it is not surprising that the poor tend not to participate in or fail CXC examinations (the key examination for admission into tertiary education or finding a job). The adult population in the bottom quintile has disproportionately fewer academic qualifications—86 percent of the poorest quintile possess no academic qualification, compared with 52 percent for the richest quintile; none of the poor had a tertiary degree, while 12 percent of the richest quintile did. Looking at it another way, the richest quintile forms the vast majority of those with degrees or those with 3 or more A levels.

Jamaica spends more on education than many countries but ends up with less satisfactory outcomes. Jamaica has been spending an average of over 6 percent of GDP on education over the last five years, more than most of its Caribbean neighbors. Moreover, this ratio as well as real spending on education has increased substantially over the last decade. Yet, its outcomes are low, as noted above (spending and outcomes are often weakly related, see Chapter 4 in World Bank 2003). In addition to the factors mentioned above, another reason for poor outcomes could be lower instructional time—Jamaica has the lowest number of classroom hours in the above sample, partly because crime and civil disturbances force school closures.

Public expenditure on education favors the better-off, largely because of the subsidy for tertiary education. Public expenditure on education is equitably distributed in early childhood, primary, and secondary education. However, tertiary education expenditure is skewed, with 77 percent going to the top quintile, which is not surprising given the enrollment patterns (see Figure 8). Per student recurrent expenditure is much higher for tertiary education (US$3464 in 1999/00), compared to US$85 in early childhood, US$313 in primary, US$1925 in special education and US$533 in secondary education. As a result, overall education spending is regressive, with the top quintile getting 34 percent, and the bottom two quintiles getting 32 percent.

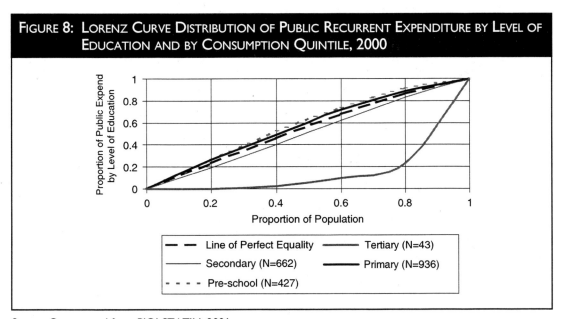

FIGURE 8: LORENZ CURVE DISTRIBUTION OF PUBLIC RECURRENT EXPENDITURE BY LEVEL OF EDUCATION AND BY CONSUMPTION QUINTILE, 2000

Source: Constructed from PIOJ-STATIN, 2001

Higher cost recovery needed in tertiary education. Given that 91 percent of tertiary students are from the top two quintiles, equality considerations are not an issue in reducing the subsidy for tertiary education. Even within tertiary education, government recovers more from teachers and community colleges than from UWI, where the students are comparatively better off. A graded increase over time in fees within the different categories of tertiary institutions will reduce inequities and generate some much-needed resources. This and other issues relating to tertiary education will be addressed in greater detail in the forthcoming Bank report on Tertiary Education in the Caribbean.

Teachers' salaries, particularly at the entry levels, have risen with public sector wages, which has distorted education spending. Wage compression has reduced the difference between the highest and lowest teacher salaries to 16–18 percent, making teacher retention difficult. Also, teacher salaries as a ratio of per capita GDP are much higher than those that prevail in the US and Latin America. The high personnel spending has led to reduced spending for instructional materials and maintenance.

The 2001 White Paper on education stresses life-long learning and quality education for all. It underscores the importance of early intervention to compensate for a negative home environment; decentralization and school-based management; increasing allocation to education to 15–20 percent of the recurrent budget. The effectiveness of education could be increased by enhancement of certain policies and some prioritization, including:

- **Focus on early learning and raise the functional literacy target to 100 percent.** Without early learning, later education is more costly and less effective and the functionally less literate are likely to become at risk.
- **Increase parental involvement and awareness and student empowerment.** Publicity and awareness campaigns are needed to inform parents about their role in child learning—such as in discouraging absenteeism, providing money for book rental, and in general creating a more conducive environment at home. Fathers need to be informed about their critical role in their sons' development and single mothers about good practices in rearing responsible children. Schools should systematically encourage students, involve them in school improvement, and provide them some discretionary funds to address pressing issues and thereby also get them more engaged.
- **Expand upper secondary education through better preparation and more places.** A cost-effective way to increase school spaces would be to buy seats in private schools that target and achieve quality improvement, rather than construct new schools. Private schools can also be paid to organize compensatory education to repeaters.
- **Improve teacher incentives and school-based management.** Teacher salaries need restructuring to reduce the salary compression, which is perpetuated by the practice of uniform percentage increase. Empowering teachers and giving them key roles in school management and planning would help.
- **Reform education finance and address the uneven quality of schools.**
  1. Allocate resources based on enrollments, not teacher positions approved. Basing grants on enrollment will allow flexibility in the use of the resources.
  2. Give special grants to schools that have large needs (for example, students reading below grade level).
  3. Increase cost recovery in tertiary education. Also, the student loan scheme should draw on private rather than public resources (the current scheme has not been financially self-sustaining), given the high private returns to tertiary education, and the high migration.

Crime and its Impact on Business

Jamaica has a strong democracy, high caliber bureaucracy and good regulatory framework. Jamaica has relatively strong democratic traditions and institutions (high level of political participation with voter turnouts of two-thirds in general elections, and a free media) and a high quality civil service (comparable to Chile, Hong Kong, France) according to cross-country surveys (see Figure 9 and Chapter 6, Table 6-1). In addition, Jamaica ranks highly in international comparisons of its regulatory framework. For example, it requires 37 days to start a firm in Jamaica, compared to 34 days in Chile).

However, strengths have not converted into comparable outcomes. Public satisfaction with government policies and government's ability to carry out its declared programs are below average in the cross-country comparisons. This public dissatisfaction could be partly explained by

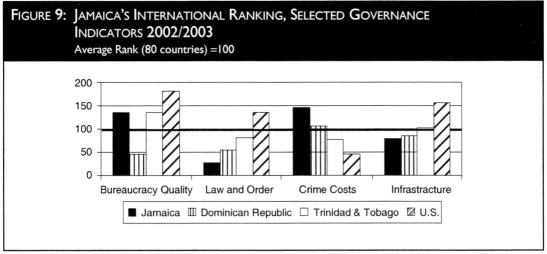

FIGURE 9: JAMAICA'S INTERNATIONAL RANKING, SELECTED GOVERNANCE INDICATORS 2002/2003
Average Rank (80 countries) =100

Legend: ■ Jamaica ▥ Dominican Republic ☐ Trinidad & Tobago ▨ U.S.

Source: See Table 6.1

the perception that quality of public service provision is below average. In addition, infrastructure quality is perceived to be low.

Unfortunately, very poor rule of law and crime negate the positive elements in the business environment. Crime has a negative effect on the development of human capital, creates incentives for migration, introduces inefficiencies into the economy, undermines the work ethic, and diverts resources from investment to crime management.

Jamaica is amongst the most violent countries in the world. In 2000, the recorded intentional homicide rate was 33 per 100,000 inhabitants (44 per 100,000 in 2001), lower only than Colombia (63) and South Africa (52). There has been a relatively steady increase in crime (as measured by the Crime Rate Index) over the decades (although the highest year for violent crime was 1980, a period of partisan political violence), with the increase in murders over the last ten years being highly visible. These trends reflect the serious social problems associated with growing urbanization, including high levels of unemployment, formation of gangs, creation of slums, and an escalation of drug trafficking.

Violence is pervasive, and hurts unemployed youth as well as business. While violence is an endemic feature of Jamaican society, it is often concentrated among the poorest in the society, and among young males, who often tend to be the victims as well as the perpetrators of violence (about 90 percent of murder victims, and more than 90 percent of the offenders are male). In a business victimization survey carried out for this report, about 42 percent of all managers felt that they were either highly likely (11 percent) or likely (31 percent) to be murdered at the workplace. Even in the context of the high murder rate in Jamaica, this is an alarming figure.

Government alone spends about 3 percent of GDP on crime control. Violent crimes cost Jamaica 0.6 percent of GDP in 2001, in terms of lost production and health expenses due to mortality and injury. Including government expenditure on crime control (defense, justice and correctional services, and police), crime results in direct costs to Jamaica of nearly 4 percent of GDP (see Table 6). Given Jamaica's fiscal position, the opportunity cost of these resources is very high, and in a less violent society at least a part of such resources could have been used for provision of critical economic and social services or infrastructure development.

The business victimization survey reveals the high costs that firms face. The costs of suffering crime and preventing crime are categorized as follows:

(i) **Firm closures.** Firms closed for an average of 3 days due to violence in 2001, and experienced losses, on average, of J$1 million (J$ 400,000 in 2000) in KMA.

(ii) **Looting.** Of the firms looted in 2001, 57 percent had losses of less than J$100,000, 19 percent losses between J$100,000 and J$500,000 and 4 percent losses between J$1 million and J$5 million.

(iii) **Maintaining security.** Private security expenditure by firms was about 2 percent of annual revenue of the average firm (or J$1 million) in 2001. These costs were as high as an average of 17 percent of annual revenue for micro-enterprises with annual revenue less than J$5 million, 7.6 percent for medium firms with annual revenue between J$10–20 million, and 0.7 percent for large firms.

(iv) **Installing security.** The cost of installing new security devices was on average 0.3–0.7 percent of the annual revenue of firms.

(v) **Cost of extortion, fraud, robbery/burglary and arson.** Average losses due to extortion, fraud, robbery and arson were highest in manufacturing and processing firms (5.7 percent of revenue) and distribution (2.5 percent). These sectors account for most of the firms in the less than J$5 million and J$20–50 million annual revenue group, where such losses are highest, about 9 percent of revenue (see Chapter 6, Table 6-6).

TABLE 6: THE ANNUAL ECONOMIC COST OF CRIME, 2001 (J$ million)	
I. Health Costs	1.3 bn (0.4% of GDP)
Public Health System	995.7
Private Citizens	254.5
II. Lost Production	0.5 bn (0.2% of GDP)
Mortality	194.1
Injury due to Crime	337.2
III. Public Expenditure on Security	10.5bn (3.1% of GDP)
Total I + II +III	**12.4 bn (3.7% of GDP)**
IV. Private Expenditure on Security	1.3% of revenue

Source: Harriott et al., 2003.

Impact on Business Practices and Prospects. In terms of qualitative/ordinal indicators of the impact of crime, the most frequently cited was the increase in the cost of providing security (see Table 7), reported by over 50 percent of firms. About 39 percent of firms indicated that crime has affected their plans for business expansion. Another 37 percent stated that crime has had a negative impact on their plans to invest in productivity improvement. Given that crime appears to be such an important factor limiting the growth of firms and limiting their investment in improvement in productivity, how do firms view their economic prospects in the next three years? About 18 percent of firms in the distributive trade reported that they expect to abandon operations in Jamaica if the crime situation does not improve. This is followed by tourism (15 percent), entertainment (14 percent), agriculture (11 percent) and manufacturing and processing (10 percent). In all cases (except tourism), firms were more likely to close permanently than to relocate outside of Jamaica. This data suggest a worst-case scenario in which GDP could decline by about 7.5 percent (calculated as weighted contributions of each sector in the economy) over the next three years, assuming that the survey above represents intentions of all firms in Jamaica.

Coping with crime strategies imply huge implicit costs. In response to the threat of criminal victimization, individuals and firms may adjust their activities in various ways such as refusing to work on a night shift and later opening times (see Chapter 6, Table 6-5), which raise the cost of capital. These adjustments may lead to reduced economic activity and loss of employment and income. Crime may create incentives for firms to relocate their operations outside of Jamaica and for individuals to migrate. For example one of the reasons for the departure of the textile factories was the inability to operate more than one shift. Crime can also lead to loss of productive time at work owing to injuries. The periodic closure of schools reduces educational quality, particularly in the poorer areas. The impact of crime on society goes beyond the purely material level. Crime and violence impose considerable psychological stress on the population, deplete social capital and generally reduce the quality of life of the people.

TABLE 7: IMPACT OF CRIME ON BUSINESS PRACTICE (%)						
	Highly Significant (1)	Significant (2)	Somewhat Significant (3)	Significant (1+2+3)	Insignificant	No Impact	Total Number of Respondents
Increased cost of security	18	17	16	**51**	11	38	300
Increased cost of services purchased	4	4	10	**18**	17	64	291
Negative impact on worker productivity	4	4	14	**22**	23	55	290
Negative impact on plans for business expansion	14	10	15	**39**	17	44	304
Negative impact on investments to improve productivity	10	10	17	**37**	16	47	301
Other	5	3	5	**13**	14	73	79

Source: Harriott et al., 2003.

The determinants of violent crimes in Jamaica. Econometric analysis (see Chapter 6, Annex 6-4) shows that the determinants of violent crimes in Jamaica are similar to those encountered in other countries (for Latin America see Fajnzylber et al., 2000): (i) negative incentives or deterrence factors, such as more imprisonment, more crimes cleared up, and tougher sentencing and (ii) positive incentives such as higher per capita income, more equality, and lower youth unemployment. Policies to reduce crime should consider both dimensions of the problem: to both increase the direct costs of committing crime (the expected punishment) and its opportunity cost (the loss of income in the formal labor market).

Policy Options. Better overall economic performance, in particular higher employment opportunities will reduce crime. Regarding the deterrent measures to control crime, even modest efforts will require additional resources from a country with a fiscal crisis and a stagnant economy. Based on the results of the survey, managers are unwilling to support increased taxes, but seem willing to provide financial support to specific collective solutions that directly affect them and over which there is some direct accountability. The policy options can be grouped under four themes:

Identify and measure the crime problem.

- Strengthen official data collection on crime.
- Conduct frequent general victimization surveys and specialized surveys on the susceptibility of crime to improve data on costs of crime, coping strategies, and to validate official data.

Improve law enforcement for crime deterrence.

- Upgrade investigative capacity of police to improve clear-up rates for violent crimes and thereby deter such crimes, and consider special measures to investigate murders (in 2001, only 42 percent of reported murders were cleared).

Improve social prevention measures to address the root causes of crime.

- Improve the quality of the school experience, especially for poor students. A significant fraction of the poor, and more so the males, tend to drop out of school, end up poorly educated and unemployed, and become susceptible to delinquent behavior. To address this, the disparities between different school types need to be reduced, and special efforts directed to schools that have large numbers of students reading below grade level (see Chapter 5). Also, school programs should be enhanced to include teaching of social and conflict resolution skills to students.

■ Form effective partnerships between the police, business and local communities, by setting common goals and sharing information.

■ Build social capital such as greater trust and lower tolerance to crime and violence, especially through interventions in the home, school and the workplace.

Apply focused interventions.

■ Target high crime urban areas, especially the Kingston Metropolitan Area, to reduce the impact of crime on the business community using a combination of measures suggested above, as was done in the case of Boston (see Chapter 6 and Annex H).

■ Target youth at risk with specific youth development programs in addition to the schooling focus mentioned above.

Improving Jamaica's International Competitiveness

Jamaica is a very open economy, with few trade barriers. It introduced capital account convertibility in 1991. It undertook significant tariff reform after 1991, which reduced the average tariff from an already moderate level of 20.3 percent to 8.9 percent in 2002. In 1991, it eliminated all quantitative restrictions and licensing requirements for exports and imports. Recent work by Dollar and Kraay (2001b) shows Jamaica as a "globalizer," meaning that it is in the top one-third of a group of 72 developing countries in terms of their increase in trade relative to GDP between 1975–79 and 1995–97. The study shows that the weighted average growth rate per capita of globalizing countries rose from 3.5 to 5 percent between the 1980s and 1990s, while that of the non-globalizing ones rose from 0.8 percent to only 1.4 percent. However, in Jamaica's case, the positive impact of trade and other structural reforms has been more than offset by other factors, resulting in disappointing GDP growth as discussed in Section V, Chapters 2 and 7, and Loayza et al. (2002).

Jamaica's competitiveness declined in the 1990s, which was reflected in loss of world export share and a lower export share of output. Figure 10 shows that Jamaica's share of world merchandise exports fell steadily from 0.036 percent in 1994 (and similar figures in the early 1990s) to 0.024 percent in 2001, a fall of one-third. This was accompanied by an even larger proportionate decline in the share of exports in GDP (in nominal terms), from 32 to 19 percent. If GDP growth was disappointing in the latter half of the 1990s, export growth was even more so. After doubling between the mid-1980s and end-1980s, merchandise exports have fallen since 1995. Manufacturing employment has declined since 1997 and manufacturing exports since 1995. Agricultural output and exports peaked in 1996, and have generally declined since then. Even the growth in tourist receipts slowed down in the second half of the 1990s.

The weak performance of exports and goods is closely linked to the behavior of the real exchange rate (REER), which is often itself considered as an indicator of competitiveness (as well as other factors making Jamaica "high-cost," see below). The REER (CPI-based), appreciated sharply from 1992–1998, with significant reversal of this after January 2002, and especially in 2003. The wage-based REER has appreciated even more than the CPI based REER, arising from the large wage increases over 1992–1998. Figures 10 and 11 show that the link between the REER and export shares is strong, and demonstrate the sensitivity of exports to the exchange rate, contrary to what is sometimes believed in Jamaica.

An appreciated exchange rate affects the pattern of growth. With an appreciated exchange rate, resources tend to flow to the more profitable non-tradables sector, leading to higher imports and lower exports. Also, overvalued exchange rates tend to affect growth through reduced produc-

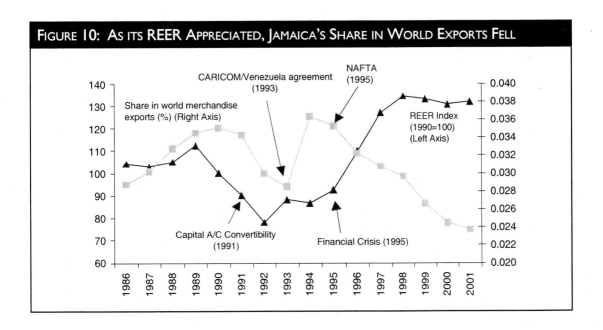

FIGURE 10: AS ITS REER APPRECIATED, JAMAICA'S SHARE IN WORLD EXPORTS FELL

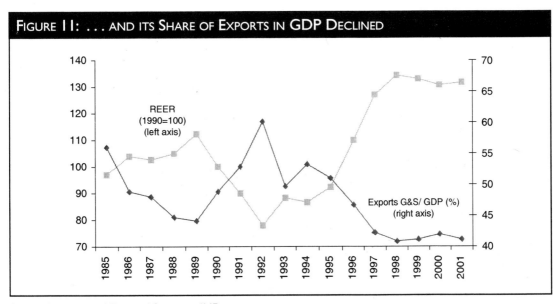

FIGURE 11: ... AND ITS SHARE OF EXPORTS IN GDP DECLINED

Source: International Financial Statistics, IMF.

tivity, since export and import competing sectors often see the most rapid productivity advances. Of course, an appreciated real exchange rate also stimulates imports, and in Jamaica's case the lower cost of food imports was probably a factor not only in depressing agricultural output but in reducing poverty.

The 1992–1998 appreciation of the real exchange rate made domestic adjustment to the tariff reduction more difficult. For example, after 1992, when tariffs were reduced as per the CARICOM agreement, the exchange rate was appreciating. A depreciation of the exchange rate during that period would have softened the competitive impact on the domestic sector. An appreciated exchange rate would also help to explain the increased pressures for protection (and the levying of increased stamp duty) since 2001 from the producers of agroproducts such as poultry, meat, and eggs.

The real exchange rate has depreciated in 2003, as a result of a substantial nominal exchange rate depreciation without significant pressure on inflation. Given the rising current account deficits (CAD) since 2001, as well as the worsening fiscal situation, pressure had been building up on the exchange rate. In the event, the nominal exchange rate did depreciate significantly in 2002 and especially in the first half of 2003. Between January 2002 and July 2003, the nominal effective exchange rate depreciated 24 percent, consumer prices rose 15 percent, and there was real depreciation of 18 percent. This behavior of the real exchange rate after depreciation is in line with recent research. According to a number of studies including one recently published in the Bank of Jamaica Research Papers (McFarlane, 2002), the pass-through factor from changes in the exchange rate to inflation has declined in the 1990s. This decline could arise from: a) the large gap between actual and potential output; b) years of low inflation, which themselves help to engender lower inflationary expectations; c) low current and projected world inflation; and d) the decline in protection in the 1990s, which has left a strong competitive pressure on prices.

The survey of exporting firms done for this report finds that export competitiveness has also been hurt by high wages, high crime, difficulties in accessing inputs, and high cost of utilities, all adding up to a high cost economy. Companies had been adversely affected by the wage increases, which exceeded productivity increases every year between 1992 and 1998, save 1994 (see Chapter 2). High crime has imposed large overhead costs on companies (see also Chapter 6)—in agroprocessing, increasing costs are incurred to ensure no drug contamination. Security costs can be as high as 5 percent of sales. Crime has also increased substantially the costs of night shifts in call centers and textiles, reducing their competitiveness with countries that work two or three shifts. In the all-important tourism industry, crime reduces the potential number of visitors and creates a need for higher costs in marketing and security. The exporting sector, as also the rest of the economy, is handicapped by slow customs procedures, which increases the cost of imported materials, including bottles and packaging materials. Small firms and start-ups have difficulty in accessing credit, because banks consider them too risky. Also, high cost and unreliable utility services have led firms to invest in expensive alternatives like stand-by electricity production.

Many of these problems are reflected in the decline of the apparel sector after 1995, which at one time had promised much, but whose exports fell off from US$533 million in 1995 to US$289 million by 2001. In the last five years, it has shed over 10,000 workers. Costs relating to labor, security, energy, along with an appreciated exchange rate, have meant that Jamaica has lost out to competitors like Haiti, the Dominican Republic, Honduras, and El Salvador, to name a few.

The adverse environment has affected even tourism, one sector that has done relatively well. Jamaica's most successful exports have been based on exploitation of natural resources, especially tourism and bauxite. Tourism, for example, continues to trade on its endowments of sun, sand, and beaches. However, tourism growth has slowed since 1995 (2.4 percent annual increase in dollar receipts over 1996–2001 compared to 9 percent over 1991–95), and Jamaica has lost market share to the Dominican Republic, Cancun and Aruba. The hotel business has been hurt by the increase in wages, the exchange rate appreciation (especially in the European market), harassment of tourists, and high security costs.

The scenario for export demand is largely favorable, in spite of erosion of preferences. Services have grown from 33 percent to 57 percent of GNFS exports over 1980–2001, mirroring similar orders of increase in world trade patterns. Jamaica's GDP is increasingly dominated by services (such as tourism and financial services), thus producing a positive congruence between world demand growth and Jamaica's production structure. In other areas including manufactures, Jamaica needs to worry less about growth areas in world trade, since it will always be a niche player and so can look to its own strengths. Finally, even though erosion of preferences is likely to hurt exports of sugar, bananas and apparel, these constitute a relatively small 11.3 percent of GNFS exports. In any case, Jamaica often does not fulfill its quota even in preferred commodities, demonstrating that its competitiveness problems are largely domestic. Other issues relating to ongoing developments in world trade in the context of Caricom's negotiations in the WTO, FTAA and with the EU will be addressed in the Bank's forthcoming report on competitiveness and trade issues in the Caribbean.

Policy options. Increasing exports and trade as well as FDI involves providing a supporting environment. In general, FDI cannot be expected to create competitiveness, and in fact foreign investors will invest in sectors and niches that they view as competitive. Improving competitiveness will involve:

- Ensuring that the recent gains and future potential gains in exchange rate competitiveness are preserved. Recent trends in the exchange rate indicate that this is possible. It will also require moderate nominal increases in wages in Jamaican dollars. At the same time, maintenance of credible fiscal policies will be required in order to prevent the possibility of an excessive correction in the exchange rate.
- Eliminating the stamp duties that are levied on selected imports, especially food, so as to limit the price increases that accompany exchange rate depreciation.
- Reducing crime, which is a major cost for exporters (Chapter 6).
- Improving the credit climate for small companies and start-ups (Chapter 3).
- Reducing the cost and providing better coverage of water and sewerage services, improving roads, especially rural roads, and the reliability of power supply, and ensuring that all these are fully financed by user charges, that is, by levying and increasing tolls and user fees on existing and upcoming infrastructure facilities.
- Improving access to imported inputs by making customs procedures more efficient.

PART II

MAIN REPORT

CHAPTER 1

GROWTH AND POVERTY REDUCTION IN JAMAICA

Poverty in Jamaica declined substantially in the latter half of the 1990s, from an estimated 27.5 percent of the population in 1995 to about 17 percent in 1999. Paradoxically, this decline occurred despite a major financial crisis and a small annual decline in measured GDP after 1995. The decline in poverty is probably due to several factors particular to the period: (a) output probably has grown somewhat faster than measured GDP; (b) the informal sector has provided incomes for many people who could not find formal sector work (see Chapter 2); (c) inflation, a "tax" on the poor, has fallen sharply; and (d) the relative price of food has fallen. In addition, rising real wages and remittances may have helped reduce poverty. However, rising real wages can cut both ways, because these, along with the appreciating real exchange rate and crime, have tended to reduce demand for labor in the formal private sector. Remittances, which have grown sharply in dollar terms, though not relative to GDP, have probably kept people out of poverty, but not contributed much to its decline.

Unfortunately, it is unlikely that the factors that reduced poverty in the latter half of the 1990s will continue to operate; indeed, the slowing impact of these factors may explain why the incidence of poverty has remained roughly constant since 1998.

A sustained reduction in poverty in the future is likely to depend on sustained growth in the Jamaican economy as well as the implementation of pro-poor policies. As cross country evidence demonstrates, on average poverty declines with growth, and poverty can be sustainably reduced with policies that encourage private sector demand for labor, improve empowerment of the poor and access to education, health and social services. Rural poverty will need special attention, since it will depend not just on improved growth in agriculture, (which will be helped by a more competitive exchange rate), but wider growth in the rural sector and better access to social services.

The chapter is divided into five sections. The first section provides a brief review of poverty trends, identifying four distinct stages. The second section presents a profile of the poor in Jamaica and the factors linked to poverty, such as large households and households headed by females, which are characteristic not only of poverty in Jamaica but in most countries. The third section examines the issue of rural poverty vs. urban poverty and finds that the rural poverty incidence is more than three times higher than in Kingston. The fourth section discusses the paradox of poverty reduction despite no measured growth in the latter half of the 1990s, examining the issues of the measurement of GDP and poverty as well as analyzing the possible impact on poverty of the reduction in inflation, the falling relative price of food, the growth in remittances and the growth in the informal sector. The fifth section summarizes and presents some suggestions for policy.

Poverty Incidence and Income Inequality

In 2001 the Jamaica Survey of Living Conditions (SLC)[1] reported that the incidence of poverty was 16.8 percent, down from 18.7 percent in 2000. The incidence of poverty in the rural areas, 24.1 percent in 2001, also declined, albeit marginally, from 25.1 percent in 2000. In the Kingston Metropolitan Area (KMA), where the poverty is well below the national average, the incidence of poverty fell to 7.6 percent, down from 9.9 percent in 2000.

BOX 1.1: MEASUREMENT OF POVERTY IN JAMAICA

Since 1989, the Government of Jamaica has been estimating poverty annually, based on a Living Standards Measurement Survey (LSMS), conducted by the Statistical Institute of Jamaica (STATIN). The survey uses a multistage stratified random sampling method to select dwellings of households in the Enumeration Districts (EDs). STATIN collects data by direct interview, on food and non-food consumption from a sample of representative households.

The absolute poverty lines used in estimating poverty in Jamaica are based on the food energy intake method and also factor in consumption of basic non-food necessities. The minimum food consumption basket was determined by the Ministry of Health based on a dietary survey of the bottom two quintiles of the population. The survey was used to develop a representative food basket that takes into account the minimum needs for energy, calcium, protein and iron. The minimum requirement was based on a PAHO/WHO recommended standard of 11,700 kcals for members of a reference family of five.

Speaking broadly, poverty in Jamaica seems to have gone through four phases (see Tables 1.1 and 1.2 and Figure 1.1). In the first phase, from independence until the first major oil price shock in 1973, it seems likely that poverty declined along with the strong growth in aggregate income. Between 1966 and 1973, the Jamaican economy grew at an average rate of 5 percent per annum, driven by the boom in bauxite and tourism, as well as fairly strong growth in a highly protected manufacturing sector. During this period, inflation averaged a moderate 7.5 percent per annum. In the second phase, from the mid-1970s to mid-1980s, it seems likely that poverty rose, especially in the mid-1980s. This period was marked by a second oil price shock in 1979, higher external interest rates, higher inflation and lower growth in Jamaica. A minimum wage policy was implemented and may have helped to double the share of the bottom quintile in consumption over 1971–1975. The increase in poverty towards the end of the period probably reflects the difficulty of sustaining poverty reduction in an environment of weak growth and high inflation.

The third phase, from the late eighties to 1998 reflects a trend decline in poverty interrupted in 1991 and 1992 by inflation and rising food prices, then again in 1995 and 1996 by the financial crisis (see Figure 1.1). A deepening of the structural adjustment process and the deregulation and liberalization of the economy marked the beginning of this period. The sharp rise in poverty in 1991 probably reflects not only the slow growth of income, massive inflation and devaluation, but also the removal of cross subsidies on food imports. However, the elimination of the Jamaica Com-

---

1. Published jointly by the Statistical Institute of Jamaica (STATIN) and the Planning Institute of Jamaica (PIOJ).

modity Trading Corporation monopoly, the removal of import food subsidies, and the real devaluation created greater incentives for domestic agriculture, which grew at an average rate of about 10 percent over the period 1992 to 1994. The possible explanations for the trend decline in poverty are: the possible underestimate of growth and the contribution of the informal sector; the reduction in the inflation "tax," which largely falls on the poor; the reduction in the relative price of food related to trade liberalization and the appreciation of the real exchange rate; and the rise of real wages. The changes in poverty during this period appear to be driven by large changes in the middle of the distribution of consumption, and not by changes around the poverty line, according to Handa et al. (2001). The food stamp program has limited extreme poverty and contributed to improving the welfare of the poor.[2]

TABLE 1.1: CONSUMPTION OF THE POOR, 1958–1988

| Year | Share of the poor Percent of Total Consumption | | Index of real per capita consumption (1988 = 100) | | |
	Bottom Quintile	Next Quintile	All Jamaica	Bottom Quintile	Next Quintile
1958	2.2	6.0	83	34	50
1971	2.0	5.0	110	41	56
1975	4.1	9.0	123	94	112
1984	4.2	9.5	102	80	98
1988	5.4	9.9	100	100	100

Source: World Bank, 1994, p. 15.

In the fourth phase, from 1998 to 2001, poverty has leveled off. The lack of further gains may reflect the leveling off of the factors that contributed to the decline in poverty noted above.

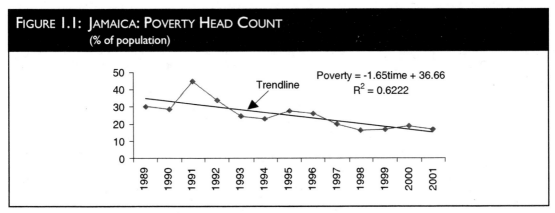

FIGURE 1.1: JAMAICA: POVERTY HEAD COUNT
(% of population)

Poverty = -1.65time + 36.66
R^2 = 0.6222

Trendline

Source: Survey of Living Conditions, PIOJ-STATIN, various issues.

In 2001, the poorest 20 percent of the population had 6.2 percent of national consumption, while the wealthiest 20 percent had 45.9 percent. This distribution of consumption would suggest Jamaica is a country with medium inequality, with less income inequality than most Latin American countries but more than most industrial countries. As shown in Table 1.1, there has been a

---

2. Ezmanari and Subbarao (1999) suggest that in the absence of a food stamp program, the poverty gap index in Jamaica would have been much worse in 1990–91. They also present evidence suggesting that in this period the program was most effective in helping the elderly poor and families with young children.

significant increase in the share of consumption of the poorest quintile of the population since 1975. However, inequality, as measured by the Gini coefficient of consumption in the SLC, has not changed much in Jamaica over the last decade, although poverty has fallen significantly and GDP growth has been negligible.[3]

	Head count Poverty Index (percent of population)	Rural Poverty (percent of population)	GINI Coefficient Consumption	Inflation (CPI, percent per year, Dec.–Dec.)	GDP Growth (percent per year)	Growth in Per Capita Real GDP J$ (percent per year)
TABLE 1.2: POVERTY AND SOCIAL AND ECONOMIC INDICATORS						
Year						
1989	30.4	40.7		17.2	7.0	6.4
1990	28.4	37.5	0.381	29.8	6.3	5.2
1991	44.6	57.2	0.397	80.2	0.8	0.0
1992	33.9	42.2	0.375	40.2	1.7	0.7
1993	24.4	29.6	0.372	30.1	2.0	1.0
1994	22.8	28.8	0.382	26.7	0.9	−0.1
1995	27.5	37.0	0.362	25.6	1.0	−0.1
1996	26.1	32.8	0.360	15.8	−1.1	−2.1
1997	19.9	27.4	0.416	9.2	−1.7	−2.7
1998	15.9	19.5	0.372	7.9	−0.3	−1.2
1999	16.9	22.0	0.379	6.8	−0.4	−1.1
2000	18.7	25.1	0.379	6.1	0.7	0.1
2001	16.8	24.1	0.384	8.7	1.7	1.2

Source: PIOJ, STATIN

Who are the Poor?

In Jamaica, the profile of the poor in the more recent SLC suggests that several interrelated factors are linked to poverty—large households, households headed by females, low educational attainment, unemployment, and dependence on rural employment—factors that are associated with poverty in most countries. About 23 percent of Jamaica's children live in poverty (PIOJ-STATIN, 2001) and they account for about half of all people living in poverty (UNICEF and PIOJ, 2000). In Jamaica, poverty also appears to be strongly correlated with social factors including: teenage pregnancy; single parenting; drug abuse; domestic violence; child abuse and delinquency, though these associations are more often the result of poverty, than its cause.

Individuals with the highest incidence of poverty are those in relatively large households, in all surveys from 1989–2001. Econometric work using data for 1999, 1997 and 1993, finds that those in larger households have a greater probability of being poor (Benfield, 2002). The link between large households and poverty is found in most countries. This probably reflects the fact that larger households have more dependents, which more than offsets any economies associated with household size in the use of durable goods. In Jamaica in 2001, the mean household size in the poorest quintile was 5.2, compared with 2.3 in the wealthiest. The geographic distribution for the 2001 JSLC showed the mean household size was highest in the rural areas at 3.62 and lowest in the Kingston Metropolitan Area at 3.19. The mean number of children was 1.27 in rural households compared with 0.96 for urban households. There is also a vicious cycle in that the poorer and rural

---

3. The lack of change in the Gini coefficient may reflect its insensitivity, and the fact that the same Gini can apply to more than one income distribution. For example, if the status of the poor improves, but the status of the middle class deteriorates, then the Gini could remain unchanged.

households tend to be larger because they are less educated about fertility and contraception and have less access to health facilities, and larger household size tends to makes the household poorer.

Female-headed households now account for about two-thirds of the households in poverty, and generally show a higher incidence of poverty in all the surveys since 1989. (The proportion of households headed by females has varied from 42 to 45 percent between 1990 and 2000). In 2001, per capita consumption in female-headed households (J$77,850) was nearly 10 percent lower than in male-headed households. The higher incidence of poverty in female-headed households is also related to the fact that female-headed households tend to be larger than those headed by males. In 2001, the average household size of the female-headed household was 3.6 persons compared with 3.2 persons for the male-headed household.

As is the case with other countries, the higher poverty incidence of households headed by females is partly explained by the correlation between households headed by females and single income households. Greater poverty incidence in female-headed households also probably reflects the higher open unemployment rates among women. In 2001, the unemployment rate among females was 21 percent, more than twice the rate for males (10.3 percent). The situation is little changed since 1990, when the female unemployment rate was 22.5 percent and the male rate 9.1 percent.

In Jamaica, the education of the household head is also a strong determinant of poverty, as in most countries. The SLC data suggest that while educational achievement is weak overall, the poor tend to have even less education. For example, the data for 2001 showed that 86 percent of the poor do not possess any academic qualification, compared to 52.3 percent of the wealthiest quintile, despite the progress since the early 1990s. Current data do suggest some hope—access to education is almost universal with 99.5 percent enrolment at the primary level (6–11 years), and 96.4 percent at the lower secondary level (12–14 years)—but it will take a while for this to work its way through the labor force. The mother's education has a significant impact on both grade attainment and current enrollment, while father's education is more important in determining current school enrollment than grade attainment (Handa 1996b). This creates the risk of a vicious cycle of low parental education and poverty leading to low education and poverty of the children. Also, poorer students get tracked into lower quality schools, which limits the benefits of education (see Chapter 5). The current data for Jamaica raise the concern of a cycle of chronic poverty, since poverty rates drop significantly only after the head of the household has completed the second cycle secondary school, and family income is the most consistently significant determinant of high school enrollment (Handa 1996b).

For policy purposes, another important dimension of poverty is the vulnerability of those close to the poverty line. Consistent with the general decline in poverty, vulnerability appears to be somewhat less in 2000 than in 1993. According to data from the SLC in 1993, of the population at or above the poverty line, 37.5 percent had per capita consumption between 0–25 percent above the poverty line. In 2000, that figure had fallen to 31.4 percent. Of the population below the poverty line, in 1993, 15.1 percent had per capita consumption 0–20 percent below the poverty line. By 2000, the figure had fallen to 10.1 percent. Regarding the sensitivity of poverty to the choice of the specific poverty line, Handa et al. (2001) used Kernel density estimates of per capita consumption to analyze the behavior of consumption distribution for several periods between 1991 and 1998 and conclude that poverty headcount rates are not sensitive to the specific choice of poverty line.

Rural vs. Urban Poverty

The incidence of poverty in the rural areas at 24.1 percent is more than three times higher that in Kingston (Table 1.3). Poverty has generally declined over time in both urban and rural areas, but at a much faster rate in the Kingston Metropolitan Area. As a result, the incidence and the relative incidence of poverty are higher in the rural areas. The stubbornness of poverty in the rural areas is reflected by the fact that in 2001, despite an almost 17 percent increase in per capita consumption in the rural areas, the incidence of poverty declined by only 1 percent (PIOJ-STATIN, 2001). Nonetheless, urban poverty tends to receive more attention from the government due to concerns that it may be associated with higher crime, violence, and other anti-social behavior that contribute to perpetuating chronic poverty by limiting access to social services including education (closing of schools) or restricting employment opportunities. This is partly due to the fact that urban poverty tends to be concentrated in inner city areas.

The incidence of rural poverty also exhibits more volatility—over 1991–2001, the standard deviation of rural poverty was 10.8, versus 6.1 for urban poverty. A cursory examination of the data suggests that when agricultural GDP growth has been high (above 10 percent) there has been a corresponding sharp reduction in the incidence of rural poverty. For example, in 1992 and 1993, when the agricultural sector grew by 13 percent and 10 percent respectively, the rural headcount ratio fell from 57.2 in 1991 to 42.2 in 1992 and 29.6 in 1993. Thus, rural poverty dropped sharply after subsidized food imports were eliminated in 1991 and agricultural production increased, but then has fallen only slowly as agricultural production fell. In 2000, when agricultural GDP contracted by 10.9 percent, rural poverty rose from 22 percent in 1999 to 25.1 percent in 2000. The volatility in the level of rural poverty is related not only to policy changes but also to the fact that the welfare of many rural people is tied directly or indirectly to the weather, rain-fed agriculture and seasonal work. Given the duality of agriculture, it is likely that small farmers constitute a large proportion of the rural poor.

Notwithstanding the above, the overall correlation between growth in agriculture and rural poverty is low (0.27), suggesting that the performance of the agricultural sector may be only a small part of the puzzle of high rural poverty. At the very basic level, this suggests that rural poverty in Jamaica cannot be fixed by only focusing on agriculture or even domestic agriculture. To be sure, much can be achieved by taking actions to increase the productivity in agriculture through improvements in research and extension as well as improving road and irrigation infrastructure. However, many of the rural poor are those left behind, who are hard to reach, including unemployed youth who are not engaged in agriculture.

TABLE 1.3: POVERTY IN RURAL AND URBAN AREAS (percent of population)											
Regions	1991	1992	1993	1994	1995	1996	1997	1998	1999	2000	2001
KMA	28.9	18.8	16.7	13.8	15.0	17.2	9.3	8.6	10.6	9.9	7.6
Other Towns	31.4	29.9	22.9	20.0	22.8	22.0	14.8	13.4	12.1	16.6	13.3
Rural	57.2	42.2	29.6	28.8	37.0	32.8	27.4	19.5	22.0	25.1	24.1
Jamaica	44.6	33.9	24.4	22.8	27.5	26.1	19.9	15.9	16.9	18.7	16.9
Rural/KMA/a	1.98	2.24	1.77	2.09	2.47	1.91	2.95	2.27	2.07	2.53	3.17

a: Ratio of rural poverty to KMA poverty.
Source: Jamaica Survey of Living Conditions, various issues.

Poverty Reduction With No Growth: "The Paradox of the 1990s"

Poverty has declined over the 1990s despite negligible or even negative measured GDP growth, as mentioned above (see Figure 1.2). The decline in poverty appears whatever poverty metric is applied to the SLC.[4] What, therefore, has been responsible for the marked reduction in poverty over this period? The following subsections discuss possible explanations for the decline in poverty over the 1990s: measurement errors in GDP and the SLC, the informal economy, real wage trends, falling inflation, falling relative prices of food, and the possible role of remittances.

---

4. The poverty gap and the severity of poverty also declined (Sanchez-Paramo and Steele, 2002).

Measurement Issues

Questions have been raised regarding both the measurement of GDP growth and the measurement of poverty. Regarding the measurement of GDP growth, some evidence suggests that both consumption growth and overall GDP growth may be underestimated. (see Chapter 2). For example, the consumption of meat and fish grew at an average annual rate of 6.4 percent between 1995 and 2001, compared with a much slower growth of 0.7 percent per annum in the previous five years; household electricity consumption also grew (see Chapter 2, Box 1). STATIN has alluded to the fact that such underestimation may be attributed not to the methodology used by STATIN but possibly to weakness in the sources of input (some from surveys) to the National Income estimates. If GDP growth has been underestimated, then the paradox may be somewhat less. If GDP growth is being consistently underestimated by, say, 1.5 percentage points per year during the latter half of the 1990s, even considering the financial crisis years of 1996 and 1997, GDP growth per capita would average about 0.3 percent between 1995 and 2000. Assuming an elasticity of −1.0 of change in the head count with respect to change in GDP growth per capita, poverty would decline, on average, by about 0.3 percentage points per year. However, this would still leave the head count poverty index well above 20 percent in 2000.

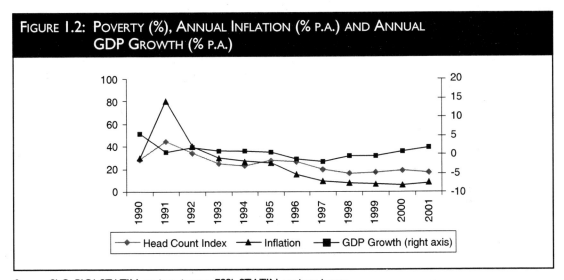

FIGURE 1.2: POVERTY (%), ANNUAL INFLATION (% P.A.) AND ANNUAL GDP GROWTH (% P.A.)

Source: SLC, PIOJ-STATIN, various issues; ESSJ, STATIN, various issues.

Questions have also been raised regarding the accuracy of the JSLC in the measurement of poverty, particularly in 1997 when the JSLC reported a significant fall in the level of poverty, from 26.1 percent of the population in 1996 to 19.9 percent in 1997.[5] Correspondingly, the ratio of consumption in the SLC to consumption in the national accounts rose from 66.7 percent in 1996 to 85.2 percent in 1997, the highest figure between 1990 and 1997 (1997 SLC and 2001 National Income and Product). However, STATIN explicitly denies any change in the methodology for the JSLC. Of course, one could interpret the sudden change to over-estimation of poverty before 1997 as well as underestimation in 1997. Nonetheless, there does seem to be a fall in poverty from the early 1990s to 1996, albeit with poverty rising after 1994, as might be expected in a macroeconomic and financial crisis. After 1997, poverty incidence falls again and then levels off, varying between 16 and 18 percent between 1998 and 2002. Overall, poverty does seem to have declined. This is in accord

_____

5. *The Jamaica Gleaner,* October 30, 1999.

with other estimates of poverty, which are generally higher than the JSLC estimates but also show a decline in poverty between 1995 and 2000 (See Benfield, 2002, for some alternative estimates).

The Informal Sector, A Residual Source of Employment

The informal sector, including the drug industry, may be a source of underestimation of GDP (see Chapter 2) and has been a residual source of employment. Employment in the informal sector (as roughly proxied by own account workers, see Annex Table A2.7) was roughly constant over the latter half of the 1990s. Although this is not a strong performance, it is much better than total private employment, which declined about 7 percent during the same period, or overall employment (including the public sector), which declined by about 3 percent. Reflecting the above trends, the share of own account workers in the employed labor force rose from 34.4 percent to 36.4 percent over 1995–2001, a figure that rises to 40.2 percent if public sector employment is excluded. Generally speaking, the informal sector tended to increase faster than the formal sector over the last three decades (Witter and Kirton, 1990; IADB, 2002). The relative growth of the informal sector may reflect the decline in demand for labor outside the public sector, reflecting the slow growth of the formal economy and in its demand for labor, discussed above. The recent changes in informal sector employment and private employment are positively correlated, suggesting that both are determined by the same factor, for example, aggregate demand. However, the *declines* in informal sector employment are generally much less in absolute size than formal private employment. These figures suggest that informal employment has helped some workers avoid poverty. To account for the fall in poverty, it is likely that informal employment and earnings from the informal sector would have to be under-reported, which may be the case, as discussed in Chapter 2. However, the general trends suggest that informal employment, as reported, cannot account for the large fall in poverty during the 1990s.

Informal sectors workers tend to have fewer years of schooling and earn less than formal sector workers. A recent study finds that, on average, informal sector workers earn about 36 percent less than workers in the formal sector (IADB, 2002). However, these workers pay no direct taxes, or licensing fees, reducing the difference in net income between the formal and informal sectors. For example, an informal taxi avoids the costs of operation associated with registering with the Transport Authority and purchases insurance for a private vehicle rather than insurance for a public passenger vehicle, which may be significantly higher. Thus, the high cost of being in the formal sector is another factor leading to the growth of the informal sector (see Chapter 3).

Rising Real Wages but Falling Employment

Another possible explanation of the decline in poverty is the increase in real wages (Table 1.4), though that increase has probably also contributed to the loss of private sector employment, particularly among females. Nominal earnings rose by 107 percent between 1995 and 2000, outstripping the CPI index, which increased by 71 percent. In the early 1990s, with the liberalization of the current account and the removal of exchange rate controls, the country suffered a series of severe foreign exchange shocks and exchange rate depreciations,[6] accommodated by loose monetary policy, all of which led to high inflation. Strong trade union pressure forced many employers into wage settlements above the high inflation rates and led some companies that could not afford the high wage settlements to fire workers, go out of business, or limit their new hiring.

In 1995, the Government embarked on a policy of disinflation, underpinned by a tight monetary policy based on base money targeting. Inflation fell from 25.6 percent in 1995 to 9.2 percent in 1997 and has remained in single digits since then. However, backward-looking labor contracts and rising public sector wages continued to raise wages in excess of inflation and real wages in large firms and the public sector rose significantly. However, employment shrank in the formal sector outside the government as a result of the rising real wages, as well as the loss of competitiveness in goods production due to the appreciating real exchange rate and the cost of crime (see Chapters 2 and 7). Over the latter half

---

6. For example, the average annual exchange rate moved from J$12.12/US$1.00 in 1991 to J$22.96/US$1.00 in 1992.

of the 1990s, formal private employment declined by about 7 percent, and female employment declined by over 30,000. In 2002, employment apparently rose, along with GDP growth, but this was almost all due to increased public sector employment—mainly short-term contracts—and there are also problems of comparability of the data (see Chapter 2). In sum, the net effect of the rise in real wages on the overall poverty headcount is difficult to establish, not only because many formal sector employees may already have been above the poverty line, but also because of the potential negative effect on employment, particularly new hires and females, who are more likely to be poor.

TABLE 1.4: MOVEMENT IN AVERAGE WAGES AND EARNINGS COMPARED TO INCREASE IN CPI

Quarter Ending	CPI Jan 1986 = 100	Increase Over Preceding Year CPI	Average Earnings Per Employee ($)	Increase over Preceding Year (Earnings)	Average Wages per Employee $	Increase over Preceding Year (Wages)
September 1995	789.2	17.6%	3,579	37.9%	2,317	25.0%
September 1996	989.0	25.3%	4,246	18.6%	2,567	10.8%
September 1997	1084.5	9.7%	5,367	26.4%	3,191	24.3%
September 1998	1175.8	8.4%	5,981	11.4%	3,369	5.6%
September 1999	1276.3	8.6%	6,751	12.9%	3,747	11.2%
September 2000	1349.3	5.7%	7,408	9.7%	4,150	10.7%

Source: STATIN, Employment, Earnings and Hours Worked in Large Establishments. Various issues

The national income data of the national accounts data corroborates the picture of improving income of formal sector workers, at the expense of profits, but also, surprisingly, a rise in the average income in the informal sector. As a percentage of GDP, compensation of formal sector employees increased from 41 percent in 1994 to a peak of 49.2 percent in 1999, before declining slightly in 2000 and 2001. At the same time, operating surplus, as a percentage of GDP, fell from 38.9 percent in 1994 to 29.2 percent in 2001 (Table 1.5).

TABLE 1.5: FACTOR INCOME SHARE

Year	Compensation of Employees, Percent increase	Compensation of Employees, percent of GDP	Operating Surplus, Percent increase	Operating Surplus, Percent of GDP	Nominal GDP Growth, Percent per year
1991	44.5	41.7	59.9	39.6	48.2
1992	76.2	39.2	96.1	41.3	87.8
1993	49.9	42.1	24.3	36.9	39.4
1994	30.3	41.0	41.4	38.9	33.8
1995	39.2	45.2	7.5	33.1	26.3
1996	24.7	47.5	10.7	30.9	18.7
1997	10.8	48.4	10.2	31.3	8.7
1998	7.4	49.1	−0.8	29.3	6.0
1999	7.8	49.2	4.5	28.5	7.6
2000	10.8	48.7	13.4	28.9	11.9
2001	7.8	48.3	10.0	29.2	8.8

Source: STATIN, National Income and Product

The Falling Inflation Tax: A Pro-Poor Policy

Another factor that may explain the reduction in poverty, despite Jamaica's slow growth is the sharp reduction in inflation, which Dollar and Kraay (2001a) have called a "super-pro-poor" policy. Many other authors also have argued that keeping inflation low is beneficial to the poor.[7] This is not surprising, since high inflation taxes the limited assets of the poor, which are mostly in currency, much more than it taxes the assets of the middle and upper classes.[8]

In Jamaica, there seems to be a strong correlation between high inflation and increased incidence of poverty (see, for example, King and Handa, 2000). Jamaica's inflation jumped from 29.8 percent in 1990 to 80.2 percent in 1991, due, among other things, to a sharp depreciation of the exchange rate, accommodating monetary policy, and the decision to allow the utilities and the Jamaica Commodity Trading Company to pass on the real cost of goods and services to consumers. The reduction in the subsidy on imports and the removal of price controls were in keeping with the strategy to liberalize the economy. In addition, the implementation of the General Consumption Tax in 1991 may have also contributed to the sharp rise in prices. During that period, the headcount poverty ratio increased dramatically from 28.4 to 44.6 percent, as shown in Figure 1.2 and Table 1.2. With the fall in inflation, poverty also fell. In the latter half of 1995, the government intensified its stabilization program. Since 1997, Jamaican inflation has been reduced to single digits (Table 1.2), and at the same time, poverty has fallen. Statistically, there is a high correlation between the poverty head count and inflation.[9]

As noted above, in the last few years, the reduction in poverty has leveled off. Partly this may reflect the leveling off of inflation at low levels. Declines in inflation from its already low levels are unlikely to generate much additional reduction in the inflation tax, and thus not have much additional effect on poverty reduction.

The Fall in the Relative Price of Food

Relative prices of food also have fallen, contributing to the reduction in poverty because of the large role that food plays in the budget of the poor (Table 1.6). According to the 2001 SLC, mean annual per capita food consumption constituted 55.7 percent of the budget of the poorest quintile compared to 36.6 percent of the wealthiest. The opening of the economy, the sharp devaluation, and the elimination of the monopoly and subsidies on food imports in the early 1990s, initially led to a rise in the relative price of food. However, since 1995, the relative price of food has fallen by about 10 percent. This fall reflects lower prices of primaries worldwide, the real appreciation of the exchange rate and the decline in trade protection. The fall in the relative price of food has reflected very clearly in the budgets of the poor—the share of the poorest quintile's household budget spent on food declined from 66 percent in 1991 to 55.7 percent in 2001. On average, the fall in relative food prices after 1995 would have helped to reduce and then stabilize the poverty ratio, especially once there were no further gains in poverty reduction to be had from reduction of overall inflation since 1997.

---

7. See, for example, Bruno and Easterly (1995). Romer and Romer (1998) have found that the income share of the poorest quintile is inversely related to inflation, using panel data. Bulir (1998) found that the effect of inflation on inequality is not linear-reductions in inflation from hyperinflationary levels lower income inequality much more than further reductions to low inflation levels.

8. The high inflation tax was partly offset by the increased availability of US dollars in Jamaica after liberalization. However, the use of Jamaican dollars, which are subject to loss of purchasing power during inflation, continues to dominate the day-to-day transactions by the poor.

9. The estimated equation is:

Poverty Head Count = 16.5 + 0.37* Inflation
"t"statistics   (7.5) $R^2_{adj.} = 0.90$

where ** signifies a variable is statistically significant at the 95 percent level or better.
The jumps in poverty and inflation in 1991 contribute to the significance of the result, but even excluding 1991 the relation between inflation and poverty is significantly positive.

The Role of Remittances

Waves of migration since the early sixties have resulted in a significant Jamaican diaspora in North America and Europe (mainly England). Strong family ties in Jamaica including dependent parents and children as well as demand for retirement real estate in Jamaica have resulted in a significant inflow of private remittances, which reached nearly US$1 billion in 2001 (see Table 1.7). Remittances are really the flip side of the massive brain drain and skills migration, which Jamaica has experienced over the past several years. In Jamaica, it is estimated that remittances from overseas average about US$700 per year for the families that receive them. Internal remittances, mainly from urban centers to rural areas are also important. Internal remittances average about J$3,000 to J$3,500 or about US$50–US$70 per transaction and tourist centers figure prominently as starting points for these flows. This income support from remittances may in fact be the means by which many families have remained above the poverty line. In the Consultations with the Poor (1999) it is reported that in some rural areas, 40 percent of households derive significant financial support from relatives working abroad or in one of the major cities.

Remittances are a significant part of the coping strategy of the poor, and may be a significant factor in reducing vulnerability but it is less clear that they explain the sharp fall in poverty after 1995. Between 1995 and 2001, private remittance inflows to Jamaica grew at an average rate of nearly 8 percent per year in US dollars. The increase may be due not only to a rise in migration, but also to the increased efficiency and security of transferring money to Jamaica that resulted from the rapid growth of the remittance companies in the mid-nineties. However, remittances have risen only about 1.5 percentage points of GDP over 1995–2001—the difference between the figures in US dollars and those relative to GDP reflects the real appreciation of the Jamaican dollar. In fact, remittances actually fell by about 2 percentage points of GDP between 1995 and 1998. Hence it seems unlikely that (recorded) remittances from overseas can explain the sharp fall in poverty.

TABLE 1.6: JAMAICA CPI ANNUAL INDEX AND RELATIVE PRICE OF FOOD

Year	All Items	Food	Food price ratio
1990	139	145.9	1.05
1991	208.1	227.8	1.09
1992	389.9	425.4	1.09
1993	447.8	473.7	1.06
1994	692.3	757.6	1.09
1995	869.3	966.6	1.11
1996	1006.9	1083.1	1.07
1997	1099.2	1179.8	1.07
1998	1185.5	1226.6	1.03
1999	1256.6	1254.81	0.99
2000	1359.7	1342.65	0.99
2001	1454.85	1388.3	0.95

Source: STATIN

TABLE 1.7: PRIVATE REMITTANCE INFLOWS
(US$ millions)

Year	Postal System	Financial System	Remittance Companies	Others	Total
1990	4.7	164.5	0	15.0	184.2
1991	2.8	170.0	0	10.5	183.3
1992	2.4	223.4	0	59.4	285.2
1993	1.8	201.2	0	128.0	331.0
1994	1.3	321.6	138.8	18.3	480.0
1995	1.4	407.0	178.1	26.1	612.6
1996	1.3	408.0	228.1	14.8	652.2
1997	1.2	387.3	253.8	18.9	661.2
1998	1.2	370.2	283.3	22.4	677.1
1999	1.2	322.8	357.0	23.4	704.4
2000	1.2	334.6	453.7	24.8	814.3
2001	1.2	372.5	566.2	25.8	965.7

Source: Bank of Jamaica

Summary and Issues for the Future

The characteristics of poverty in Jamaica are similar to poverty in most developing countries. The poor are more likely to be members of larger households, in female-headed households, have less education, and employed in the rural sector—agriculture or fishing.

Poverty in Jamaica has fallen substantially over the 1990s, despite negligible or negative measured GDP growth, owing to a confluence of factors particular to the period. First, it is possible that output has grown somewhat more than measured GDP (see Chapter 2). Second, the informal sector and the underground economy have continued to provide employment, which may be one of the factors in the underestimate of GDP. Third, inflation, a "tax" that particularly hits the poor because of their use of currency, has fallen. Fourth, the relative price of food has fallen, reflecting the falling price of imported food because of both trade liberalization and the appreciation of the currency. In addition, rising real wages (arising partly from backward indexed wage contracts, and partly from strong union pressure) and remittances may have helped reduce poverty. However, the impact of rising real wages on poverty is mitigated by the likelihood that many formal sector employees already had incomes above the poverty line and because the rising real wages (along with the appreciating real exchange rate) contributed to a decline in formal sector employment that particularly affected females. Remittances have grown sharply in dollar terms, but their effect on poverty seems to be one of maintaining incomes, rather than raising people out of poverty.

For the period 1989–2001, a strong statistical relationship exists between poverty and real GDP, inflation, and the relative price of food.[10] This relationship explains relatively well not only the sharp rise in poverty in 1991 but also the observed fall in poverty (see Figure 1.3). According to that relationship, the elasticity of the head count with respect to GDP (percent change in the headcount divided by the percent change in GDP) is 2.8, a relatively large figure by international standards. This elasticity implies a ten-percent increase in real GDP would reduce the head count by the relatively larger figure of 28 percent, i.e., from the 17 percent currently to 12 percent. A ten-percentage point fall in inflation would reduce the poverty head count by 3 percentage points, i.e., from 17 percent to 14 percent and a ten-percentage point reduction in the relative price of food would reduce the poverty head count by almost 4 percentage points, i.e. from 17 percent to 13 percent. Of course, these estimates reflect both any underestimate of GDP growth and the other factors that were occurring during the decade and their correlation with the three variables.[11]

Unfortunately, it is unlikely that the macroeconomic factors that contributed to the recent poverty reduction and offset the impact of slow growth on GDP will continue to operate in the next few years. Indeed the slowing impact of these factors may explain why the incidence of poverty has leveled off since 1999. Further gains from falling inflation and lower relative food prices are unlikely—inflation has leveled off and the real exchange rate has begun to depreciate. Only further reductions in protection of agriculture, such as cuts in stamp duties, are likely to limit rises in relative prices of food. Growth of the informal sector has helped maintain employment and contributed to unmeasured GDP growth, but it is unlikely to grow rapidly without faster growth in measured GDP. Whatever the impact of rising real wages has been, it is unlikely that employers will be able to continue to give wage increases in excess of inflation and productivity, given the openness of the economy and associated competitive pressures. Pressures for wage increases not justified by higher productivity are likely to continue to reduce employment and to slow growth,

---

10. The estimated equation is:

Poverty Head Count = 48.1 − 0.0036** Real GDP + .030** Inflation + 37.8* Rel Price of Food (base = 1.0)
"t" statistics   (−2.8)   (6.4)   (1.9) $R^2_{adj.}$ = 0.90

where ** signifies a variable is statistically significant at the 95 percent level or better, * at the 90 percent level or better. Real GDP is measured in millions of J$ in 1986 prices, inflation is measured in percentage points per year from December to December, and the Relative price of food is measured with 1988 as the base year equal to 1.0.

Estimates using the real exchange rate instead of the relative price of food were not quite as good in statistical terms, perhaps reflecting the fact that the relative price of food reflects changes in protection as well as the real exchange rate. Estimates using real GDP per capita were nearly as good in statistical terms, but yielded improbably high estimates of the relationship between GDP and poverty.

11.   For example, the estimated impact of inflation included both the decline in the inflation tax and the extent to which real wage increases caused by "backward looking" labor contracts reduced poverty.

FIGURE 1.3: JAMAICA: POVERTY HEAD COUNT ACTUAL AND REGRESSION PREDICTION

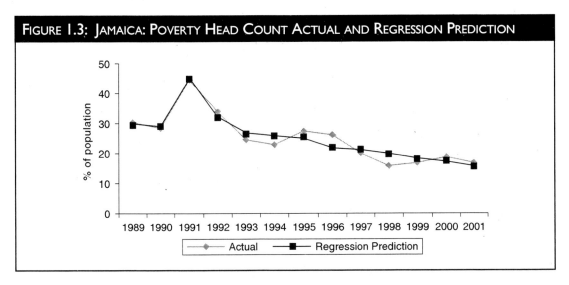

Source: Poverty data from SLC, PIOJ-STATIN.

especially since the need for fiscal stringency will reduce the public sector's demand for labor. Remittances may play a greater role in poverty reduction in the future, assuming remittances continue to grow in dollar terms and the real exchange rate depreciates. Finally, it should be noted that in all countries poverty becomes harder to reduce as the proportion of people in poverty decline. A closely related point, as suggested by international experience, is that the elasticity of poverty with respect to GDP declines as the level of GDP rises.

Future sustained reduction in poverty is therefore likely to depend on sustained growth in the Jamaican economy as well as the implementation of policies to ensure that the poor are empowered to take advantages of the opportunities that arise from increased growth. A recent World Bank study, based on cross-country regressions, suggests that on average the income of the poor rises one-for-one with overall growth (Dollar and Kraay, 2001a).

It will also be important to ensure that Jamaica's growth is pro-poor—that growth raises the income of the poor at least as much as average income growth, if not more. The poor face a number of problems in benefiting from growth alone. This is illustrated by the aforementioned World Bank study, which implied that in half the countries, income of the poor rose less rapidly than overall growth. As in most countries, Jamaica's poor are more likely to be members of larger households, be in female-headed households, have less education, and be employed in the rural sector—agriculture or fishing. In Jamaica, poverty also appears to be strongly correlated with social factors including: teenage pregnancy; single parenting; drug abuse; domestic violence; and child abuse and delinquency, though these associations are often the result of poverty, rather than its cause. As the cross-country evidence demonstrates, policies that promote growth in demand for labor, and access to education, health and social services (as discussed in Chapters 2, 5, and 7), can help to reduce poverty, reduce the vulnerability of the poor and allow the poor to take advantage of opportunities that are generated when the economy grows. Policies that address structural rigidities in factor markets will also be important to ensure that Jamaica's growth is broad-based.

Rural poverty is also an issue that should be addressed. The incidence of poverty in the rural areas, at 24.1 percent, is more than three times higher than that in Kingston. However, the low correlation between the fortunes of agriculture and the level of rural poverty suggests that rural poverty issues are much broader than agriculture alone and the non-farm productive sector may require attention. There is therefore need for a comprehensive rural strategy that embraces the multidimensional nature of rural development, including addressing issues of governance, infrastructure and the cost of credit.

CHAPTER 2

UNDERSTANDING GROWTH IN JAMAICA

Jamaica's measured GDP growth was low in the 1990s while, paradoxically, measured investment was high.[1] Average growth actually was negative in the period 1996–2001 as output fell in agriculture and manufacturing. Jamaica's lack of growth is often explained by the financial crisis (discussed in Chapter 4) and the poor external climate, which offset the gains from the liberalization of the early 1990s. In addition, the appreciation in the real exchange rate, which arose from the post crisis stabilization, and the rise in real wages hurt tradable goods production especially. Another factor in the loss of competitiveness has been the cost of crime. Even tourism, priced in US dollars, has grown slowly and suffered a decline in market share, as the rising costs in dollars limited growth and cut into the earnings of investors and the government from tourism. Rising government consumption also burdened the economy. GDP growth may have been underestimated, however. Much of any underestimation of growth appears to be in services, which are always difficult to measure, and in the informal sector. Nonetheless, growth, even adjusting for a possible underestimation of 1–2 percentage points per year, was low.

At the same time, much of the investment of the early 1990s has produced little output, suggesting the capital stock is overestimated and the high recent investment rate was concentrated in particular sectors that, while profitable, may suffer from distortions. Investments made in the early 1990s are often underutilized currently, because of overbuilding, high costs measured in foreign currency, and difficulties of running multiple shifts in a high crime environment. Some capital was also destroyed in hurricanes. Investments in security of course yield no measured additional output and, indeed, crime may reduce the productivity of the existing capital stock by reducing multiple shift operations. Recent investment was concentrated in hotels, mining, telecommunications, and housing, where in some

---

1. This report does not explore issues relating to volatility of income and growth, which small, open economies like Jamaica's are susceptible to. Volatility arises from frequent natural disasters, openness to trade, and lack of economies of scale. Small size also limits the ability to establish institutions that would normally help manage exposure to shocks. For more details on volatility in the Caribbean countries at both the macro and household levels, see World Bank (2002c).

cases measuring output is not easy and in some cases distortions may have reduced investment's contribution to production in the national accounts, even though it yielded benefits to the investor.

Whatever growth occurred, it did not generate much employment—private sector employment has fallen, particularly in the formal private sector. This decline seems related to the loss of external competitiveness and the large increases in real wages, which fed back into a loss of competitiveness (discussed in Chapter 7). Slow growth in employment opportunities and the high crime have probably contributed to the massive migration of secondary and tertiary graduates, which in turn raises the issue of the large subsidy to higher education.

Generating higher growth will not be easy. The informal sector has only limited potential without growth in the rest of the economy and does not present many opportunities for productivity gains. Ultimately, growth will depend on a policy environment that increases external competitiveness as well as key infrastructure investments.

Slow Growth, High Investment, Low Employment Generation

Although poverty has declined recently, Jamaica's recent GDP growth has been negligible, as it was over most of the last 20 years and was actually negative in 1996–1999 (Table 2.1). The only exception to slow growth was the latter half of the 1980s. During the 1990s, Jamaica's per capita GDP growth was in the lowest quartile of countries (Loayza et al. 2002 data base); its TFP growth was amongst the lowest in Latin America and the Caribbean (Annex Table A2.5). GDP growth turned positive in 2000 and was 1.7 percent in 2001 and 1 percent in 2002, but this barely offset the decline over the previous four years.

TABLE 2.1: JAMAICA—GDP GROWTH, EMPLOYMENT GROWTH AND INVESTMENT RATES: 1981–2001

| | Average | | | | 1996 | 1997 | 1998 | 1999 | 2000 | 2001 | Average |
	1981–1985	1986–1990	1991–1995	1996–2000							1996–2001
	Percent per year										
GDP growth	0.1	4.9	0.9	−0.7	−1.3	−2.0	−0.5	−0.4	0.7	1.7	−0.3
Employment growth	1.7	2.6	1.5	−0.6	−0.4	−1.4	0.7	−1.0	−1.1	0.6	−0.4
	Percent of GDP (nominal)										
Gross Cap Formation % GDP	20.4	22.7	27.8	27.8	29.7	29.8	26.7	25.1	27.6	30.1	28.2
Construction % GDP	10.0	10.8	13.1	12.2	12.6	12.2	12.0	12.4	12.0	12.2	12.2
Machinery & Equip. % GDP	7.3	7.8	9.9	10.9	12.8	10.8	10.2	9.1	11.7	13.4	11.3
Transport % GDP	3.1	3.4	4.3	4.5	4.2	6.6	4.3	3.5	3.7	4.3	4.4
Public Investment	8.0	6.9	5.0	3.9	5.6	5.1	2.7	3.1	2.9	—	—
Private Fixed Cap Formation	12.4	15.8	22.8	23.9	24.1	24.7	24.0	22.0	24.7	—	—

Memo:						
Sources of Growth 1991–2000	Estimated GDP Growth	Est. Contrib. to Growth:	Capital Growth	Emp. Growth	Growth of Total Factor Productivity	(Residual)
Loayza et al. (WB sources and estimates)	0.3		1.9	1.4	−3.0	
Bartelsman (STATIN Sources and estimates)	0.7		1.2	0.3	−0.8	

Sources: National Income Product 2001, STATIN; Economic and Social Survey, PIOJ, various issues; WDI/GDF Central database, World Bank.

Some general explanations for slow growth in the 1990s are well known—the financial crisis that followed the excesses of the late 1980s and early 1990s and the consequent monetary tightening, which left a massive, costly debt overhang (Chapters 3 and 4). In addition, the external climate deteriorated. These macroeconomic developments seem to have more than offset the potential effects of the substantial trade and capital account liberalization of the early 1990s (Chapter 7).

A recent cross-country study quantifies these explanations and can account for most of the slow growth.[2] The study finds that the decline in the growth of GDP per capita from 1980–89 to 1990–1999 (−1.9 percent per year according to World Bank data) can be almost completely accounted for by the negative impact of the financial crisis and higher inflation ("stabilization issues" accounting for −1.3 percent per year). These problems almost completely offset the positive impact of structural reforms (1.45 percent per year) that opened up the economy and reduced government consumption. This left growth to be determined by the negative influence of external factors (−0.7 percent per year) that affected all countries, and the cyclical reversion and convergence of the Jamaican economy back from the unusually high growth in latter half of the 1980s (−1.2 percent per year; see Annex Table A2.6 and Loayza et al. 2002, Table II.4).

The study's comparison of changes within the 1990s sharpens these conclusions somewhat. In the latter half of the 1990s, the empirical results suggest even greater negative impacts from the financial crisis (reflecting more years of financial crisis), the burden from rising government consumption, and the increasing overvaluation. Meanwhile the positive impact of the structural reforms wears off. External conditions continue to have a similar negative effect on growth. There is no cyclical rebound, because growth in the early 1990s was similar to the long run trend (see Annex Table A2.6).

The question of course, is what does this study imply for the future—when will stabilization efforts be able to stop, given the high debt level, when will international conditions improve, and what new structural reforms are needed, since those of the early 1990s have already begun to wear off.

Turning to sector level data, both agriculture and manufacturing output actually declined in the late 1990s. Poor weather and increased competitive imports at the appreciated real exchange rate hurt agriculture (though, as discussed in Chapter 1, lower priced agricultural imports helped reduce poverty). Textile production has declined by nearly 75 percent since its 1995 peak, as textile exporters left for Mexico, Haiti, and the Dominican Republic. The reasons usually given for their departure are not only better access to US markets in some of the other countries but also lower wage costs, lower infrastructure and security costs and less shipping problems (Chapter 7). Tire production has also shifted, to Trinidad and Tobago.

Only the transport and communications, power, and tourist sectors have grown rapidly since 1996. The tourist sector is heavily dependent on Jamaica's natural resources—location and natural beauty. It is perhaps less dependent on cost competitiveness and productivity than other sectors. Nonetheless, an appreciated real exchange rate means that prices in foreign exchange have to be higher to cover local costs, thereby reducing tourist arrivals and the country's earnings on its sites and its taxes. Financial services have grown since 1997 but are only back to the 1995 level. Moreover, though on a sounder regulatory base, the sector's assets are now largely government

---

2. Loayza, et al, 2002. The study's approach is a cross-country estimate of possible factors that are associated with growth, of the type used by Lucas, 1988 and Barro, 1991. In this approach, the "average" impact (coefficient) of various possible supply and demand factors on growth are estimated using cross-country data. Of course, the average impact of these factors includes the impact of the "average" policy response to them by the sample countries. For example, a financial crisis typically would be accompanied by certain monetary and fiscal policies, to a greater or lesser degree, which in turn would affect growth. These estimated "average impact coefficients can then be multiplied by the values of the variables in a particular country to see how well its growth can be "explained."

debt (Chapter 4). The real imputed bank service charge, a deduction from the sum of sector GDP, has grown nearly 40 percent since 1995, and its calculation may need some reconsideration—if it grew only as fast as sectoral GDP, then real GDP growth would be nearly one percentage point per year higher.[3]

Despite the slow GDP growth and high real interest rates/large debt overhang, the estimated rate of gross fixed capital formation is and has been fairly high. Gross fixed capital formation averaged nearly 28 percent of (nominal) GDP over the last decade and rose to nearly 30 percent in 2001 (Table 2.1). Jamaica's average investment rate was in the top quartile of countries in the 1990s, and well above the average investment rate of about 21 percent across countries (Loayza et al. 2002 database). Though the investment rate did decline toward the end of the 1990s, after the financial crisis, the average investment rate from 1996–2000 was nonetheless higher than in the 1980s. Moreover, new foreign direct investment, which is equal to about 12 percent of investment (excluding privatizations and retained earnings), has remained strong, which is usually a good indicator of favorable market conditions.[4]

Within investment, machinery and equipment investment has held up surprisingly well after the crisis and is concentrated in telecommunications, tourism, and bauxite mining. Machinery and equipment investment represented a higher fraction of GDP recently than the average in either 1990–1995, or the 1980s. This is in spite of the real appreciation of the exchange rate. In US dollar terms, imports of machinery and equipment were about 80 percent higher in 1999–2001 than in 1991–1993.

Construction also has held up well, but there appears to be a shift to housing and the informal sector. Real value added in construction, which is associated with formal construction activity, has fallen much faster than GDP, almost 13 percent in 1999–2001 compared to 1993–1995. Government investment has declined over the 1990s as a percentage of GDP, being crowded out in the budget by rising debt servicing and wage costs (see chapter 3). Housing starts, though down since the mid-1990s, have held up surprisingly well because of public sector activity. On balance, these figures suggest a slight fall in the ratio of real construction to real GDP in the latter half of the 1990s, as compared to the constant ratio of nominal construction to nominal GDP that is reported in the investment figures.

Employment has grown slowly and actually declined in the latter half of the 1990s (Table 2.1). This decline reflects both discouraged workers and the rise in open unemployment as employment in the formal sector grew slowly. Moreover, labor has shifted into the government sector, while private sector employment declined except for own-account workers. Moreover, migration, notably of those with tertiary education, is large. Labor force issues are discussed more fully in below.

The Supply Side of Growth

Jamaica's slow reported GDP growth and high investment rates imply low, if not negative, aggregate productivity growth. Although questions can be raised about the measurement of outputs and inputs, discussed in the next sections, the calculation also raises important issues for the future.

The negative aggregate productivity growth shows up formally in the traditional, Solow (1957) approach of analyzing the sources of GDP growth in terms of the contributions of the

3. For the 2002 GDP estimates, revisions were made to remove a portion of the imputed service charge associated with household consumption from the product side of the estimates and include it in consumption estimates. Improvements have also been made in the deflation technique.

4. Relating foreign direct investment to investment in the national accounts is difficult. In addition to the issue of foreign purchases of public sector enterprises (not a new investment), there are problems relating retained earnings to investment. Moreover, foreign owners of firms may borrow locally to make investments.

growth of capital and labor and "total factor productivity," which is really a residual.[5] Application of the standard Solow growth model to Jamaica suggests that (total) factor productivity declined 2.5 percent per year in the 1990s (Table 2.2, column 1). The decline in aggregate productivity is even worse if adjustment is made for the estimated increases in human capital, which tend to raise the growth rate of (effective) labor (Table 2.2, column 2). On the other hand, the decline in total factor productivity is much less, when adjustment is made for informal sector employment and capital growth is disaggregated and depreciated more rapidly (Table 2.2, column 3).

Negative productivity growth could come from diminishing returns or from the costs of crime. In the bauxite industry, there may indeed have been a decrease in productivity—more inputs are needed to make up for the decreasing physical productivity of the mines,

TABLE 2.2: JAMAICA ESTIMATES OF SOURCES OF GROWTH 1991–2000

	Loayza et al		Bartlesman
	1	2	
Growth (average % per year) of			
Output	0.3	0.3	0.7
Capital	4.7	4.7	3.2
Labor	1.6		
Labor adj. for Human Capital		2.3	
Labor adj. for Informal Employment			0.5
Total Factor Productivity	−2.5	−3.0	−0.8

Memo
| Labor Output Elasticity (share of labor) | 0.60 | | 0.63 |

Loayza Sources:
Output and Capital: World Bank (2002b), capital based on updating of Nehru and Dhareshwar (1993)
Labor: ILO and ECLAC

Bartlesman Sources:
Output, Capital, and Labor: STATIN; Labor adjusted by reducing non-formal labor by 60 percent.

although the profitability of the investment may still be high.[6] However, in most industries, technology seems to have remained at least constant, if not improved. It is possible that increasing investment in security and crime prevention, which does not add directly to output (see discussion below and in Chapter 6), could generate a decline in aggregate productivity growth.[7]

---

5. Solow, 1957. In Solow's model, GDP growth is definitionally equal to the growth in capital and labor multiplied by their output elasticities and an unexplained residual that is called total factor productivity growth. Formally: Growth of GDP = a Growth of Capital + (1−a) Growth of Labor + Residual
where a = % change in GDP/% change in Capital,
1− a = % change in GDP/% change in Labor.
These elasticities may be estimated or, more commonly, are simply assumed to be the shares of capital and labor. In addition, it is usually assumed that the output elasticities of capital and labor sum to one (by definition the shares do); if there are economies or diseconomies of scale then their total would exceed or fall short of one, and the empirical application of the equation would tend to generate positive or negative residuals. Questions have been raised about the application of the formula because of theoretical problems in computing an aggregate stock of capital, and empirical problems of: (i) estimating the output elasticities (often simply taken as the income shares of labor and capital, which not only raises questions about the implicit assumption of competitive factor markets but also the empirical problem of splitting the earnings of the self-employed into returns to capital and labor), and (ii) estimating the base year capital stock and the rate of depreciation to be used under the permanent inventory method of computing the annual stock of capital as last year's capital stock less an assumed rate of depreciation, plus investment.
6. Bartlesman, 2002, using heroic assumptions about the allocation of the total capital stock, estimates that aggregate productivity has fallen in the mining industry somewhat faster than in the rest of the economy. Note even if productivity in the mines fell, investment would still be profitable, if world prices of bauxite are expected to rise faster than the productivity of the mines declines, power costs fall, or the industry receives tax concessions.
7. Note that the issue is not whether productivity is low, but whether productivity growth is negative—in other words, declining productivity. Underutilization of facilities such as tourist hotels for much of the year will contribute to low productivity, but to declining productivity only if the degree of underutilization is

Whether these investments are large enough to lead to a decline in estimated productivity growth in the aggregate is not clear.

The estimate of falling productivity, as well as the high rates of presumably profitable new investment, raise the issues of measurements of GDP, capital and labor, as discussed below. These issues of measurement are not sterile discussions; they raise important issues about the kind of economy Jamaica is turning into and the problems of raising growth.

Jamaica's GDP Growth may be Underestimated

A number of factors suggest that Jamaica's GDP growth is underestimated.[8] Underestimation of GDP growth would reduce the apparent paradox of high investment (and increasing foreign direct investment) despite low measured GDP growth. It would also reduce the paradox of low growth and rapid poverty reduction.

One indicator that GDP growth may be underestimated is the large difference between consumption growth in the GDP accounts and the annual household Survey of Living Conditions.[9] Between 1995 and 2001, estimates of real per capita consumption from the household survey grow by 3.8 percent per year, while real per capita consumption in the GDP accounts declines by 1.5 percent per year (see also Chapter 1). Corroborating evidence for an underestimation is the decline in poverty in the latter half of the 1990s according to the household survey (Chapter 1). The difference between the estimates of consumption in the survey and GDP naturally raises the question of which is a better estimate.[10] Some independent real indicators of consumption, such as apparent consumption of meat and fish, purchases of electricity, and cars and trucks licensed, all seem to be growing much faster that would be the case if GDP per capita had fallen (see Box 2.1).[11]

---

increasing over time, on which there is no evidence. In the case of investments in security, they would add to the capital stock and be multiplied by the average elasticity of output to generate a contribution to output, but no increase in measured output in GDP, in other words negative factor productivity.

8. Again, the issue is not whether GDP is underestimated, but whether the degree of underestimation has increased over time. With regard to the growth models discussed above, an underestimation of GDP growth would mean that total factor productivity growth (the residual in the Solow approach) would be more positive and Jamaica's growth would show a larger unexplained residual in the cross-country approach.

9. Jamaica's GDP estimates are largely based on estimates of value added by industry. On the demand side, nominal values of government spending, estimated investment, and net exports of goods and services are obtained directly. Consumption is estimated using a commodity flow method, then adjustments are made to equilibrate the demand and production side of the accounts. If the resulting estimate of consumption were increasingly underestimated, then GDP (value added in production) probably would be increasingly underestimated. Note that remittances, which are important in Jamaica, are not, by themselves, an explanation of why consumption, and thus production, may be underestimated. The reason is that when the additional purchasing power provided by remittances is translated into consumption, the goods that are consumed must either be produced or imported. Hence, the issue is not remittances per se, but the extent to which the estimates of production and net imports match up with independent estimates of demand, including an independent estimate of consumption that includes consumption financed by remittances.

10. The ratio of consumption in the survey to consumption in the GDP accounts varies substantially from year to year, with 1995 consumption in the survey the smallest fraction of consumption in the national accounts. (Nominal) consumption in the survey grows much faster than (nominal) consumption in the national accounts after 1995, as shown in Table 2-2 in the 2000 SLC. One explanation may be a change in the survey methodology, but the 1997 SLC specifically denies any change in the methodology, as noted in Chapter 1. Of course, one explanation of the difference in the growth rates between the survey and the national accounts is that the national accounts are increasingly underestimating GDP; another is that the national accounts underestimated the severity of the recession in the crisis. Unmeasured output, plus the rapid growth of remittances, are both potential sources of income that can be spent on consumption, part of it produced in the poorly recorded sectors.

11. Also, Jamaica's current consumption of infrastructure services like electricity, air transport, telecommunications, seem to suggest that the *level* of GDP may be underestimated (Ehrhardt et al. 2003).

BOX 2.1: CONSUMPTION INDICATORS

Purchases of a number of commodities seems to have grown fairly fast in the 1990s, despite falling measured GDP per capita. These figures suggest consumption and thus GDP growth is underestimated.

These figures are estimated separately from both the GDP accounts and the SLC, and thus provide something of an independent check of the other two estimates. These are all luxury goods, with income elasticities of demand typically above 1. Hence consumption probably should have fallen if GDP per capita declined. To some extent purchases may have risen because of relative price effects, but these goods all have a domestic component. Also, as income distribution appears to have changed little (Chapter 2), it is unlikely that shifts in income distribution could explain these growth rates of consumption.

Jamaica: Real Indicators of Consumption: Average Annual Growth Rates

	1990–1995	1995–2001
Meat & Fish Apparent Cons.*(tons)	0.7	6.4
Power Sales (kwh)	3.9	6.5
Household Consumers of Power (number)	4.5	4.3
Cars & Trucks Passing the Fitness Test (number)	8.3	8.5

Source: STATIN, *Economic and Social Surveys*
*Apparent Consumption = Production + Imports − Exports.

On the production side of the national accounts, the basis for the GDP estimates, STATIN generally does an excellent job of applying standard methods on the formal sector. Specifically, STATIN estimates of real GDP are largely based on the standard methodology of applying value added coefficients to indicators of output growth or deflating value added by output prices. In other words, input and output prices are generally assumed to move together, although improvements are continually being made in deflation techniques. Thus, in the formal sector, one potential explanation for the possible underestimation of Jamaican growth may be the differential movement of output and input prices, perhaps leading to mis-estimates of real value added, which is the difference between real outputs and real inputs. However, a recent study carried out for this report suggests that taking into account differences between real output growth and real input growth makes little difference in estimates of real GDP growth (Havinga 2002). STATIN plans to shift to separate deflation of both outputs and inputs (double deflation) in the future, depending on the availability of data.

Service output is inherently more difficult to estimate than goods output, particularly in an open economy like Jamaica. Services represent about 70 percent of the economy. The main growth sectors have been telecommunications (10.5 percent p.a. average growth in the period 1995–2001), transport (4.5 percent per annum), and hotels (2.5 percent per annum growth). Nonetheless, their growth may be underestimated, particularly since part of the income in telecommunications and hotels (tourism) is reported overseas.[12] The growth in tourism seems surprisingly low. There is also the knotty theoretical issue of the treatment of increases in real wages or spending on services, in sectors where the growth in value added is estimated by growth in employees (government) or numbers of visitors (tourism).

Another potential explanation of the possible underestimate of GDP growth may be an underestimate of illegal and informal activities, which are difficult to measure in all countries. As the media widely reports, the drug trade is an important activity in Jamaica. However, according

---

12. The charges on fixed line, international calls are split between the two countries; the division on international cell phone calls is defined in contracts, and the imputation of both items for purposes of national accounts may need a reassessment. Tourist packages are typically paid offshore.

to the United Nations, the level of Caribbean drug exports has not changed much since the early 1990s, and Jamaica has lost its share in marijuana sales (UNODC, 2003). Of course, the drug trade by its nature is difficult to estimate. However, if the UN estimate is correct, then the drug trade may account for an underestimate in the level of GDP of, perhaps, 15 percent, but not much of an underestimate of growth. In contrast, informal and underground production may have increased as a result of the imposition of the General Consumption Tax in 1991. Red tape and bureaucracy in setting up businesses, which often generate complaints, may also have led to the growth of unrecorded production, although there is no direct evidence that bureaucratic bottlenecks have increased over the 1990s. Finally, as is well known, not only has the share of GDP in services risen but, since 1995, so has the share of the own account workers and micro and small establishments in the private labor force, where output is difficult to measure. On the other hand, the number of own account workers has not increased since the mid-1990s, according to the employment survey. Hence, whatever growth has taken place in the sector would appear to reflect higher per capita incomes.

STATIN has made attempts to include estimates of the informal sector in the GDP accounts, using different approaches in different sectors. In agriculture, the drug trade is not included, but attempts are made to estimate small farmers' production. In manufacturing, STATIN notes that it begins its estimate of output with data on firms with more than 10 employees but then adds in estimates of the output of smaller firms based on data from income taxes, commodity flows, and the surveys of household expenditures, living conditions, and the labor force. More important issues may exist in the construction and services sector. Services have grown relative to goods production and are inherently more difficult to estimate than goods output. For example, estimates of distributive trade are based on commodity flows and historic margins, which may need review. Again, the issue is whether this activity has increased relative to GDP over time. Real estate and business services also are always hard to estimate. In Jamaica, the level of estimated imputed rents of owner occupied housing seems low compared to other economies (Havinga, 2002), particularly given the apparent shift to housing construction suggested by the decline in value added in formal construction in the national accounts. However, the growth of imputed rents over time, slightly higher than GDP growth, may only be slightly underestimated. Finally, there is the complicated issue of estimating and attributing the imputed margins of the banking sector, which in Jamaica is estimated directly (FISIM) and then subtracted from the total of sectoral outputs to calculate GDP, rather than imputed on a sector-by-sector basis. As noted, it may be desirable to revisit the estimation of this variable, given that the estimated value rises sharply in real terms over the decade (despite the problems in the banking sector) and correspondingly lowers the real GDP growth by about one percentage point per year.[13]

One often-used indicator of the underground economy is the ratio of currency to GDP (Feige, 1990), a ratio that has increased by about 74 percent in Jamaica since the early 1990s and 28 percent relative to the late 1980s (see Table 2.3).[14] Moreover, this increase has occurred despite the legalization of US dollar deposits and currency holdings in 1991, with the establishment of capital account convertibility. Given the expected rates of return, there should have been a substitution of US currency for Jamaican currency, which in turn suggests that total currency usage has grown even faster than the growth of Jamaican currency would suggest. Ignoring the growth of holdings of US dollars, if we assume, conservatively, that say two-thirds of the rise of Jamaican currency usage over the 1990s reflects a response to continued concerns about the banks, falling inflation, and other factors, then the remaining one-third would be associated with the relative growth of unmeasured activities. This would imply that nominal, and real GDP in 2000 was underestimated, relative to 1990, by between

---

13. See Havinga, 2002, and various STATIN publications for details on sectoral estimates of output.
14. While part of the increase over the early 1990s might reflect the concern over weakness of financial institutions, that concern should largely be gone by the end of the 1990s, after the government effectively guaranteed financial sector liabilities and then established a formal deposit insurance fund in 1998.

TABLE 2.3: JAMAICA: THE RISE IN CURRENCY HOLDINGS, 1991 TO 2001					
	Average 1987–89	Average 1991–93	Average 1999–2001	Ratio '99–'01 / 1987–89	Ratio '99–'01 / '91–'93
Currency (June)/GDP (percent)	3.7	2.7	4.8	1.28	1.74

Source: Bank of Jamaica.

nine to twenty-five percent (depending on whether the comparison of currency holdings is with the late 1980s or early 1990s).[15] This in turn would imply that real GDP growth from 1990 to 2000 averaged almost 1–3 percent per year, presumably concentrated in the post-crisis years.

To summarize, there are some indications that Jamaica's GDP and GDP growth are underestimated. The rapid growth of consumption in the SLC and of some physical products and electricity usage is one such indicator, another is the rise in the use of currency. There are the standard difficulties of estimating informal activities and service output, compounded by the open nature of Jamaica's economy. There is also the issue of the large rise in the estimate of the real imputed banking services. Adjusting for an underestimate might raise GDP growth by perhaps 1–2 percentage points per year. This is a better growth rate, but not an outstanding growth performance. Moreover, much of this growth may have come in informal activities, where future productivity growth is likely to be small. The next two sections discuss the measurement of capital inputs and the growth of employment and its implications for future job growth.

Capital Inputs

Jamaica's high investment rates may reflect rapid growth of real wages and the appreciation of the exchange rate, but the effective growth of capital also may be overestimated, thus suggesting an underestimate of the increase in total factor productivity. Rapid growth of real wages encourages substitution of capital for labor, and a more capital intensive/less labor intensive growth path. Similarly, an appreciating real exchange rate reduces the relative price of imported machinery and equipment, which represents almost all of Jamaica's investment in machinery and equipment, and thereby encourage investment. Thus, the pattern of price movements in the labor market and the exchange market may have contributed to a rising capital intensity in Jamaica. However, increasing capital intensity does not explain the negative growth in total factor productivity; the explanation probably lies in overestimates of the growth of capital stock and its productivity.

---

15. The argument is as follows: the ratio of currency to measured nominal GDP in 1999–2001 is 28 (74) percent higher than if 1987–88 (1991–93) ratio prevailed. If all of the difference were due to a relative increase in the informal sector/underestimate of GDP, this would imply nominal GDP was underestimated by 28 (74) percent in 1999–2001, compared to the earlier years. Assuming prices rose the same in the informal and formal sectors, this would further imply all of the difference was due to an increasing underestimate of real GDP. Of course, some of the increase in currency use may be attributed to the public's concerns about the banks and some may be attributed to the fall in expected inflation. In addition, the informal sector probably uses more currency than the formal sector (Feige, 1990), so its relatively faster growth would create an additional rise in the ratio of currency to nominal GDP. Suppose simply that only about one third of the rise in the currency ratio is due to the relative growth of the informal sector, two thirds due to concerns about the banks, the fall in inflation, and the higher use of money by the faster growing informal sector. (The alternative is to estimate this split by imposing a more sophisticated model and assumptions about the relative size of the informal sector in the base year and assumption or estimates of the income and inflation elasticities of currency demand in the two sectors, see Bennett, 1995 for an example applied to Jamaica in the 1980s). This would imply that the underestimate of real GDP had increased by between 9 and 25 percent since the early 1990s, and growth was underestimated between 0.9 and 2.9 percent per year compared to a constant rate of underestimation of the informal sector. Presumably, GDP was also underestimated in 1990 and some of the money stock was used for these activities. But this calculation shows how much the non-included activities rose faster than a constant rate of underestimation, based on the rise in the use of currency.

One possible source of overestimating capital growth is the use of too low a base year capital stock and too low a depreciation rate, which translate into an overly rapid growth of capital.[16] The comparison of the two recent estimates of capital stock growth above gives some idea of the issue. The Loayza et al. (2002) capital stock estimates, taken from earlier World Bank estimates of capital stock in all countries using common assumptions on depreciation, are substantially greater the Bartelsman (2002) estimates which are based on a more detailed breakdown of investment, and depreciation rates and initial capital stock, all specific to Jamaica.[17] As a result, Bartlesman's figures imply a smaller growth in capital, a correspondingly smaller difference between the weighted sum of inputs and the growth of output and, thus, a less negative figure for total factor productivity growth.

Hurricanes are a particular issue for measuring capital stock in Jamaica, as they reduce the capital stock and imply much of the investment is simply for replacement. In Jamaica, and other Caribbean economies, the weather probably makes the depreciation rate of capital stock not only higher, but also more variable than can be accounted for by a low, steady, depreciation rate. Bartlesman's capital stock estimates include a relatively high average depreciation rate to account for hurricanes.

A second, standard problem in estimating capital stock is capacity utilization, a potentially important problem in Jamaica after the financial crisis. As the number of manufacturing and financial firms have declined, real non-housing rentals have declined by about 20 percent since 1995, according to the national accounts. Some of the buildings constructed in the building boom of the late 1980s and early 1990s are still partially empty. In addition, the aforementioned departure of textile producers has left empty the buildings in the export zone, which are only gradually being converted to other uses. More generally, capacity utilization of machinery as well as structures may have declined due to the recession in aggregate demand. Adjusting the capital stock for such changes in capital utilization would imply a much slower growth of capital and a higher growth of total factor productivity than the figures shown in Table 2.2.

Another issue is the concentration of new investment in sectors such as housing and hotels where its productivity, in terms of GDP, may be reduced by distortions. For example, housing is desirable for the welfare of the population, but adds to future GDP only by the imputed value of owner occupied housing.[18] The economic productivity of housing may be less than directly productive investment because of the lower taxes on owner occupied housing services that encourage housing investment, relative to plant and equipment, and by direct subsidization of housing access. In hotels, differential taxes and tax incentives may generate "over investment" because of individual profit rates that differ significantly from the investment's contribution to output (Artana and Navajas, 2002). To generate an aggregate capital stock including housing and other activities, the value of investment must be weighted by their relative productivity, not relative prices. Thus, to the extent that the share of housing has increased in investment, the capital stock has grown less rapidly than the sum of investment weighted by relative prices.

Low productivity of investment in security against crime is particularly pertinent to Jamaica (see Chapter 6). While such investment can reduce the impact of crime on the business that invests in it, from the standpoint of the economy its future productivity is negligible. Moreover, the threat of crime also tends to reduce the productivity of all investment, by making multiple shift work unattractive to the workers. Hence, increasing crime could lead to a reduction in total factor productivity.

---

16. In the standard, permanent inventory method of computing the growth of capital, there is always an issue of estimating a base year capital stock (if one does not exist) and a depreciation rate to calculate the growth rate of capital—if a low base year capital stock or a low depreciation rate are used, then the growth of capital will be too high (capital deepening), the contribution of capital to growth will be overestimated and the growth of total factor productivity will be underestimated.

17. Bartelsman (2002), divides investment into six types, applies specific depreciation rates for each based on US GDP methodology (which takes into account obsolescence), adjusts depreciation upward to allow for hurricanes, and then cumulates the estimates from 1960 onward to get a capital series for Jamaica, which implies a thirty percent lower estimate of capital than in Loayza et al. (2002).

18. As noted above, the GDP attribution for owner-occupied housing in Jamaica seems low by international standards.

In sum, the growth in capital stock may indeed be overestimated by Jamaica's high investment rate. A key issue for future growth is to increase the productivity of the investment. Reduction in crime, as discussed in Chapter 6, will help to reduce the need for relatively unproductive investment and increase utilization rates. Increases of domestically oriented investment and housing are unlikely to be very productive, especially once the large investment boom in telecommunications is completed. Hence, increased productivity of investment is likely to depend on encouraging greater competitiveness in traded goods.

The Labor Force and Growth

The slow growth of employment in Jamaica over the 1990s suggests that GDP growth, whatever the degree of underestimation, has been too slow to generate rapid growth in employment demand. As can be gleaned from Table 2.4, employment has grown at an average rate of less than 0.3 percent per year from 1991–2001. Even before the crisis fully hit, over the period 1991–1996, employment grew less than 6 percent, while the rate of unemployment rose. From 1996 to 2001, when Jamaica was undergoing a crisis and then recovering, employment actually fell by over 2 percent. While employment did rise somewhat in 2001 and 2002 (1.3 percent and 1.6 percent respectively), at roughly the same rate as average GDP growth over the two years, it remains to be seen if this increase is transitory. The entire increase of about 21000 people between 2000 and 2002 owes to the increase in public employment and there are also issues of statistical comparability of the data.[19]

Other aspects of the labor force confirm the slow growth of employment opportunities (Table 2.4 and Annex Table A2.7). The labor force actually declines between 1996 and 2001, suggesting a withdrawal of workers from job seeking. Within employment, employment in the goods producing sector has fallen at an increasing rate over the 1990s (Table 2.4), much faster than goods output. Female employment has fallen, largely reflecting the loss of jobs in the textile industry. Public sector has increased by about 11,000 jobs, perhaps indicating an implicit counter-cyclical policy of employment. However, private employment has fallen even faster than total employment, with a loss of some 50,000 jobs since 1996. Only own-account employment has been stable, and hence has become an increasing share of the employed since 1996.

Surprisingly, average wage and salary earnings (in large establishments) have risen strongly despite the fall in employment—a fact that suggests that this part of the labor market does not seem to be working very well and that employers may even have reduced their hirings and increasingly substituted capital for labor because of high wage demands supported by strong unions. Between 1995 and 2000, average real weekly earnings in Jamaican dollars have more than doubled (a compound growth rate of 16 percent per year—PIOJ, ESSJ various issues), and, in US dollars, earnings have almost doubled. These wage increases are probably a factor in the falling labor intensity of output, decline in labor demand and the loss of competitiveness in goods production. As shown in Chapter 7, growth of wages in excess of productivity has been a major factor in the loss of exports, particularly apparel exports.

The slow growth of employment opportunities has added to the push of crime and the pull of high foreign wages in encouraging emigration from Jamaica. Despite restrictive immigration policies, estimated emigration rates to the US and Canada have averaged over 20,000 per year in the

---

19. Until 2000, the labor force and employment numbers were based on an average of four surveys in each year. In 2001 and 2002, only two surveys were done, January and April in 2001, and April and October in 2002. These changes raise the issue of comparability of the data with those of previous surveys, owing to possible seasonal effects, as discussed in PIOJ, 2002 ESSJ, page 21.3. In addition, the 2002 survey incorporated a new sample frame to increase the falling response rate of interviewees, as well as a new sample design, thus affecting comparability with earlier surveys. In 2001, employment rose by 1.3 percent compared to the same January–April period in 2002. In 2002, employment rose 1.6 percent, but this could be seasonal. More importantly, it was the large increase in public employment (mainly short-term contract workers relating to flood damage, other capital projects, and for the Electoral Office and the Population Census) that was almost entirely responsible for the increase in overall employment.

TABLE 2.4: JAMAICA: LABOR FORCE INDICATORS, 1991–2000 (Annual Averages, thousands of workers)	1991	1996	2000	2001	2002
Labor Force	1073	1143	1105	1105	1125
Employed	908	960	934	939	954
o.w. Agric. Mining, & Manufacturing	348	324	270	268	261
Construction & Services	560	636	664	672	694
o.w. Female Employment	390	407	381	385	402
Male Employment	518	553	552	555	553
o.w. Own Account		338	332	337	322
o.w. Private Sector	812	868	828	837	834.5
o.w. Public Administration	96	92	106	103	120
Unemployed	165	183	172	165	170

Source: Economic and Social Survey, PIOJ, Government of Jamaica, various issues.

1990s (PIOJ, ESSJ various issues, based on US and Canadian data, data include students), though emigration has slowed recently, perhaps reflecting tightening immigration restrictions in these countries. Even though general migration to Canada and the United Kingdom has slowed, migration to the United States under family reunion provisions continues. Emigration at this rate means that migration absorbed much of the potential growth in Jamaica's labor force during the 1990s. In addition to permanent emigration, a policy of temporary migration to the United States for hotel and farm work accounts for over 10,000 temporary emigrants per year.

The outflow of educated people is especially large and has been less affected by the tightening of immigration restrictions. Bratsberg and Terrell (2002), using 1980 and 1990 US census data, find that the weighted average migration rates of male Jamaican workers top all 67 countries in both years in the United States. By contrast, in Singapore, which has about 3 million people, migration rates of those with primary and secondary education in 1980 and 1990 were below 1 percent, and the rates of those with tertiary education was 2.5 percent in 1980 and 4.8 percent in 1990. (Bratsberg and Terrell, 2002, Table A2, p. 195–196). An estimate based on the 1990 US census suggests that some 90,000 Jamaicans with secondary education and 66,600 with tertiary education were living in the US in 1990.[20] These figures overestimate the "brain drain," since some of these Jamaicans probably received part of their education in the United States.[21] Nonetheless, these figures suggest that in 1990, between 25 and 30 percent of Jamaica's secondary graduates and over two-thirds of its tertiary graduates were in the United States (Carrington and Detragiache, 1998, Table 2).

More recently, Jamaican nurses have now become an important part of health services in the United States. There have been systematic recruitment efforts from the United Kingdom and New York City for Jamaican teachers. A rough estimate of the total migration, made by comparing to the numbers of resident tertiary graduates shown in the household surveys to the number of graduates over the 1990s, suggests that the equivalent of about 80 percent of tertiary graduates in the 1990s had emigrated.[22]

---

20. Carrington and Detragiache, 1998. Migrants are defined as foreign-born residents over 25 years of age, excluding graduate students.

21. In the early 1990s, an estimated 5000 Jamaicans were enrolled in US, UK and Canadian undergraduate and postgraduate studies, including two-year colleges (Buttrick, 1994).

22. Note that these migration figures suggest that the growth of human capital, which is typically estimated between censuses by graduation rates (for example Loayza et al. 2002), is substantially overstated for Jamaica (see also Chapter 5).

The large emigration of educated Jamaicans raises the issue of the high cost of educating university students who then migrate. For many Jamaican students, the cost of secondary and tertiary education is largely paid by the state—fees, though a burden on middle class households, cover only about a fifth of secondary and tertiary education's costs. Thus, the Jamaican taxpayer is not only subsidizing the education of people from higher than average income families and who will have higher than average incomes once they graduate, but who will not even pay taxes on those incomes, nor provide any benefits to the community in terms of teaching/nursing. It is true that the emigrants send remittances (though some of these "remittances" may be drug-related payments). However, the remittances are only a small fraction of the income they earn and they are taxed only when spent. Moreover, the remittances tend to appreciate the real exchange rate, making exports of goods and services less profitable and thus dampen the demand for labor in Jamaica.

Raising Growth in Jamaica

Growth has been negligible in Jamaica in the latter half of the 1990s, despite high investment rates. The foregoing discussion suggests that GDP growth in Jamaica is probably underestimated, because of the growth of informal, underground and illegal activities. However, the upward adjustment of growth could be 1–2 percentage points per year, enough to turn the growth of aggregate productivity positive (at least according to some estimates), but still not an impressive performance. Much of the growth in (recorded and unrecorded) GDP is in the informal sector where productivity growth is likely to be low in the future. Meanwhile investors in such sectors as textiles and tires have left Jamaica. Jamaica seems to have lost competitiveness in goods production because of world conditions, but also because of the appreciating real exchange rate and rising real wages. As a result, investments previously made in these sectors, and in pre-crisis building construction, are now substantially underutilized and do not represent fully productive elements of the capital stock.[23] There is also an issue that investments and salaries to deter crime do not contribute much to the national output as measured. GDP growth and investment in the latter half of the 1990s has been in natural resource-based sectors like tourism, transport, and bauxite, which have lost less competitiveness at the current exchange rate and wage rates.[24] In these sectors, plus telecommunications, investment is profitable and they have attracted most of the non-housing investment and the foreign investment in Jamaica.[25] Even in these sectors there may be some underestimate of GDP growth.

The rate and characteristics of Jamaica's growth did not generate a rapid growth in employment. Only public sector employment has grown, private sector employment growth has been negative, because of the fall in female employment. The labor market also appears to be functioning imperfectly, with high wage demands depressing labor demand and probably generating some substitution of capital for labor.

While average outcomes in education are poor and limit productivity gains, migration continues to be large, suggesting that tertiary education, in particular, performs relatively well. Migration offsets the potential improvement in the quality of the labor force, at least at the higher skill level (see Chapter 5). Canada, the United States, and the United Kingdom actively recruit skilled Jamaican workers like teachers and nurses. High crime rates may be a factor contributing to migration.

High rates of emigration are likely to continue, as long as the United States and Canada continue to accept Jamaican graduates as immigrants. Moreover, such emigration raises the issue of the brain drain, and methods of recouping at least some of the large amount of public sector expenditure to educate these students (Chapter 5).

Generating higher growth in tradables is the key to growth in Jamaica's open economy but is likely to be difficult because of the country's high costs. Dependence on further growth in the informal sector and further increases in public sector employment is not a viable strategy for improving

---

23. Calculations of the capital stock also need to reflect the damages from recent major hurricanes.

24. In natural resource based sectors, higher wages and appreciated exchange rates reduce the incomes to the owners of the natural resources and the taxes that government can levy on their use.

25. Some investors in these sectors may also have been attracted by tax concessions.

economic performance. Yet expanding tradables will be difficult without tackling distortions. The impact of past exchange rate appreciation (despite significant real appreciation since 2002) and high wage increases in the 1990s continues to keep costs high compared to Asia or regional competitors. Capital costs are high because of the debt overhang and government demands for finance, and the high overheads necessitated by high crime rates and security costs. As a result, imports have substituted for most manufacturing production, other than that protected by transport costs, and some agro processing. Some exports do occur to the other Caribbean countries but that is a slow growing market. Other exports are to the niche market of Jamaicans overseas but, for instance, exports of Red Stripe beer pale in comparison to the success of Mexico's Corona. Export-oriented textile production shifted to the Dominican Republic, Honduras, Haiti, among others, and to Mexico after the formation of NAFTA (see Chapter 7), a loss in GDP of about 1 percent. Banana and sugar exports are largely made possible by quotas given by importers that are gradually being reduced. Sugar is largely a public sector operation and the attempt to privatize it collapsed because of the unattractive exchange rate, but some of the private sector firms are said to have substantially lower costs. In other sectors, the attempts to take advantage of the good telecommunications and English language skills for IT-related industries run into high labor cost and the crime issue (night time workers need to be transported to and from their homes). The bauxite industry is still a major contributor to exports, but low world prices and the falling productivity of the old mines are reducing its dynamism. Tourism is competitive because of the climate and beaches and it continues to bring in substantial foreign investment, even with higher wages, partly because much of the competition is elsewhere in the Caribbean, which also has high wages in U.S. dollar terms. However, the benefits that tourism brings are somewhat eroded by the subsidies and tax concessions offered by the government. The crime issue, or the perception that there is a crime issue, also limits tourism growth. Indeed, in the second half of the 1990s, growth of tourism has slowed, and Jamaica has lost out to popular destinations such as the Dominican Republic.

Policies that improve international competitiveness and increase productivity are thus the key to growth in Jamaica's open economy. Improving competitiveness means wage growth much more in line with productivity; a reduction in crime to reduce its associated overhead costs; better customs services, so smaller firms can access imported inputs better; and a reduction in the tax and interest rate burden imposed by the public sector. A gradual nominal depreciation would tend to increase competitiveness: the pass through into prices is likely to be limited by the weakness of the economy and low inflation in recent years, according to recent research. The resulting depreciated real exchange rate will reduce the local component of costs in US dollar terms and thereby stimulate output in agriculture, manufacturing and tourism. The events of 2003 have demonstrated that a real depreciation is possible—in the first half of 2003, the nominal exchange rate depreciated about 15 percent, but consumer prices rose about 7 percent, leading to a real depreciation of 11 percent. This real depreciation also demonstrates the enhanced credibility achieved by the central bank in recent times, and that credibility will continue to be key to maintaining the gains in exchange rate competitiveness. It is also important to note the while depreciation will benefit agriculture by raising prices of imported foodstuffs, it will hurt poor urban consumers and raise the burden of external debt. A one-time, step devaluation alone is unlikely to sustain export growth. Sustained growth in exports will depend on policies that generate a perception that exports will be kept profitable for some time and therefore investment in outward oriented production will pay off. Finally, better infra-structure will also be needed. In addition to general infrastructure improvements, infrastructure will be needed to maintain tourism's dynamism and decisions will need to be made: a) whether to improve infrastructure in existing tourist areas or start new ones, and b) how to pay for it. Unless growth picks up, the demand for labor will continue to grow slowly and migration (labor export) will continue.

REDUCING THE FISCAL AND DEBT BURDEN

In the early 1990s, Jamaica made considerable progress in its fiscal affairs. Tight fiscal policy was part of the overall macroeconomic strategy to stabilize the economy and stimulate economic growth. From 1990/91 to 1995/96, the government ran a fiscal surplus and a significant primary surplus (the difference between revenue and non-interest expenditure), although these surpluses declined over the period. These surpluses, plus Paris Club and bilateral debt restructurings, reduced the total public sector debt from US$5427 million (US$3942 million external) in 1990/91 to US$4435 million (US$3070 million external) in 1995/96; the ratio of debt to GDP declined from 138.3 percent in 1990/91 to 85.9 percent in 1995/96.

The financial crisis of the mid-1990s, together with the rising government wage bill and falling revenue over 1996/97 to 1997/98 (relative to GDP), have worsened the fiscal and debt position dramatically. It is possible that the trends in revenue and expenditure would have worsened the debt position even without the financial crisis. However, in response to the massive financial crisis, the government replaced all of the financial institutions' weak lending with government debt. This policy protected the depositors, but generated a massive Government debt increase. The resulting interest costs, together with the deteriorating underlying balance, have reversed the fiscal gains of the first half of the 1990s and 1999/00–2000/01, even despite cuts in government investment that would have been desirable for growth. Recent domestic and external shocks have only served to exacerbate the already weak fiscal situation.

Primary surpluses of more than 10 percent of GDP are needed just to sustain the current, high debt to GDP ratio of about 150 percent. A lower primary surplus (6–7 percent of GDP) would only stabilize the debt if the debt were lower by some 50 percentage points of GDP.

Reaching fiscal and debt sustainability are critical to a return to sustained growth, hence the near-term challenge for the government is to chart and maintain a transparent course to improved fiscal and debt indicators in what is likely to be a less friendly external economic environment.

The chapter is organized as follows. The first section examines the current fiscal situation as well as its evolution since the early nineties. The second section analyzes the issues of debt sustainability given the current structure of the debt and in the context of the current macroeconomic policy framework. The third section briefly examines one of the imperatives of fiscal policy going forward—the challenge of reducing and improving government expenditure. This is an area where more detailed analysis is required, and will be taken up in the Bank's forthcoming Public Expenditure Review. The fourth section deals with the other imperative of fiscal policy—raising revenue in a weak economy with a large informal sector and where the tax rate is already relatively high. The fifth section looks at the legal and institutional framework for the management of fiscal policy and concludes that the legal and institutional framework is essentially sound with need for only fine-tuning.

The Government Budget

Jamaica currently faces significant challenges in its fiscal affairs. The fiscal targets for 2002/03 were missed by large margins—the outturn for the central government deficit was 8 percent of GDP, compared with a target of 4.4 percent, and the primary surplus was 8 percent of GDP against a target of 10.4 percent. Given the increase in the total debt to about 150 percent points of GDP, and very low GDP growth, the fiscal deterioration poses significant challenges.

From a longer-term perspective, Jamaica's fiscal position has deteriorated significantly since the mid-1990s, interrupted by an improvement from 1999–2001. The deterioration is mainly the result of: a) a massive rise in interest costs, much of it due to debt arising from the financial crisis and b) a nearly as large a rise in the wage bill. Government expenditures rose from 25.6 percent of GDP in 1994/95, to 32.6 percent in 1996/97 and then, after stabilizing at about 33 percent of GDP until 2001/02, rose sharply in 2002/03 to 37.6 percent of GDP. Meanwhile, revenues rose from 28.6 percent of GDP in 1994/95 to about 30 percent of GDP in 2000/01 and 2002/03 (although they deteriorated over 1996/97 to 1997/98). The worsening deficit and the corresponding worsening of the already high ratio of debt to GDP naturally have raised questions of debt sustainability.

Between 1991/92 and 1995/96, Jamaica's central Government's operations were in surplus (Figure 3.1). Expenditures roughly tracked revenues. However, as a percentage of GDP, the fiscal surplus was falling because nominal GDP was growing somewhat faster than revenues due in part to high inflation. The overall public sector balance was in surplus. However, the Government surplus was preserved in 1995/96 only by postponing several expenditure items, which contributed to the deficit in the 1996/97 budget (1996 ESSJ).

In 1996/97, both the Government's interest costs and wage bill rose significantly, by 2.7 and 2.4 percentage points of GDP, and continued to rise in most years thereafter. Other non-capital expenditure also rose in 2001/02 and 2002/03, after being compressed for four previous earlier years. As a result of these trends, the government has increasingly been forced to borrow not only for capital spending but also current spending.

The rise in interest costs initially reflected a rising real interest rate. After 1996/97, interest costs also rose because of rising debt, as the Government absorbed the costs of the financial crisis including FINSAC debt (Table 3.1) and took on some other contingent liabilities. Adding to the concern is that the 2 percentage points of GDP increase in interest costs in 2002/03 came at a time when U.S. interest rates had fallen to thirty year lows. Partly the rise in 2002/03 is explained by the greater dependence on domestic debt, as domestic rates are higher in nominal terms than international rates. Nonetheless, the sharp rise in interest costs raises a concern that the Government is facing a rising risk premium for domestic borrowing.

The rise in the ratio of wages and salaries to GDP that began in 1996/97 reflected both higher real wages and the growth of employment (see Chapters 1 and 2). After a sharp increase in 1996/97, the higher ratio of wages to GDP was roughly maintained, despite continued growth in the public sector labor force, until 1999/00. In that year, the wage bill was lowered from 11.5 percent to 10.5 percent of GDP, a figure that was maintained in 2000/01, contributing to the falling deficit and rising primary surplus. However, since then, the ratio of Government wages and salaries to GDP has increased about 1 percentage point of GDP per year. In part, the recent increases reflect the pol-

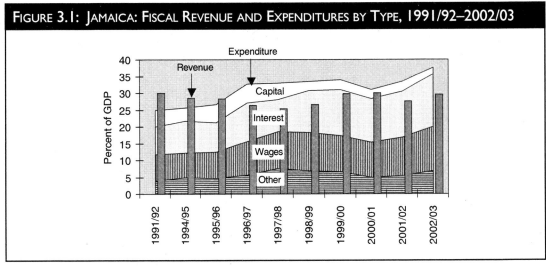

FIGURE 3.1: JAMAICA: FISCAL REVENUE AND EXPENDITURES BY TYPE, 1991/92–2002/03

Source: IMF.

icy of raising civil service wages to 80 percent of comparable private sector wages, but there has been no offsetting reduction in overstaffing. The net result is that Government wages and salaries are now nearly 6 percentage points of GDP higher than they were in 1994/95 (over 8 percentage points higher compared to 1992/93).

Wages and salaries have increased from less than 30 percent of expenditure in the first half of the 1990s to nearly 34 percent of (a much higher) expenditure today. Interest costs have risen from about 33 percent of expenditure in the first half of the decade to nearly 42 percent of (a much higher) expenditure in 2002/03.

Meanwhile, the Government has reduced its investment (as a percentage of GDP) to offset partially the rise in wages and salaries and in interest costs—a crowding out of investment *within* the budget (Figure 3.1). Government capital expenditures have fallen from over 4 percent of GDP in the first half of the 1990s (and over 5 percent between 1995/96 and 1997/98), to only 2 percent of GDP today, that is, from about 17 percent of total expenditure in the first half of the decade to only 5 percent currently. And, while the Government debt has not crowded-out overall investment much, in terms of the overall investment ratio, the increased availability of government debt and the segmentation of the credit market has probably affected small borrowers, who are riskier and unable to access foreign markets (see Chapter 4 for further discussion).

TABLE 3.1: JAMAICA FISCAL OPERATIONS 1992/93–2002/03
(% of GDP)

	92/93	93/94	94/95	95/96	96/97	97/98	98/99	99/00	00/01	01/02	02/03p
Central Government Balance	3.7	3.0	3.1	1.8	−6.3	−7.6	−6.9	−4.2	−0.9	−5.7	−8.0
Revenues and grants	27.3	28.3	28.6	28.3	26.4	25.4	26.6	29.8	30.0	27.6	29.6
Tax 1/	24.0	25.8	26.0	25.7	24.3	23.7	25.0	26.9	26.7	25.0	26.4
Non-tax 2/	2.2	2.1	1.8	2.1	1.7	1.4	1.3	2.7	2.8	2.1	2.9
Grants	1.1	0.4	0.9	0.6	0.4	0.3	0.2	0.3	0.5	0.5	0.2
Expenditures	23.6	25.3	25.6	26.5	32.6	33.0	33.5	34.0	31.0	33.3	37.6
Wages and salaries	4.6	8.7	7.2	7.7	10.1	11.1	11.5	10.5	10.5	11.5	13.0

(continued)

TABLE 3.1: JAMAICA FISCAL OPERATIONS 1992/93–2002/03 (CONTINUED)
(% of GDP)

	92/93	93/94	94/95	95/96	96/97	97/98	98/99	99/00	00/01	01/02	02/03p
Interest	8.0	8.3	9.6	8.7	11.4	9.4	12.4	13.8	12.8	13.7	15.7
Domestic	4.2	5.0	6.6	6.0	8.9	7.2	10.2	11.6	10.2	10.9	11.8
External	3.7	3.3	3.1	2.7	2.5	2.2	2.2	2.2	2.6	2.9	3.8
Other expenditures 3/	5.6	4.2	5.0	4.7	5.5	7.5	6.9	6.6	5.0	5.4	6.9
Capital expenditures	5.4	4.1	3.8	5.4	5.6	5.0	2.7	3.0	2.8	2.7	2.0
Rest of public sector balance	−1.6	−0.1	0.7	0.2	0.9	−1.6	−4.0	−3.0	−4.7	−1.1	−1.3
Operating balance of public enterprises	3.0	1.6	2.7	−0.4	0.3	0.8	1.3	1.1	0.4	0.5	1.3
FIS/FINSAC balance 4/	0.0	0.0	0.0	0.0	−0.3	−2.1	−5.2	−4.4	−4.6	0.0	0.0
Bank of Jamaica operating profit/loss	−4.6	−1.7	−2.0	0.6	1.0	−0.3	0.0	0.3	−0.5	−1.7	−2.5
Total public sector balance	2.1	3.0	3.8	2.0	−5.3	−9.2	−10.9	−7.2	−5.6	−6.8	−9.3
External financing	−0.7	0.7	0.5	−1.5	−0.9	1.1	−0.8	−1.2	3.6	7.0	−3.3
Domestic financing	−1.5	−3.6	−4.2	−0.6	6.2	8.2	11.7	8.4	2.0	−0.1	12.6
Banking system	−2.7	−4.3	−1.4	3.5	−1.2	18.6	8.4	2.7	4.2	7.8	8.1
Others	1.3	0.6	−2.8	−4.1	7.4	−10.4	3.3	5.6	−2.2	−7.9	4.5
Adjusted central government balance 5/	3.7	3.0	3.1	1.8	−6.3	−8.7	−12.3	−8.3	−5.5	−5.7	−8.0
Central government primary balance	11.6	11.4	12.7	10.5	5.2	1.8	5.5	9.6	11.8	8.0	7.7
Public sector primary balance	14.6	13.0	15.4	10.2	5.4	2.6	6.8	10.7	12.2	8.6	8.9
Memorandum items:											
Non-financial public debt (end of period) 6/	114.0	122.5	110.1	85.9	79.1	102.3	115.7	132.7	131.9	130.6	148.5
Domestic	21.5	19.9	32.6	26.4	35.4	59.3	73.1	90.0	83.6	78.2	89.8
External	92.5	102.6	77.5	59.5	43.7	43.0	42.6	42.8	48.3	52.4	58.8

Notes:
1/ Includes bauxite levy
2/ Includes capital revenue
3/ Includes statistical discrepancy
4/ Includes interest due and capitalized during the year up to 2000/01
5/ Includes FINSAC interest payments on a full year basis
6/ The public sector debt is defined to include central government domestic and external debt and domestic and external debt guaranteed by the government. It excludes government securities held by public enterprises and external debt held by BoJ.
p Figures for 2002/03 are preliminary.
Source: IMF.

Towards Sustainable Debt

The rising ratio of debt to GDP in Jamaica raises questions of its sustainability. In 1996/97, Jamaica had a Government debt to GDP ratio of 79 percent, already a fairly high ratio by international standards.[1] However, the financial crisis, the economic contraction, and the increasing fiscal deficits and

1. In 1991/92, the debt to GDP ratio rose to 181 percent, from 138 percent in 1990/91, owing to the significant depreciation of the exchange rate from J$8.4 per US dollar in 1990/91 to J$24.8 in 1991/92. The external debt stock in US dollar terms actually fell from US$3,942 million in 1990/91 to US$3,787 million in 1991/92, but rose from 100 to 163 percent of GDP. The decline in the debt ratio to 79 percent in 1996/97 was achieved through: debt reduction under the Enterprise for the Americas Initiative, debt cancellations from the British and Netherlands Governments, and debt rescheduling under a Multi-Year Rescheduling Arrangement with the Paris Club, in 1991 and 1993.

the resulting increased borrowing have led to a sharp rise in debt, relative to GDP. In particular, the fiscal cost of the financial crisis exacerbated the adverse debt dynamics so that by 2000, debt was about 130 percent of GDP (Table 3.1 and Figure 3.2). Most of the increase in debt was domestic, replacing private credits in the banks, and today Government debt is the counterpart of more than half of Jamaican banks' deposits, as discussed in Chapter 4. By 2002, fiscal tightening and greater reliance on offshore borrowing (which is less costly in the context of an appreciating real exchange rate) had reduced the ratio of debt to GDP slightly. However, with the significant fiscal slippage in 2002/03, depreciation in the exchange rate, and higher interest rates, the ratio of debt to GDP rose to nearly 150 percent of GDP, one of the highest ratios in the world, with domestic debt about 90 percent of GDP and external debt about 60 percent of GDP.[2]

The structure and composition of debt has changed significantly since 1991 (Table 3.2). The share of domestic debt in total debt has risen from 8.3 percent in March 1992 to 60 percent at the end of March 2002, owing in large part to the financial crisis and its ensuing impact on the deficit. Initially, most of the increased domestic borrowing has been through Local Registered Stocks (LRS) and Treasury Bills. LRS stocks rose from 61 percent of domestic debt in March 1992 to 72 percent by March 2002. Treasury Bills issuance reduced after 1994/95, and their share in domestic debt fell from 27.3 percent in March 1992 to 5.4 percent in March 2002. As the domestic capital market developed in the mid-nineties and the government moved to lengthen the term structure of its domestic debt, long-term bonds became more important. Consequently, the share of bonds increased from about 4 percent in March 1995 to 21.4 percent in March 2002.

Apart from this, the Jamaican banking system, which is emerging from the financial crisis of 1995/96, has more than one-third of its assets consisting of Government debt (which, net of Government deposits, represented about 45 percent of deposits in banks in June 2003, see Chapter IV). The rest of the financial system (merchant banks, brokers, building societies) also has a large holding of Government debt.

The share of external debt has fallen from 91.7 percent in March 1992 to 40 percent in March 2002. Its structure has also changed, with the share of concessional debt (bilateral and multilateral) falling from 85.5 percent in 1991/92 to 52.6 percent in 2001/02. Reflecting increased access to the international capital market, the share of private creditors in total external debt grew from

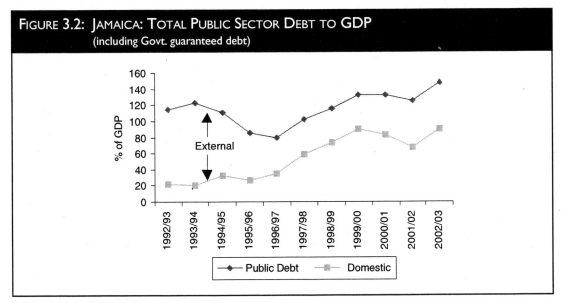

FIGURE 3.2: JAMAICA: TOTAL PUBLIC SECTOR DEBT TO GDP
(including Govt. guaranteed debt)

Source: IMF; See Table 3-1.

2. Note that external debt figures do not include short-term external debt.

TABLE 3.2: JAMAICA—DOMESTIC AND EXTERNAL DEBT, AND STRUCTURE OF EXTERNAL DEBT, 1991/92–2001/02

	1991/92	1994/95	1995/96	1996/97	1997/98	1998/99	1999/00	2000/01	2001/02
Total Debt J$Mn	113,041	170,807	193,843	198,205	219,214	262,303	308,688	380,641	497,083
Domestic Debt J$Mn	9,359	50,139	57,675	85,181	101,540	139,204	175,323	215,084	300,201
% Share	8.3	29.4	29.8	43.0	46.3	53.1	56.8	56.5	60.4
External Debt US$Mn	3,786	3,612	3,402	3,223	3,223	3,216	3,165	3,624.27	4,135.29
% Share	91.7	70.6	70.2	57.0	53.7	46.9	43.2	43.5	39.6
Share of External Debt (%)									
Multilateral	35.5	35.9	35.3	33.1	35.0	33.0	32.3	30.7	27.3
Bilateral	50.0	52.6	53.3	53.2	45.3	44.2	41.9	31.8	25.3
Private Creditors	14.5	11.5	11.4	13.8	19.6	22.9	25.8	37.5	47.4
Commercial Banks	9.0	8.5	8.7	8.7	8.8	4.8	4.3	4.2	2.2
Other	5.5	2.9	2.7	1.9	1.5	0.9	1.2	5.6	5.2
Bonds	—	—	—	3.1	9.3	17.1	20.4	27.8	40.0

Source: Ministry of Finance

14.5 percent in 1991/92 to a high of 47.4 percent in 2001/02 (Table 3.2). It is also noted that bonds accounted for the bulk (40 of 47.4 percent) of the share of private creditors.

Reaching fiscal and debt sustainability are critical to a return to sustained growth, but primary surpluses of more than 10 percent of GDP are needed just to sustain the current, high debt to GDP ratio of 150 percent. Table 3.3 (which shows the debt-stabilizing primary surplus under alternative assumptions about interest rates, inflation, growth[3]) shows that this is the case under plausible future scenarios for growth and interest rates (for example, growth of 2 percent, nominal interest of 18 percent and inflation of 8 percent). Moreover, the required surplus is extremely sensitive to growth and interest rates, and it is worth noting that the Government in June 2003 floated 2 and 5 year LRS at about 34 percent (implying a real rate of about 25 percent). For example, given the stock of debt, a 1 percentage point increase in the nominal interest rate increases the required primary surplus by about 1.4 percentage points of GDP. Similarly, an increase in growth by 1 percentage point would reduce the debt-stabilizing primary surplus by about 1.5 percentage points of GDP. As the table also shows, it is possible to trade off higher inflation for a lower primary surplus, but this depends on limited movement in the interest rate—if the interest rate rises with inflation, then there is no tradeoff.

The debt stock is also sensitive to the exchange rate, given that external debt is about 60 percent of GDP, and about 20 percent of domestic debt is indexed to the US dollar. In the simple model above, the initial exchange rate is factored in through changes in the initial debt to GDP ratio. A rough rule of thumb is that a one Jamaican dollar depreciation versus the U.S. dollar results in an increase in total debt by 1 percent of GDP. To mitigate this, real exchange rate depreciation (which will help improve competitiveness) would need to be accompanied by growth and productivity enhancing measures, and preferably reduction in real interest rates.

Reducing the debt stock will of course demand higher primary surpluses. In order to meet its target of reducing the debt to about 123 percent of GDP by the end of 2005/06, higher surpluses of about 15–17 percent of GDP will be needed (assuming 2 percent growth, interest rates of 15–17 percent, and inflation of 8 percent).

---

3. It should be noted that these projections assume that Jamaica will not be subject to adverse shocks, such as those it has had to contend with since the events of September 11, 2001. Adverse shocks could erode confidence and put pressure on the currency and upward pressure on interest rates, both of which would increase the level of debt.

TABLE 3.3: PRIMARY SURPLUS/DEFICIT (% OF GDP) REQUIRED TO STABILIZE THE STOCK OF PUBLIC DEBT

d = 150	g = 0		g = 1		g = 2		g = 4	
	f = 8	f = 6	f = 8	f = 6	f = 8	f = 6	f = 8	f = 6
i = 10	2.8	5.7	1.3	4.1	−0.2	2.6	−3.1	−0.3
i = 12	5.6	8.5	4.0	6.9	2.5	5.4	−0.4	2.4
i = 14	8.3	11.3	6.8	9.7	5.2	8.1	2.2	5.1
i = 16	11.1	14.1	9.5	12.5	7.9	10.9	4.9	7.8
i = 18	13.9	17.0	12.3	15.3	10.7	13.7	7.6	10.6
i = 20	16.7	19.8	15.0	18.1	13.4	16.5	10.3	13.3

Note: g: real growth rate; d: debt to GDP ratio; i: nominal interest rate; f: inflation.
Source: World Bank staff estimates.

Fiscal slippage, to a primary surplus of 6–7 percent of GDP, would lead to a rise in the debt to GDP ratio. A primary surplus of 6–7 percent of GDP, would, under assumptions mentioned earlier (growth 2 percent, interest 18 percent, inflation 8 percent), only stabilize debt if the debt were lower by some 50 percentage points of GDP. Such surpluses, while still high, would be more manageable. Lower required surpluses could free up resources for critical economic and social investment, crowd-in private investment and create a virtuous growth cycle that would further improve debt dynamics.

To summarize, the current debt of about 150 percent of GDP needs primary surpluses of over 10 percent of GDP just to stabilize the debt, at interest rates much lower than the ones currently prevailing. Reduction of the debt to 123 percent by 2005/06 would further increase the required surpluses. A lower primary surplus (6–7 percent of GDP) would only stabilize the debt if the debt were lower by some 50 percentage points of GDP.

Reducing and Improving Government Expenditure

A key element in reducing Government expenditure is control over the wage bill, which now accounts for over a third of Government expenditure. Rising real public sector wages are inconsistent with a sustainable debt ratio and a slow-growing economy, unless public sector employment is reduced, in percentage terms, by more than the real wage increase. Allowing real public sector wages to fall may provide a temporary reduction in the growth of public wages and salaries, but it is not a sustainable way to reduce wage and salary expenditure relative to GDP. Typically, falling real public wages and salaries generate political pressure for an increase and, once the catch-up is granted, the ratio of public wages and salaries to GDP returns to, or even exceeds, the original level.

The four major ministries of Finance, Education, National Security and Health accounted for over three quarters of the total public sector employment and 90 percent of recurrent expenditure in 2001/02, up from 82 percent in 1991/92. Therefore, attempts at controlling or reducing total recurrent expenditure would need to focus on these key ministries. However, this is a complex issue that bears detailed investigation. For example, the nine-fold increase in the budget of the ministry of national security reflects the response to the increased levels of crime since the mid-nineties. As a result, the strength of the police force has increased by 1068 since 1991 to 7,033 in 2000. Over the same period, the number of registered nurses in the health ministry increased by only 330. Any attempt at reducing or controlling expenditure in the public sector must necessarily focus on the details of the expenditures within each ministry vis-à-vis the specific mandate of the ministry. In addition, it may be possible to rationalize some functions across ministries. For example, it may be possible for some ministries to outsource some specialized services such as auditing or procurement. While more work is needed on this (to be taken up the Bank's forthcoming Public Expenditure Review), it would appear that significant reduction in public sector employment would need to be accompanied by organizational and efficiency gains.

BOX 3.1: A TALE OF TWO PRIVATIZATIONS

Jamaica's privatization program began in 1981 as part of a general effort to reduce the role of the government in the economy. However, privatization as part of a more distinct strategy of liberalization and private sector led growth started in the mid eighties. This box highlights two privatization experiences in Jamaica—the sugar industry, which despite significant preparatory work was considered a failure; and the telecommunications company that, in spite of initial problems, is considered an overall success.

Privatization in the Sugar Industry

In 1994, a private sector consortium, including the transnational Tate & Lyle, a local merchant bank and a local distillery group, acquired the majority stake of the Sugar Company of Jamaica (SCJ). The government retained minority participation through the holding of 49 percent of the shares. The sale of the mills was highly transparent and all stakeholders were fully informed of the process of privatization. It was envisaged that privatization would lead to lower production costs through improvements at the field and factory levels. However, in October 1998, approximately four years after privatization, the Jamaican government re-acquired the SCJ, due in part to the financial crisis and the heavy debt carried by the company. The re-acquisition made the government once again the major player in the sugar industry.

The failure of the sugar industry under private ownership has in large measure been blamed on the revaluation of the exchange rate in 1997. Government's retention of a significant share (49 percent) after privatization may have also weakened the incentives for the private sector to persevere in pursuing the tough reform measures that may have been necessary to turn the industry around. The fiscal cost of the re-acquisition (with working capital deficiency of over J$3 billion or 1 percent of GDP) and operations of the sugar mills has been significant

Privatization in the Telecommunications Industry

In 1988, the Government of Jamaica privatized the provision of basic telephone services with the sale of licenses to Cable and Wireless Jamaica Limited. It is clear that not enough attention was paid to the establishment of an adequate regulatory framework. Perhaps in its effort to maximize revenue or woo investors, Jamaica granted the privatized telephone company a twenty-five year concession on local and competitive international services that guaranteed a rate of return exceeding industry norms.

Notwithstanding the regulatory issues, there were many gains from the privatization in the telecommunications sector. The most immediate gain was the significant investment by the monopoly C&W to expand service in the sector. After liberalization in March 2000, mobile phone accounts grew from 144,000 to 1.2 million by 2002, and penetration rates were higher than several developed countries. In March 2003, the sector became open to competition in all aspects of telephony. The macroeconomic impact of the privatization and liberalization of the telecommunication sector has been quite considerable. Since the liberalization of the sector, more than US$400 million has been invested. The reduction in the local telecommunication cost facilitated the development of several information technology-related services and has reduced at least one of the disadvantages faced by Jamaican firms (see Chapter 7).

Lessons Learned

These two episodes of privatization with sharply contrasting results, along with privatization experiences around the world, highlight three potent lessons for future privatization: (1) the necessity to create incentives for the private sector to take full control, which avoids the creation of contingent fiscal liability for the government, either through occasional bail-outs or through the outright re-acquisition of the privatized entity; (2) the importance of a predictable planning environment for the private sector (the revaluation of the exchange rate in 1997 must have been a major shock for the new investors in the sugar industry); and (3) the importance of carefully considering the regulatory framework a priori, to encourage early competition that would enable reaping of the larger economic benefits of competition. The overall fiscal benefits of early competition may outweigh the one-time gains to revenue of a sale with regulatory concessions.

The government has made progress on the privatization agenda but the experience has been mixed (see Box 3.1) and the government still has substantial holdings in some entities, including Air Jamaica,[4] mining companies, the power company and the sugar industry. In addition, there are a number of relatively small enterprises that remain in the public sector in activities such as agriculture and tourism, which could be transferred to the private sector. The proceeds from the sale of shares or privatization of these entities could be used to write down the debt, although the proceeds are likely to be much smaller than in the past. In addition, the transfer of the entities to the private sector could reduce the risk of contingent liability even though it would not eliminate it, as the case of Air Jamaica has proved.

Achieving a more sustainable debt burden and improved Government expenditure will depend not only on lower public expenditure, but more public investment within that expenditure, focused in sectors that are critical for creating the enabling environment for private sector investment and growth. Government expenditure has increasingly become current expenditure, as noted above. However, development depends to some degree on more infrastructure investment. Cross-country evidence suggests that infrastructure tends to encourage ("crowd-in") private investment. Of course, such infrastructure investment can be financed by reasonable user charges or other revenues linked to debt servicing, allowing the Government, or a public entity, to repay the debt taken to carry out the investment.

While private investments have substituted for some traditionally public infrastructure in Jamaica, notably telecommunications, power and more recently toll roads, public infrastructure investment will be important in stimulating growth. In recent years, the government's capital investments have been focused on roads and water supply but significant investment has also been made in the information technology and tourism sectors. Table 3.4 gives the sectoral shares in the government's planned Public Sector Investment Program up to fiscal year 2003/04. Economic infrastructure has been accorded high priority, getting over 50 percent of the total investment. Included in this are significant investment in major roads (maintenance, rehabilitation and new construction); airports (including investments pursuant to the divestment of the Sangster's airport) and seaports. In an effort to finance priority infrastructure, the government has also resorted to "deferred financing," where private contractors are asked to arrange their own financing for government projects on which they bid, thus avoiding a direct budget outlay. However, this creates contingent liabilities for future budgets..

The government's social investment has been focused on education and housing. Other social infrastructure, which includes a significant outlay for the Lift Up Jamaica Program and the Social and Economic Support Program (SESP), account for a major share of social investment. Given the current tight budget, the government may need to review its investments in housing given the involvement of the National Housing Trust and a fairly well-developed mortgage market.

Raising Revenue: Taxes and User Fees

Revenues are about 27 percent of GDP (taxes about 25–26 percent of GDP and non-tax revenue about 2–3 percent of GDP). Compared to other developing countries, Jamaica has a fairly high revenue base, particularly compared to Latin American countries (Table 3.5). The distribution of revenue is shown in Annex Table 3.3. Forty percent of tax revenue comes from income and profit taxes, which have been about 10 percent of GDP in recent years. Of the income and profit taxes, more than half comes from withholding tax on incomes (PAYE) and about 20 percent from with-

---

4. The Government recently re-acquired Air Jamaica, which was privatized in 1994 and in which the government retained 30 percent. Before the re-acquisition in 2003 the government had provided several guarantees for loans to the privatized entity. Indeed, by 2000 the government had injected about US$133 million into the privatized airline and had increased its share to 45 percent.

TABLE 3.4: JAMAICA PUBLIC SECTOR INVESTMENT PROGRAM, 2000/01–2003/04
(percentage share by sectors)

	2000/01	2001/02	2002/03	2003/04
Directly Productive	3.2	4.3	4.3	3.5
Agriculture	2.3	2.7	2.8	2.1
Mining	0.04	0.1	0.1	0.1
Tourism	0.9	1.6	1.4	1.4
Economic Infrastructure	52.6	58.8	39.9	27.6
Transport & Communication	27.8	23.2	12.1	8.5
Power & Energy	6.1	13.4	7.3	7.1
Water Supply & Sewage	5.5	5.1	6.4	4.3
Other Economic Infrastructure	13.2	17.0	14.1	7.6
Social Infrastructure	24.8	25.6	30.0	26.9
Education	5.4	5.9	8.1	4.8
Health	1.4	0.8	1.7	1.3
Housing	7.5	8.2	8.6	10.6
Other Social Infrastructure	10.4	10.7	11.7	10.2
Administration	18.9	10.2	23.4	40.5
Total PSIP excl. on-lending	99.5	99.0	97.6	98.5
Funds & Loans	0.5	1.0	2.5	1.5
Total PSIP and on-lending	100.0	100.0	100.0	100.0

Source: Jamaica Medium Term Strategy, Planning Institute of Jamaica

held taxes on interest. About seven percent comes from taxes on profits of companies, which have been falling steadily as a percentage of GDP since the mid-1990s. The Education Tax, 1 percent of GDP, is also a kind of withholding tax that is paid by employers on the wage bill. The General Consumption Tax (GCT, Jamaica's version of the VAT) produces 7 percent of GDP, nearly 40 percent from imports. However, the GCT has declined nearly one percentage point of GDP since the mid-1990s. The Special Consumption Tax (SCT) (imported goods) accounts for nearly 3 percent of GDP. Tariffs still account for about 2.5 percent of GDP, and the bauxite levy has fallen to 0.4 percent of GDP reflecting lower levels of production as well as lower prices. Capital revenues have been erratic reflecting the fortunes of both the financial performance of the selected public sector entities and the government's divestment program.

Given the already high tax rate, revenue measures have increasingly focused on: (a) increasing compliance through plugging the loopholes in the tax system and (b) increasing user fees to reflect the economic cost of providing government services.

Since the early 1980s, Jamaica's tax system has undergone significant reform in order to achieve the multiple objectives of simplicity, equity, and effectiveness and to make the system more capable of stimulating investment and economic growth. There has been significant simplification of personal income tax, moving from a marginal rate of 57.5 percent in 1980 to a flat rate of 33.3 percent in the mid-eighties, and then to a flat rate of

TABLE 3.5: GOVERNMENT REVENUES/GDP

Selected Countries, 2000, %	
New Zealand (1999)	32.9
Barbados	32.7
Singapore	32.7
Jamaica	**27.0**
Mauritius	21.4
Dominican Republic	16.1
Costa Rica	12.2
El Salvador	12.1

Source: IFS, IMF.

25 percent (as well as a minimum exempt income level) currently. The GCT, the Jamaican version of the value added tax, was put in place in 1991.

The growth of the informal sector, in part, to avoid taxes, has tended to reduce the tax base. For example, the growth of the informal sector probably has contributed to the decline in the GCT as a percentage of GDP. The question is how best to bring the informal sector into the tax net, in order to level the playing field between informal and formal firms. As noted above, most of the tax revenue comes from withholding taxes or taxes on external trade, which firms in the informal sector bypass. Reducing the GCT rate is unlikely to bring enough firms into the tax net to offset the loss of revenue from lower rates. Further simplification of the tax system, including the merger of some taxes such as the Education Tax and the National Housing Trust Tax with income tax may provide an additional incentive for more small informal sector business to come into the tax net, as their transaction cost for tax compliance would be much lower.

Through amendments to the Revenue Administration Act and the introduction of the Taxpayer Registration Number (TRN) system, considerable progress has been made in increasing the number of registered taxpayers. However, this registration has been on a purely voluntary basis and may exclude many who operate in the informal sector. One approach to increasing the coverage of the informal sector, as well as to increase the revenues from personal income taxes, would be to use a system of indicators, such as motor vehicle licenses and overseas trips, to identify individuals who are not in the tax net. However, this will imply increased costs of tax administration.

Recent work by Artana and Navajas (2002) has pointed to a number of areas in which the design of the tax system could be improved, including:

- the multiple tax rates and exemptions for GCT, which cannot be explained by equity reasons and which impose significant administrative burdens.
- the tax bias in favor of debt financing relative to equity financing.
- the additional payroll taxes, including HEART, NHT, and Education Tax, which impose further taxes on labor and which may encourage firms to use labor saving technologies in an economy where unemployment and informality is high.

Significant subsidies exist in the tax code. For example, the Investment Tax Credit means that some firms do not pay their share of taxes, and this may generate misallocation of resources. Firms receiving the Investment Tax Credit receive benefits that may reduce the cost of purchasing an asset by 20–40 percent, compared to other firms. Moreover, beneficiary of the Investment Tax Credit also is allowed to depreciate 100 percent of the asset's purchase price, a further subsidy.

A particular concern relates to the tourism sector, where firms may receive subsidies and ad hoc exemptions from taxes. Agreements between the Caribbean countries have attempted to limit these incentives to potential investors in hotels. However, in practice, it appears that investors still receive incentives, setting up a competition between countries that reduces their ability to generate returns from their valuable natural assets.

Significant opportunities exist to raise non-tax revenues, notably fees for tertiary education. As discussed in Chapter 5, fees are relatively low, especially given the high quality of the education. About 80 percent of the graduates emigrate (Chapter 2), depriving the Government of the possibility of recouping even part of the subsidy from income taxes. Although most of the graduates are from middle or upper income families, a system of fellowships and loans will need to be created to ensure access by poorer students.

If the government is to bring about the fiscal adjustment necessary to reverse the adverse debt dynamics, the government may need to increase tax revenues to about 30 percent of GDP over the next five years or so. Compliance on GCT has improved over the last few years with the introduction of the tax reform program but compliance on income tax is lagging, partly due to the large size of the informal sector. Tax revenue could therefore be increased without raising the tax rate if more of the informal sector is brought into the tax net. Compliance may be improved through further simplification of the tax system and through the abolition of some tax incentives as well as some exemptions. In its 2003/04 Budget presented in April 2003, the Government has attempted to raise significant additional tax revenue amounting to about 3 percent of GDP, targeting increased taxation of imports and vehicles, and a widening of the GCT base.

Fiscal Institutions and Governance

Jamaica is considered to have a sound legal and institutional framework for fiscal management. Two recent studies rank Jamaica as the best (Alesina et al. 1996) or the second best (Stein et al. 1998) in the region, in terms of its fiscal institutions.

The overarching legal framework is the Constitution but there are other key pieces of legislations such as the Financial Administration and Audit Act (FAA), the Public Bodies Act. The consolidated Fund is entrenched in the Constitution of Jamaica.[5] The law requires that all the revenues collected by government be placed in the Consolidated Fund. This provision gives the government full control of the revenue inflows.

Sections 115 and 116 of the Jamaican Constitution deals with the budget including the responsibility for the Estimates of Expenditure and the authorization of expenditure. The Constitution authorizes that estimates for each new financial year be presented to Parliament before the end of the ongoing financial year. The Constitution also specifies that the estimates of expenditure must be separated into "statutory expenditure," mostly debt service,[6] and money needed for other expenditure to be met from the Consolidated Fund. The Constitution further states that statutory expenditure must not be voted on by Parliament and must be paid out of the Consolidated Fund without further authorization by Parliament. Consequently, debt servicing has a first call on revenues and is neither under the discretion of the Minister of Finance nor Parliament.

Section 117 of the Constitution deals with the control of expenditure from the Consolidated Fund. The section states, inter alia, that money must not be paid out of the Consolidated Fund without a warrant (written authorization) from the Minister of Finance. In addition, for further control, the section provides that the Finance Minister can only authorize expenditure out of sums of money granted by the Appropriation Law for items of expenditure lawfully charged to the Consolidated Fund. This applies to all cases of expenditure with the exception of: (a) payments for debt service, including interest and amortization and (b) advances from a contingency fund which has been established by law.

In sections 120, 121 and 122 of the Constitution, provisions are made for the establishment of the office of the Auditor-General (AG), including the terms of appointment, the tenure of office and the functions of the Auditor-General. The Auditor-General's function is to examine and report on all government accounts at least once per year. The Auditor-General is to report directly to the speaker of the house.[7] The independence of the Auditor-General is Constitutionally established in Section 122 (3) of the Constitution. However, the AG's department may be considered to be lacking independence in two regards: (i) the budget of the AG department passes through the Ministry of Finance and Planning before submission to the legislature, and (ii) control of personnel actions is substantially maintained by the Public Service Commission (World Bank, 2001a).

The Public Accounts Committee (PAC) of Parliament also plays a critical role in the audit process. The PAC consists of nine members of Parliament and is chaired by a member from the

---

5. This section of the Constitution requires a two-thirds majority in Parliament to change it.

6. This includes any expenditure which the Constitution says must be met from the Consolidated Fund or from the general income and assets of Jamaica, and any payment made to service the public debt and any money set aside for the repayment of debts (sinking fund, or that money which is set aside for the gradual repayment of debts, also redemption monies, monies to be recovered by agreed, regular payments) and all other costs involved in the management of the public debt.

7. The Auditor General's department itself is audited by the Ministry of Finance and Planning, in accordance with section 122 (4) of the Constitution.

opposition. The Public Accounts Committee considers reports of the Auditor-General on the accounts of the Government and other organizations that are within the purview of public audit. It may invite the Accounting Officer of ministries to attend public hearings to give explanation, evidence or information. Following the hearings, the PAC presents an annual report to Parliament.

The Financial Administration and Audit Act expands and clarifies Chapter VIII of the Constitution dealing with Finance and provides the legal framework for the management of funds appropriated (approved) by the House of Representatives.

The Budget Process

The budget process/cycle in Jamaica is controlled by the Ministry of Finance and Planning and involves a number of steps, illustrated in Box 3.2.

A recent assessment of the budgetary process by the World Bank Country Financial Accountability Assessment (CFAA), 2001 confirms the strength of the budgetary process but also points out some adjustments that would improve efficiency and transparency.[8] These adjustments include: (i) reducing the overlaps and duplication of functions and dispersion of oversight and policy-making responsibilities within departments dealing with the budget process; (ii) reducing the complexity of the current Program budget format to increase transparency and usefulness of the estimates; (iii) strengthening the government's corporate planning process, and integrating it into the budget process; and (iv) clarifying the classification of capital expenditure that is now classified as recurrent expenditure because ministries do not include such expenditures in the post-completion plan of projects; and (v) improvement in the transparency of cash management.

In addition, the current use of Cash Basis Accounting provides a limited picture of financial activity that could adversely affect the decision-making process. A switch to accrual accounting would reduce these risks.

The CFAA also found incomplete recording of assets and liabilities, and a lack of financial management guidance. Two key constraints also exist in the efficient and effective reporting of the use of public resources (KPMG, 1999). First, the time gap between high level and detailed information. The aggregated results for revenues, expenditure and liabilities are available immediately after the fiscal year ends, but the details are not available until twelve months after. Second, delayed reporting of actual transactions. Actual expenditures are usually recorded a year after they occur. The use of estimates as opposed to actual amounts prevents holding the ministries fully accountable for the financial results.

In its assessment of the auditing of government activities, the CFAA was generally positive as many of the recommendations from the Cowater Study regarding the auditing of government departments were being implemented. In respect of the Auditor General's Department, the CFAA indicated that its capacity and its independence were two of the more important remaining issues to be tackled.

In addition to issues of prudent management of expenditures, management of direct and contingent liabilities is also important. Explicit and implicit contingent liabilities have also been created by the government on its own behalf or on behalf of other public sector entities or even entities that have been privatized. These contingent liabilities have caused budgetary problems, and include debt write-offs for the National Water Commission (approximately J$6 billion), the Coffee Industry Board (J$2.7 billion) and the Sugar Industry (J$600 million) as well as guarantees of about J$9 billion of domestic debt. More recently, in May 2003, a J$6.3 billion loan external loan (90 million euros) was guaranteed by the Jamaican Government for the sugar industry.

Management of the overall fiscal balance is also made difficult by the lack of monitoring and reporting of non-central governments accounts on a timely basis. The CFAA noted that the GOJ budget only includes about 50 percent of the 140 public enterprises and that not all public enterprises are monitored. Since the central government is ultimately responsible for the debt or other

---

8. See also KPMG, 1999.

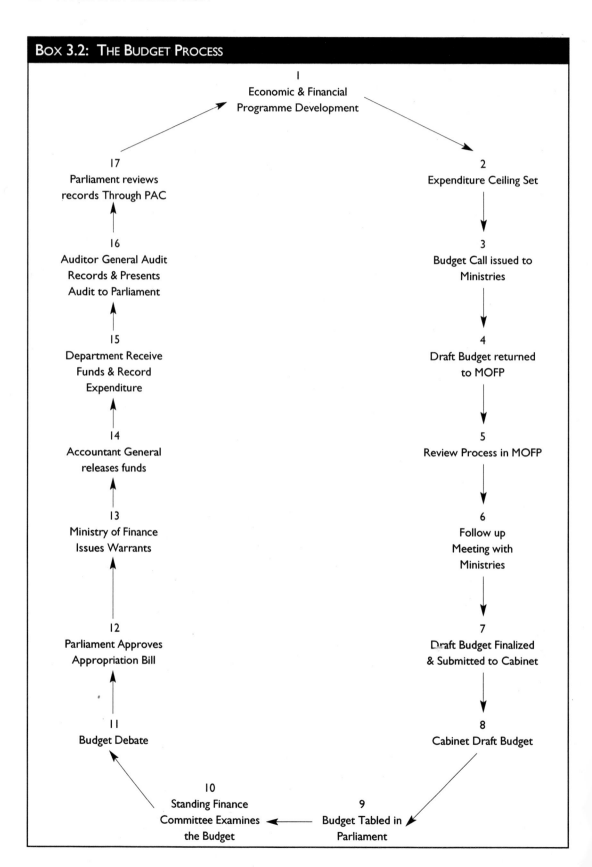

BOX 3.2: THE BUDGET PROCESS

1 Economic & Financial Programme Development

2 Expenditure Ceiling Set

3 Budget Call issued to Ministries

4 Draft Budget returned to MOFP

5 Review Process in MOFP

6 Follow up Meeting with Ministries

7 Draft Budget Finalized & Submitted to Cabinet

8 Cabinet Draft Budget

9 Budget Tabled in Parliament

10 Standing Finance Committee Examines the Budget

11 Budget Debate

12 Parliament Approves Appropriation Bill

13 Ministry of Finance Issues Warrants

14 Accountant General releases funds

15 Department Receive Funds & Record Expenditure

16 Auditor General Audit Records & Presents Audit to Parliament

17 Parliament reviews records Through PAC

TABLE 3.6: FISCAL RISK MATRIX

Liabilities	Direct (obligation in any event)	Contingent (obligation if a particular event occurs)
Explicit Government liability as recognized by law or contract	▨ Foreign and domestic sovereign borrowing (loans contracted and securities issued by central government) ▨ Budget of the Governor General ▨ Budgetary Expenditure ▨ Budgetary expenditures legally binding in the long-term (civil servants' salaries and pensions)	▨ Central government guarantees for non-sovereign borrowing and obligations issued to local government and public and private sector ▨ Umbrella state guarantees for various types of loans (mortgage loans, student loans, agriculture loans, small business loans) ▨ State guarantees on private investments (such as Air Jamaica) ▨ State insurance schemes
Implicit A "moral" obligation of government which reflects public and interest group pressure.	▨ Future public pensions (as opposed to civil service pensions) if not required by law. ▨ Social security schemes if not by law (Social Safety Net) ▨ Future health care financing if not by law ▨ Future recurrent cost of public investment	▨ Default of local government, and public or private entity on non-guaranteed debt and other obligations ▨ Liability clean-up in entities under privatization ▨ Banking failure ▨ Environmental recovery, disaster relief (floods, hurricanes, and riots)

liabilities of non-central government accounts, incomplete reporting of such accounts increases the difficulty of managing the fiscal balance.

In moving towards achieving and maintaining fiscal stability, there is need for the government to establish a budgetary planning framework that identifies and classifies the full range of fiscal liabilities, both direct and contingent, as well as the associated risk. See, for example, the fiscal risk matrix developed by Polackova et al. (1999) and illustrated in Table 3.6 above. The establishment of the Jamaica Deposit Insurance Corporation (JDIC) addresses directly the implicit contingent liability related to banking failure, although there remains the issue of funding it promptly in the event that its own resources are drawn down. Some provisions have also been made for the contingent liability associated with Bank of Jamaica losses. However, there is need for provisions related to contingent liability from riots, floods and hurricane damages as well as contingent liabilities from non-central government operations (such as National Water Commission (NWC) and Air Jamaica).

REVITALIZING JAMAICA'S FINANCIAL SYSTEM

Jamaica's growth and development are affected by the debt overhang from its enormous financial crisis. The crisis, one of the largest in the world (in terms of GDP), was resolved relatively quickly and has led to a significant improvement in regulation and supervision of the financial system, but also to a huge increase in an already large public sector debt. This debt burdens the economy, investment, and the public sector, crowding out private sector credit and public investment, as discussed below and in the previous chapter, and thereby limits Jamaica's growth. Increasing credit to the private sector, particularly small and medium industries that are potential exporters, and home loan mortgages, will depend on a primary surplus that reduces the importance of public sector debt in the financial system, and improved credit information systems to help reduce the risk of lending, particularly to smaller borrowers, and better systems of collateral execution to protect creditors' rights and increase the incentives to repay debt promptly. Given the large share of Government debt in the financial system (in banks equal to about 45 percent of deposits), maintenance of Government solvency is critical to maintaining the solvency of the financial system. Without continued public confidence in the Government's ability to service its debt, which backs the majority of deposits, a run could develop on the banks and the currency that would lead to a new crisis.

The Causes of Jamaica's Financial Crisis[1]

The fundamental causes of Jamaica's financial crisis were a privatization of financial institutions without much regard to the owners' capacity to withstand crises and a liberalization of financial markets, both in the context of weak regulation and supervision, followed by a tightening of monetary policy to contain the resulting credit boom and inflation. In the late 1980s, the Government

---

1. See also the discussion in World Bank (2000a); World Bank (2002e); and Naranjo and Osabela (2002).

85

began to privatize the banks that had been nationalized in the 1970s, as part of its general privatization strategy. However, the privatization was largely limited to domestic investors, who did not have large resources that could be called upon in the event of a crisis, particularly as they were subject to the same risks as the Jamaican economy.[2] Regarding liberalization, in the late 1980s, the Government largely reversed the interest, exchange and credit controls, and the high reserve requirements that had characterized financial sector policy earlier.

Regulation and supervision of the financial system was weak, however. Most countries, including Jamaica, did not consider financial regulation and supervision to be a major issue in the 1970s and 1980s. After banks were nationalized, political and social objectives, rather than prudential considerations, sometimes affected Government policy toward the financial system. Regulation of non-bank entities was given even less attention. The 1992 legislation to strengthen supervision of deposit-taking institutions did not provide sufficient sanction and intervention powers to bank supervisors, even for banks that were using the liquidity facilities of the Bank of Jamaica. Instead, power to fine an institution remained with the courts and power to sanction with the Finance Minister, who sometimes granted exemptions to prudential regulations and laws. Regulation of non-bank institutions remained lax.

In this environment, a huge credit boom developed, typically a predictor of a crisis. Commercial bank assets multiplied seven times between end-1990 and end-1995, merchant banks four times, and building societies nearly 10 times (Table 4.1). The share of loans in real estate and tourism increased. Various new institutions sprung up, often linked to old institutions under a conglomerate head, in response to easy entry regulations and to take advantage of regulatory arbitrage.[3] Insurance companies created deposit-like instruments (lump-sum or investment policies) where 1 percent or less went to insurance and the rest went to investments in real estate and other high risk assets.

TABLE 4.1: JAMAICA'S FINANCIAL SYSTEM 1990, 1995, AND 2001

	1990			1995			2001		
	No.	Assets	% Assets	No.	Assets	% Assets	No.[a]	Assets	% Assets
Commercial Banks	11	17,328	62.3	11	121,325	61.1	6	239,087	68.0
Non-Banks		10,469	37.7		77,271	38.9		112,745	32.0
Merchant Banks	21	4,527	16.3	25	17,334	8.7	13	15632	4.4
Building Societies	6	3,058	11.0	32	29,084	14.6	5	50448	14.3
Credit Unions	80	812	2.9	82	4,098	2.1	66	17279	4.9
Life Insurance Cos.	10	2,072	7.5	12	26,755	13.5	7	29386[b]	8.4
Total Assets		27,797	100.0		198,596	100.0		351,832	100.0
% of GDP		86.5			100.6			100.8	

Source: Bank of Jamaica, Life Insurance Company Association
Notes: a. Number of institutions refers to 1999
       b. 2000

The credit decision and the institutions themselves were weak according to a post-crisis study by FINSAC (Financial Sector Adjustment Company Ltd., the agency created in 1997 to deal with the institutions). Lending was often highly concentrated and substantial lending to related parties

---

2. Citibank and Nova Scotia Bank were already present and it is not clear that other foreign banks might have been interested. Jamaica's largest bank, National Commercial Bank (formerly Barclays International Bank which had been nationalized in 1977) was transferred to the public in stages, starting with the sale of over 40 percent of the shares in 1986. The Workers Savings and Loan Bank was privatized in 1991.

3. For example, after reserve requirements were imposed on merchant banks, which had grown in number in the 1980s, the number of building societies, which had no reserve requirements (and were only lightly supervised), increased from 6 in 1990 to 32 in 1995.

occurred. Lending also demonstrated little understanding and evaluation of risk. Loan decisions were overly dependent on collateral, particularly real estate that proved to be overvalued and illiquid, rather than projected cash flows (although these too would probably have been overstated). Maturity mismatches were common. Non-performing loans were underprovisioned. These weakness led to a crisis as GDP growth remained low and then the unsustainable boom in asset prices reversed.

The rise in credit was unproductive not only in terms of the inability to meet loan terms but in a macroeconomic sense. Although the rate of investment increased in the first half of the 1990s (in nominal terms), GDP growth fell sharply compared to the late 1980s (Table 4.2). Thus, in both micro- and macroeconomic terms, the allocation of the large increases in credit seems to have been unproductive.

TABLE 4.2: JAMAICA—FIXED CAPITAL FORMATION AND GROWTH 1986–2001
(percent of nominal GDP, except as noted)

	Average 1986–1991	Average 1992–1996	Average 1997–2001
TOTAL FIXED CAPITAL FORMATION	22.3	28.5	27.7
CONSTRUCTION	11.0	13.3	12.2
TRANSPORT EQUIPMENT	3.6	4.3	4.5
OTHER MACHINERY & EQUIPMENT	7.7	11.0	11.1
Agricultural Machinery & Equipment	0.4	0.3	0.3
Industrial Machinery & Equipment	2.5	3.6	2.7
Other Machinery & Other Capital Goods	4.9	7.1	8.1
	1986–1991	1991–1996	1996–2001
Average Real GDP Growth	4.8	0.9	0.0

Source: STATIN.

In the mid-1990s, the Government tightened monetary policy,[4] thereby reducing the high inflation that had been associated with the boom. The combination of the slow growth, poor investments, and the high real interest rates led first to illiquidity of some institutions, then to insolvency, as the weakness of their lending was exposed. Particularly hit were the insurance companies, which in turn borrowed from their related banks, thereby triggering problems in the banking sector. The interventions began in the Blaise Group, a small financial conglomerate in 1994, then the Century National Bank (where problems had actually begun in 1992, and which had received injections of liquidity equivalent to about 2 percent of GDP by 1996), and then spread across the system.[5]

Dealing with the Crisis

Jamaica's financial sector crisis was one of the costliest in terms of GDP (Figure 4.1) worldwide, but its clean-up was one of the quickest. The high costs of the crisis reflected the banks' substantial use of Bank of Jamaica's unsecured overdraft facility, and the Government's 1997 blanket guarantee of institutions' liabilities, implemented by FINSAC. The Government tried to limit its liability in the first two institutions that failed but in 1997, concerned about deposit runs, it issued a blanket guarantee

---

4. Before 1995, the Government had also made some attempts to tighten monetary policy, for example between 1989 and 1991 it re-instituted credit ceilings (dropped again in 1991), raised the liquidity requirement, and discontinued payments on reserves. The tightening probably induced financial conglomerates to undertake regulatory arbitrage to avoid the tightening, for example by relying more on deposits in merchant banks and building societies and deposit-like instruments sold by insurance companies.

5. The FIS (Financial Institutions Services), created in 1994, handled the problems in the first two institutions, before the creation of FINSAC.

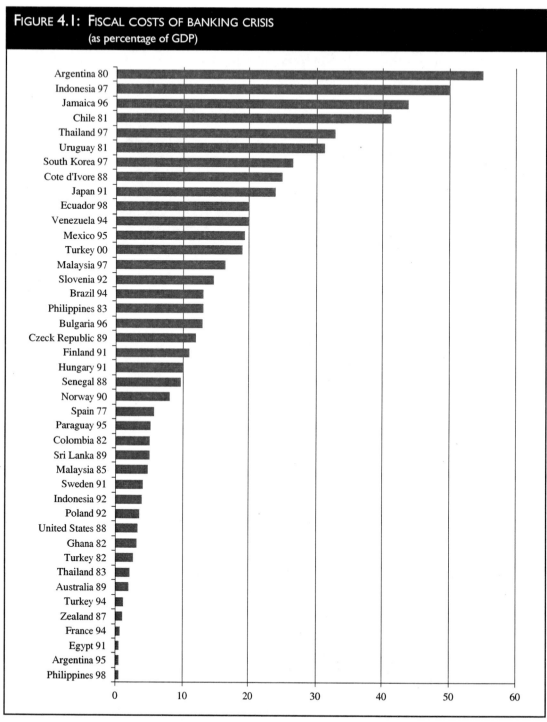

FIGURE 4.1: FISCAL COSTS OF BANKING CRISIS
(as percentage of GDP)

Source: World Bank estimates

that was implemented by FINSAC. In March 2001, the Government took over the FINSAC. bonds issued to the banks and the insurance companies (valued at J$142.7 billion or 42 percent of GDP at that time) and it is servicing this debt.[6] Note that FINSAC debt to the banks was treated as "other credit" in Bank of Jamaica statistics until 1998 and as "private credit" by the IMF until 2001, which understates the amount of public sector debt in the banking system in those data sources until those years.

FINSAC's resolution of the crisis was one of the world's fastest. In July 2002, about five years after its creation, the Government closed FINSAC operations for practical purposes.[7] FINSAC took over about 172 financial institutions including banks, merchant banks, building societies, and insurance companies and their subsidiaries. In the most important cases, FINSAC merged deposits from banks, merchant bank and building society depositors, together with FINSAC bonds into Citizens/Union Bank and National Commercial Bank, then sold these banks to Royal Bank of Trinidad & Tobago Holdings and AIC Barbados (a subsidiary of AIC Canada), in 2000 and 2002 respectively. Regarding insurance companies, FINSAC transferred the deposit-like instruments into Nova Scotia and Scotia Trust, along with an equivalent amount of FINSAC securities. It has sold Life of Jamaica to Barbados Mutual Assurance and its minority stakes in Island Life, Dyoll Insurance, and few small companies, as well as its preferred shares in Victoria Mutual Building Society are being divested. Altogether FINSAC liquidated 74 companies, with liquidation of a further 84 pending. Most assets taken over by FINSAC have been either liquidated by FINSAC or sold; the proceeds were partially used to reduce FINSAC debt.[8]

Results of the Crisis Resolution

The crisis and its resolution in Jamaica had a smaller effect on GDP than it did in East Asia but, unlike the Asian countries, growth did not even return to the previous, low trend three years after the crisis. Crisis resolution in Jamaica also has led to a much stronger financial system, with much better regulation and supervision, but a system that is more concentrated and dominated by fewer banks and system that is performing less intermediation because the assets corresponding to the deposits are now largely government debt (arising from the crisis) rather than private credit.

Growth in Jamaica's growth fell much less during its crisis than was the case in East Asian countries, although Jamaica's crisis was bigger (relative to GDP) than the East Asian countries except for Indonesia (Figure 4.2). However, Jamaica's post-crisis growth remained similar to, or even less than the low levels of the first half of the 1990s, until 2000, while in East Asia growth has resumed and largely recouped all of the losses. Indeed, Korea, which is generally regarded to have cleaned-up its financial system and its corporations the most rapidly of the Asian economies, seems to be back on its original growth path.

As a result of the crisis and its clean-up, Jamaica's financial system is now even more dominated by banks. The role of merchant banks and insurance companies has reduced substantially (Table 4.1).[9] All intermediaries hold much more public sector debt than before the crisis and the share of private sector credit has fallen dramatically (see the next section for a discussion). The increased role of well-known international banks, and the large holdings of government debt in the system have reduced

---

6. In September 2002 Government it also took over the FINSAC debt to the Bank of Jamaica (roughly J$31 billion) and it is accruing interest at market rates on this debt.

7. FIS is handling the wind-up of the few FINSAC's assets that were not liquidated by July 2002.

8. The Beale group purchased about J$68 billion of non-performing loans (including accrued interest) and is liquidating them with the Government retaining a share; so far about J$1.2 billion has been received by the Government. FINSAC also liquidated about J$30 billion in assets, the remaining assets are in the process of sale or have been leased with an option to buy. Recovery rates are obviously low and unlikely to reduce the net cost of the crisis much.

9. The reduction of the role of insurance companies and the growth of banks, particularly the international banks, partly reflects the shift of insurance companies' deposit-like liabilities to Bank of Nova Scotia and Scotia Trust.

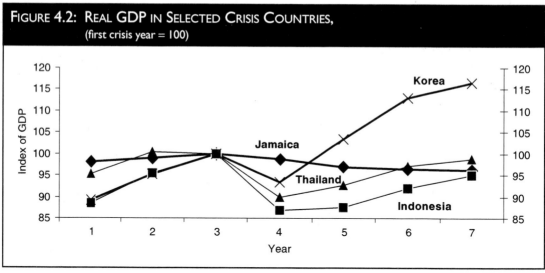

FIGURE 4.2: REAL GDP IN SELECTED CRISIS COUNTRIES,
(first crisis year = 100)

Source: International Financial Statistics, IMF.

systemic risk since the crisis. International banks with a reputation to protect are likely to lend prudently and resolve any problems themselves, without the need for Government injection of funds, as they did during the crisis.[10] Of course this depends on the Government's not attempting to tax their activities excessively, a problem that has occurred in Argentina recently. Jamaica's bank balance sheets have been cleaned up, but this is largely the result of larger government debt holdings and, to a lesser extent, a reduction in lending except to the best clients. More Government debt means less risk of NPLs, smaller risk of runs on individual banks, and less cost of resolving any crisis in an individual bank, providing the public continues to have confidence that the government will service its debt at par.[11]

With fewer institutions and the corresponding increased concentration of non-mortgage lending in fewer banks, competition in lending has probably decreased (see World Bank 2000a, Annex IV). This is particularly true since the funds available for lending to the private sector are limited by the large stock of government debt in the system and its large annual increases, as discussed below.

What might have been done differently to resolve the crisis? Without question the speed of the eventual clean-up by FINSAC was excellent. Before the crisis, the weakness of regulation and supervision and the access to liquidity from the Bank of Jamaica may have contributed to the weak lending quality, the unsustainable boom, and the eventual cost of the crisis. The access to liquidity may also have permitted insiders to "loot" their banks. If weak institutions had been intervened sooner and the costs paid up-front, then the unsustainable boom probably would have been smaller, and the eventual costs of the crisis less.[12] The need for prompt corrective action and acceptance of the

10. Partly, of course, the international banks were not subject to liquidity crises because deposits shifted to them, as typically happens in systemic financial crises.

11. In a single bank with large government debt holdings, the loss of capital (for example because of market losses) would mean that Government intervention required little additional issue of new government debt to comply with the guarantee. Of course, the Government might need to provide cash to cover possible deposit outflows, but it should be able to do this without greatly disturbing monetary policy provided it can access markets and the run is to other banks and not on the currency, i.e. confidence in the Government and the currency remains. This analysis suggests that runs on individual banks are probably less likely than previously, though some of the foreign banks experience runs in the case of problems in their home countries. Of course, the key issue is continued confidence in the Government and the currency.

12. Legal and regulatory constraints made prompt intervention difficult; these constraints have now been eased, as discussed below.

initial losses to avoid bigger losses later, is a lesson that has been repeated over and over in crises since the U.S. Savings and Loan crisis, but governments seem to have difficulty in facing these costs until they are overwhelming.

Once the Jamaican crisis became obviously large, decisions had to be made quickly with limited information. With the benefit of hindsight and the experience that has been accumulated with crises since then, it is easier to suggest alternatives than it was at the time in the midst of large short run pressures. Nonetheless, some comments on the initial response to the crisis are probably worthwhile. First, it is important to understand clearly that the key issue in crisis decision-making is the allocation of the cost of the non-performing loans, which of course are unlikely to be measured very precisely. Generally speaking, owners of financial institutions need to be the first to bear the costs, but the amounts they have at risk (their capital) are limited. Hence, the issue soon comes down to whether depositors will bear the cost, or taxpayers and future investors (in terms of higher interest rates) will bear the cost. In Jamaica, the eventual decision was to guarantee all liabilities, despite the lack of any Government legal obligation, which meant that taxpayers and future generations would bear the cost. The Government could have refused to accept any obligation, which would have transferred all the costs to the depositors. A limited Government support of depositors and holders of deposit-like obligations of insurance companies, such as was tried in the case of the Blaise group and Century National Bank (which had been allowed to continue existence by large borrowings from the Bank of Jamaica), would have reduced the cost of the crisis to the taxpayers compared to the blanket guarantee. However, concerns about capital flight and depreciation, perhaps excessive, led to the blanket guarantee. An alternative to the blanket guarantee would have been another approach to force depositors to bear some of the cost—the forced conversion of, say, time deposits into long-term, marketable instruments bearing below-market interest rates. The banks could have been permitted to do this, in effect making their depositors equity investors in their portfolios, or the Government could have issued such bonds, which would have lowered the cost compared to the actual approach. Either way, the depositors would have borne some of the cost, but would have had access to (a reduced amount of) their deposits if they needed liquidity, through the market for the instruments. Whether this approach would have been legally possible in Jamaica is not clear, but it is not clear that this would have been more difficult legally than the blanket guarantee, though certainly less attractive politically. In addition, complicated as it might have been, some reduction in the cost might have been made by crossing deposits with defaulting borrowers, given the large amount of connected lending that seems to have occurred. This crossing of deposits and bad loans might have been facilitated by the substitution of marketable instruments for bonds.

The Debt Overhang and its Effects

Jamaican public sector debt, already large before the crisis is now almost 150 percent of GDP; domestic debt is about 90 percent of GDP, largely reflecting the replacement of financial institutions' loans by government debt. The resulting 45 percent ratio of Jamaican Government debt to total bank deposits is one of the highest in the world. This debt reduces the risk of the banking system, as long as confidence is maintained in the government's capacity to service the debt at par, but the stock and the flow of debt crowds out new lending to the private sector, particularly to SME and riskier clients. This has led to pressures to resort to government directed credit with all its risks. A large primary surplus, and better information, particularly on smaller borrowers, is needed to limit the flow of new debt and increase the availability and reduce the cost of credit to the private sector.

Jamaican public sector credit typically has represented about 50 percent of commercial bank deposits, about 36 percent of assets, and about 25 percent of GDP in the last few years. In contrast, private sector credit represents only about 25 percent of commercial bank deposits, 18 percent of assets, and 10–12 percent of GDP (Figure 4.3). These recent figures are roughly a reversal of the 1994–1995 figures, when private credit represented about 20 percent of GDP and public sector credit less than 5 percent.

A similar story of increased government debt, reduced private credit is true for merchant bank and building societies. In the merchant banks, loans and advances have fallen by 50 percent in Jamaican dollars, equivalent to a drop from 3 percent of GDP in 1994 to less than 1 percent of assets in 2001. The building societies' new mortgages in 2001 were only about 10 percent larger in nominal terms than in 1996; they fell from 0.3 percent of GDP to 0.1 percent of GDP. Meanwhile their stock of Government securities rose 75 percent in nominal terms. With the decline in mortgages from banks and building societies, the Government has become the main provider of housing finance since the mid-1990s.

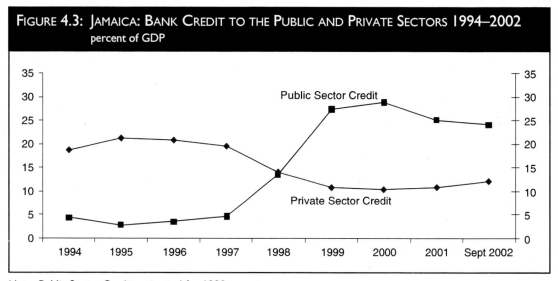

FIGURE 4.3: JAMAICA: BANK CREDIT TO THE PUBLIC AND PRIVATE SECTORS 1994–2002
percent of GDP

Note: Public Sector Credit estimated for 1998.
Source: Bank of Jamaica; IFS, IMF.

The Jamaican ratio of net Government debt to bank deposits (45 percent in June 2003) is one of the highest in the world (Table 4.3). In addition, public enterprise debt represents another 10 percent of deposits. Like Jamaica, most of the countries that have a large percentage of Government debt to GDP have experienced financial crises. In these countries, restoration of financial sector solvency after the crisis, by replacing private non-performing loans with Government debt, means financial solvency depends on the ability of the Government to service its debt or to roll it over. Confidence in the financial system thus depends on the public's confidence in the Government's debt servicing capacity.

Casual observation and some cross country evidence from some 86 developing and industrial countries suggest a negative relationship between total public sector debt (as a percentage of GDP) and GDP growth (Figure 4.4). This empirical result is something of a replication of other work that shows a positive empirical relationship between growth and the size of credit to the private sector (relative to GDP) across countries.[13] Clearly, many of the countries with large public sector debts have had financial crises, and part of the explanation for the negative correlation between public sector debt and growth may be the lengthy work-out of the crisis and an associated deterioration of the investment climate. Financial institutions are no doubt cautious in making new loans to individuals and firms that had large non-performing debts, and in some cases still have them to asset management companies (an issue that does not apply to Jamaica). The negative relationship between public sector debt and GDP is relevant to Jamaica for three reasons, however.

---

13. Levine and Levos (1988).

First, the large stock of public debt mostly represents the claims on the future tax receipts and borrowing power of the government, not any addition to the country's productive capacity. The public sector debt did replace non-performing loans to the private sector, and the uses to which these loans were originally put still exist—in this sense there is some overestimate of the impact of the crisis and public debt on the *stock* of private credit. But these loans were obviously not productive—that is the main reason for the crisis. As discussed above, the macroeconomic returns for Jamaica of the rise in credit and investment rates, was negative. And, from the microeconomic standpoint, the recovery rates on the non-performing loans (including repayments made by the borrowers even if the loans were not productive)

TABLE 4.3: GOVERNMENT NET CREDIT STOCK/ DEPOSITS, BANKS, 2000 (percent)			
Korea	−3.6	Philippines	22.7
Chile	−3.1	Hungary	23.0
Thailand	1.4	Pakistan	24.6
Malaysia	2.3	Morocco	26.5
Peru	3.2	Argentina	30.8
S. Africa	4.9	India	34.6
Czech Rep.	4.9	Russia	35.3
China	6.0	Jamaica (June 2003)	45.1
Egypt	7.8	Brazil	43.3
Venezuela	8.2	Mexico	48.8
Bangladesh	10.9	Algeria	50.6
Poland	14.8	Indonesia	56.3
Colombia	16.4	Turkey	64.7
		Average	22.3

Net Credit Stock = Claims on Gov. − Gov. Deposits
Deposits = Demand + Time Deposits
Source: International Financial Statistics, IMF.

and the collateral have been less than 20 percent. So, on balance, there has been a rise in public sector credit, and a displacement of private credit, which has its own effects on future growth.

Second, in Jamaica, some bankers have expressed the view that the high rates on government debt and deposits may have reduced the relative incentive for potential entrepreneurs and may have even turned some of them into *rentiers*. With fewer entrepreneurs, there is likely to be less growth.

Third, there is the standard problem of crowding out of private investment (see Chapter 3). Jamaica's public sector debt overhang (and the other countries with a large public sector debt overhang) must be refinanced, along with the interest on it. This has a continued negative impact on growth by displacing potentially new private borrowing. Unlike the repayments of private sector loans, which, if they had been performing, would have been relent to new borrowers, or to the same borrowers for new uses, the public debt is simply rolled over along with much of its interest cost, depending on the size of the primary surplus of the government. The refinancing of the interest absorbs much of the nominal increases in deposits. Thus, much of the additional deposits simply go to finance the stock of debt and its interest, not more productive investment. Correspondingly, private sector lending by Jamaica's financial sector has barely begun to return to its previous relationship with GDP.[14]

Jamaican public sector debt probably crowds-out private sector borrowing through both the interest rate and credit rationing based on risk. Public sector debt is naturally attractive to banks— it carries no risk of non-performance, and no capital requirement (the risk weight is zero)— relative to private sector debt. But this is a relative attractiveness that simply determines the *spread* between credits to the public sector and credits to the private sector. The *level* of (real) interest rates is determined first by the needs of the public sector to finance its amortizations, its interest costs, and its annual deficit. If a lot of public sector debt service needs to be rolled-over

14. Interestingly, in Jamaica the rate of (nominal) investment has not declined much, despite the squeeze on private credit. This suggests that more investment is being self-financed, or financed offshore than earlier.

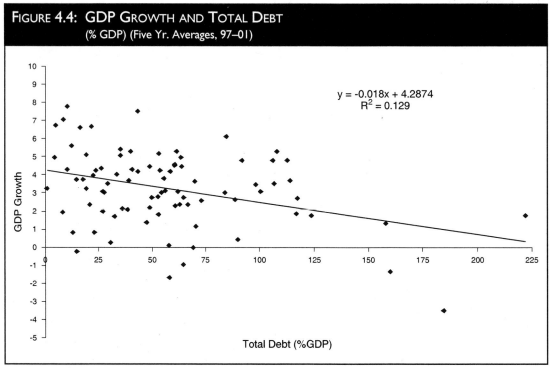

FIGURE 4.4: GDP GROWTH AND TOTAL DEBT
(% GDP) (Five Yr. Averages, 97–01)

$$y = -0.018x + 4.2874$$
$$R^2 = 0.129$$

GDP Growth

Total Debt (%GDP)

Source: International Financial Statistics, IMF.

and a primary deficit financed, then the (real) interest rate is higher than if a smaller amount is needed.[15] The deposit rate may also be driven up in these circumstances. A higher rate on public sector debt and higher deposit rates in turn mean a correspondingly higher rate for the private sector, crowding-out enough private borrowers to reduce the total of inelastic public demands for credit and private demands for credit to what the financial system can supply by mobilizing deposits.[16] Higher rates also tend to drive private borrowers off-shore and to borrow in foreign exchange locally to reduce their costs—interest rates and spreads are both lower in foreign exchange than in Jamaican dollars.[17] Currently short-term offshore borrowings (largely private) are a much higher percentage of GDP (12 percent) than in the past, and these of course go mainly to the least risky, best known clients.

---

15. The Government has been running a primary surplus in terms of current revenue and current spending, but even after deducting the primary surplus, the interest costs have often been similar to or even larger, as a percentage of GDP, than the nominal GDP growth rate. Moreover, the Government has also taken over the FINSAC debt, so the ratio of debt to GDP has increased compared to 1998/99.

16. The public sector can reduce these impacts on the domestic financial system, and reduce its borrowing costs, by borrowing offshore, as the Government of Jamaica has done. However, this strategy is limited by the country lending limits in private markets and the multilateral institutions and involves a currency risk.

17. Multilateral firms, such as those in bauxite and telecommunications typically raise much of their funding offshore. To the extent that such firms have become more prevalent in Jamaica, the demands upon the local financial market for private sector credit may be less than in the past. The tourism industry is basically a franchise operation for local investors, and they continue to depend heavily on the local financial system. Bank loans for tourism, though not keeping up with the growth of deposits, have risen 25 percent since 1995, helping to finance the increase in capacity by large hotels. However, casual observation suggests that smaller hotels have lost access to local finance and never had offshore finance.

Of course, Jamaica's crisis and the lack of recovery may also widen the spread between public sector debt and private sector debt, or simply screen out potentially riskier borrowers. After the crisis, banks and other lenders naturally have been concerned over potential borrowers' repayments. Hence, the banks probably not only charged higher spreads over government debt to the same borrowers, but reduced their lending to riskier borrowers (and they have less funds to lend because existing borrowers are not repaying, adding to this effect). The result tends to be a rise in the average measured spread (for a group of less risky borrowers) and an exclusion of credit to riskier borrowers, for example small and medium borrowers.[18]

Jamaica's interest rates over the 1990s seem to reflect these considerations. The crisis, tight money, concerns about devaluation, and the need to cover government deficits were associated with higher real average lending rates by the banks in the early part of the 1990s (Figure 4.5). After the crisis, real rates (and spreads over deposit rates) widened further and presumably only the best borrowers were able to raise money locally. With the stabilization of the exchange rate, some private borrowers even went offshore for bank loans. Gradually, however, average lending rates have fallen and spreads have narrowed back to their pre-crisis levels. However, the smaller amount of private sector credit, relative to GDP, suggests that the composition of the private sector borrowers may be less risky, on average, than in the past. Longer-term private offshore borrowing has now died out, although short-term borrowing offshore has risen to about 12 percent of GDP compared to less than 10 percent in the early 1990s.

The lack of private credit thus reflects crowding-out by the overhang of the debt crisis. Despite government primary surpluses and Government offshore borrowing to take advantage of low international rates and reduce the pressure of the debt overhang on the domestic economy, the stock of private credit in the banks currently is only about 12 percent of GDP. Foreign short-term borrowing has provided some respite for some borrowers and in fact is now more important, relative to GDP, than credit from the banking system. But both sources of funds are limited to the best customers.

While credit alone cannot be a leader of a private sector recovery—it makes little sense to lend to companies with poor repayment prospects—it is still natural to ask what could be done to increase the availability and quality of credit to the private sector?[19] First, it seems likely that as long as the public sector debt is large and growing, then it will continue to crowd out private credit, especially for small firms. Large firms still have access and may be able to borrow abroad. Hence, a basic issue is reducing the growth of public sector debt, both of the government and other public entities, whose debt has increased dramatically.

Second, credit registries can provide better information to allow financial intermediaries to distinguish between borrowers who are likely to repay their debts and those that are likely to

---

18. This result assumes the increase in the average spread to the remaining borrowers is greater than the spread that prevailed for the riskier borrowers that are excluded.

The Bank of Jamaica's Analysis of Commercial Banks' Loans and Advances indicate that total loans have increased roughly 50 percent since 1994. Within this total, loans to agriculture, manufacturing and the professions are now less in Jamaican dollars than they were in 1994, and loans for construction are down by nearly half. Loans for tourism and personal loans have more than doubled, and loans for transport, storage and communication have increased 50 percent. Loans to non-government public entities are five times larger, and loans to the central government (not counting treasury bills or LRS) are 250 percent of their 1994 levels. Of course, these shifts in the distribution of loans probably reflect not only crowding out, but the growth of the real economy. Credit cannot substitute for poor real prospects. The sharp growth of personal loans, most of which occurred in two bursts, 1994–1996 and 2000–2001, probably reflects the increased emphasis on consumer banking by banks all over the world, a type of lending that has proved to have surprisingly low risk and high returns. In some cases, small and medium firms have used personal loans and credit card debt for funding.

19. Monetary policy of course can stimulate private investment, but Jamaica's capacity for monetary policy is limited by its openness. Moreover, monetary policy's main impacts often come on construction and housing projects and, as discussed in Chapter II, a stock of underutilized buildings still exists.

default at the slightest downturn of their prospects, they also can improve access to credit. Credit registries that allow financial intermediaries to see even small borrowers' credit histories are a way to improve intermediaries' ability to distinguish between good borrowers and bad borrowers. They also provide incentives for borrowers to repay, to maintain a good credit record. Small borrowers, by repaying, can develop the intangible asset of a good credit record. Credit registries can also be used as collateral registries to help lenders see what collateral has been pledged. Finally, credit registries are also a way of increasing competition in lending, which is one reason why lenders are so reluctant to contribute information on their good borrowers to such an institution, and why Government often have to promote their formation.

Third, improve collateral execution, perhaps by creating special courts for debt disputes and bankruptcy. Surveys show dissatisfaction with the courts' performance on commercial issues.

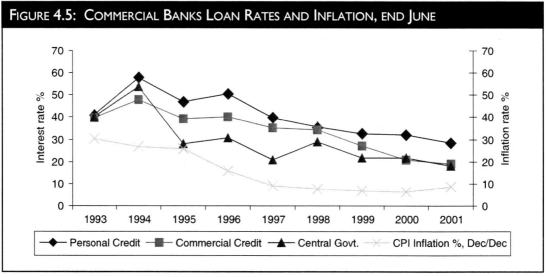

FIGURE 4.5: COMMERCIAL BANKS LOAN RATES AND INFLATION, END JUNE

Source: Bank of Jamaica; IFS, IMF.

The Jamaican Government also has tried to channel credit to the private sector through Government financial institutions. Public sector institutions have become the main financers of housing— while down somewhat compared to 1995–1997, public sector financed housing starts and completions are more than twice as high as in 1994. In addition, the National Investment Bank of Jamaica and the Jamaica Development Bank have provided increased direct and second-tier credits to the private sector, partly funded by the reduction in reserve requirements of the banks. To some extent, all these loans can be considered as "pump priming"—providing credit when the private financial institutions may have overreacted to the crisis. However, these institutions have had poor recovery records on their direct lending, which may be related to concerns that have been expressed in Parliament regarding the use of credits for political purposes. To the extent that the direct lending of these institutions is not repaid, the credits must be considered a poor allocation of resources and the government will have to issue new debt to cover the institutions obligations, further crowding-out private sector credit of the banks. The indirect lending of these two institutions, through the banks, probably has less risk, but the ceilings on the interest rates for loans financed by this facility mean that banks find these funds unattractive, except to finance loans to very low-risk borrowers.

The Post-Crisis Improvement in Financial Sector Regulation, Supervision and the Solvency Issue

The Government has improved financial sector regulation and supervision greatly since the crisis, a further contribution to reducing systemic risk, arising from the financial system. In the banking sector, minimum capital requirements were raised to 10 percent of risk weighted capital (1999); recognition of non-performing loans was tightened to 3 months (best practices) from 6 months; stronger guidelines were issued for provisioning, loan renegotiation, suspension of accrued interest on non-performing loans and loan write-offs; and limits on connected lending and concentration of lending have been introduced. In 2001, the Bank of Jamaica carried out an assessment of its compliance with the Basel Core Principles, led by the IMF, which concluded that supervision was fully compliant with 11 principles, largely compliant with 8, materially non-compliant with 5, and non-compliant with 1. To address the areas of weakness, the Bank of Jamaica has drafted prudential regulations on county risk (although Jamaican banks are not currently exposed to country risk), market risk, and consolidated supervision.

The Bank of Jamaica has received increased powers of bank intervention and independence of supervision. It can now impose penalties for technical breaches of sanctions and has the power to temporarily assume management of deposit-taking institutions. However, the Finance Minister retains the power to approve and transfer licenses (with a recommendation from the Bank of Jamaica), revoke licenses, and bar persons from participation in bank management. The Bank of Jamaica has also continued to strengthen its "ladder of enforcement," which includes recognition of problems at an early stage, prompt corrective actions, steps to minimize systemic effects, and a list of the sanctions that will be imposed by Bank of Jamaica.

To strengthen consolidated supervision, the Bank of Jamaica has since received powers to carry out consolidated supervision that includes non-bank institutions in banking groups. It has also signed an MOU with the Financial Services Commission that supervises securities and insurance, and received legal sanction for sharing information with supervisors. It also participated in the creation of the Financial Regulatory Council, a coordinating body for financial regulation and exchange of information, chaired by the Governor of the Bank of Jamaica.

Regarding non-bank intermediaries, the Government has enacted an Insurance Law to serve as the basis for regulation and supervision in the sector. The Government in 2001 also created a Financial Services Commission to regulate and supervise securities, insurance and pensions. The Bank of Jamaica is also developing a framework for regulation and supervision of credit unions. Improvements in the regulation of pensions are also being considered, a potentially important issue given the aging of the Jamaican population.

Jamaica's strengthening of bank regulation and supervision has corrected many of the problems prior to the crisis and identified in the assessment of the Basel Core Principles. However, many of these changes that have been implemented address issues that will only become important as the overhang of the crisis decreases much more. For example, risk-weighted capital requirements, income recognition and provisioning of loans, and risk management of lending are not major issues given the large share of public sector debt in the system. Work on assessing market risk is desirable, given the large share of government debt in assets, but the Bank of Jamaica must carefully tread a narrow path between allowing institutions to take reasonable risks and outlining what is prudent and imposing costs on imprudent behavior (for example in terms of capital). Consolidated supervision is also not a big issue currently, given the reduced role of non-bank intermediaries and the rise in their holdings of government debt and foreign assets, though it could become one in the future. Of course, consolidation of debtors' accounts within the banks and a supervisory assessment of the degree to which a bank's risk management considers this consolidation are always important.

Two issues—cross-border supervision and harmonization of laws and regulation—could be important in the short run. Given the importance of foreign ownership in banking and insurance, the sharing of information with foreign supervisors is important and will need to be pursued. In a number of countries, problems faced by foreign banks in their home countries have turned into problems for offshore operations of these banks. Harmonization of laws and regulations within Jamaica also could be an issue, given the numerous changes in banking laws and regulations that have occurred since the crisis. The Government is considering such an omnibus law, and the Bank of Jamaica has made proposals for a draft. As noted above, pension regulation is also becoming an issue.

Post-crisis, the solvency of Jamaica's financial system has become heavily dependent on the public sector's solvency, and less on the private sector's servicing of its debt that is the usual focus of supervision. The full bailout of the depositors after the crisis, by replacement of all bad private debt with Government debt, has left total Government debt at about 45 percent of deposits. Hence, Government's capacity to either rollover its debt or service it out of the budget is critical to the banks' capacity to cover the interest costs of their deposits, and will depend on improving the ratio of the Government's primary surplus to its debt service.

CHAPTER 5

IMPROVING EDUCATION OUTCOMES

Jamaica's Government spends six percent of its GDP on education, and real expenditure on education has doubled in the last ten years. Enrollment has expanded remarkably, and was near universal for 6–14 year olds as early as 1989, and 95 percent for 12–14 year olds from the poorest quintile. Yet, education outcomes leave much to be desired—about 30–40 percent of grade 6 leavers are functionally illiterate. Only 30 percent of those who appear pass the Caribbean CXC mathematics examination in grade 11, lower than most Caribbean countries. Jamaican-educated workers receive amongst the lowest returns in the US labor market. Poor education outcomes may be one factor limiting productivity gains in Jamaica, both in absolute terms and also as compared to other Latin American countries (see Chapter 2). Cross-country evidence shows that higher quality education makes workers more productive, increases returns to education and creates incentives for more private investment in education (World Bank 2003).

Much of the problem stems from poverty. Poor students get tracked into lower quality schools, have higher absenteeism, face a more difficult home environment, see lower enrollment after age 14 (owing to lack of seats in schools) and higher dropouts, and end up far less educated. All this creates a vicious cycle of youth at risk, especially males, and unemployment and poverty. Tackling these problems would involve a coordinated approach that would address issues of school quality of below-average schools, increase school space after grade 9, and pay special attention to those falling behind and reading below grade level.

The next section discusses the international evidence on private and social returns to education, and suggests that quality of education matters as much as the numbers. The second section discusses the expansion in education coverage in Jamaica, but suggests that it came at the cost of quality. The third section presents evidence on social returns to education in Jamaica, and makes a case that even social returns are positive. The fourth section discusses poverty, enrollment, student achievement, and the quality of schools, and the linkages therein. The fifth section shows that rising expenditures do not guarantee outcomes, and also demonstrates the unequal distribution of expenditures in tertiary education. The sixth section concludes with some policy options to improve the effectiveness of education, building on the 2001 White Paper of the Government. It is worth noting here that international experience shows that improving education outcomes is likely to be a slow and difficult process, and is rendered more complex in Jamaica by the strong linkages of education with poverty and social factors.

The International Evidence on Private and Social Returns to Education

Protagonists of the human capital approach hold that education enhances skills that improve human productivity and, thereby, economic growth. While there is strong empirical evidence on the positive private rates of return to investment in education, the micro-macro link between education and economic growth remains contentious.[1]

Using data from around the world, Psacharapoulos (1994) and Psacharapoulos and Patrinos (2002) find that private returns are higher than social returns only when the social costs (public subsidies for education), but not social benefits, are accounted for. Overall, the average return to an additional year of schooling is 10 percent. Over the last 12 years, the average education return declined by 0.6 percentage points, owing to the increase in the supply of educated labor outstripping the demand. Private returns increase with higher levels of education and are higher for those working in the public sector than the private sector. Social returns are higher in primary than in secondary education, which, in turn, are higher than those in tertiary education. Social returns are higher for women than for men, and lower for countries with higher levels of GDP per capita.

In the same vein, Topel (1999) argues that the key is not whether schooling raises aggregate output but whether the social returns to human capital formation *exceed* private returns. The arguments for the social returns being lower than private returns include: (i) education signals innate ability and does not enhance productivity; and (ii) public sector over-hiring of educated workers distorts the labor market. The arguments to the contrary include the following: (i) worker productivity depends on co-workers' education as much as own schooling (particularly in team-based production); (ii) schooling promotes technology adoption and technological innovation; (iii) educated women have lower fertility rates, and their children have better health and education outcomes, thereby leading to inter-generational mobility; and (iv) schooling may reduce crime and other anti-social behavior (Jamison, 2002). In other words, high social benefits are likely to have a positive impact on economic growth, directly or indirectly.

Using cross-country data, Pritchett (2000), however, finds no relationship between increases in human capital attributable to rising educational attainment of the work force and the rate of growth of output per worker.[2] He attributes this finding to three possible reasons: (i) perverse institutional/governance environment that encourages rent seeking behavior of educated people; (ii) rapid decline of marginal returns to education as the supply of educated labor outstripped demand; and (iii) low educational quality that creates no human capital. However, some recent work by Temple (1999) finds that increases in educational attainment are correlated with growth, once outliers in the data are removed. Barro (2001) also finds that the amount of schooling has a positive and statistically significant relationship with growth.

That quality matters should not come as a surprise. Regressing 1960–1990 growth on a standard set of factors (including schooling quantity), plus a new measure of educational quality (scores from international mathematics and science tests), Hanushek and Kimko (2000) find quality to be a positive and statistically significant determinant of economic growth. This is corroborated by Barro (2001), who finds a large, positive impact of educational quality on growth. These findings also appear to affirm at least Pritchett's third point on the importance of the quality of education.

---

1. The cross-country empirical investigations typically use either the level or change in the level of education as the independent variable to explain the growth of economic output. The summary of the debate draws from Jamison's (2002) literature review.

2. The findings of these cross-national data are the average results, derived from imposing a constant coefficient; in practice, the development impact of education on growth will vary widely across countries.

This brief review highlights the complexity of the relationship between education and growth. It is already apparent, however, that the quality of education matters as much as the number of people who receive education. Also, even if the relationship between education and growth were still open to question, the long-term social benefits of quality education would appear to be significant.

Progress in Education Coverage, But Quality Suffered

As part of the nation-building process, Jamaica's education plan in the 1960s emphasized making primary education accessible to all and expanding post-primary opportunity, and this was furthered by the socialist-oriented People's National Party (PNP), which came into power in 1972. Primary education was made free in public schools in 1973. In addition to building new schools, public financing (subvention) was extended to schools previously operated by private groups and missionaries.

Due to this early emphasis on primary education for all, Jamaica attained near-universal primary enrollment by the early 1980s, much sooner than most developing countries or countries of similar income levels. This is remarkable considering the rapid growth of the primary school-going population from the 1960s through the end of the 1980s. However, enrollment expansion came at the cost of quality (see below). Across schools, there was wide variation in size, student-teacher ratios, teacher qualifications, availability of teaching and learning materials, and the conditions of school buildings. Many schools were put on double shifts. In order to make places available to an ever-increasing number of children, automatic promotion became the norm, which, unfortunately, has led to many children moving through the system without learning the requisite skills.

The coverage of secondary education remained limited until the 1980s, necessitating rationing of secondary school places through a national examination held after completion of primary education. The Common Entrance Examination was introduced in 1953 to select the most promising students for the academically oriented secondary schools, while the less prepared students were tracked into practical or pre-vocational schools.[3] Over time, a multiple track system came to be established to cater to students of different abilities.

In spite of the shortcomings of the system, the sustained focus of policy on education resulted in practically universal enrollment of all children between 6 and 14 by 1989; as many as 95 percent of adolescents between 12 and 14 from the poorest quintile enrolled in school (PIOJ, 1990).[4] The 1990s saw enrollment expansion in early childhood education, senior secondary education, and tertiary education. This was facilitated by a decline in the 1990s of about 6 percent in the school-going population at the primary level, and 4 percent at the secondary level (MOEYC education statistics, various years).

---

3. In pre-independence days, missionaries ran secondary schools, later known as the Traditional High Schools. The government extended public financing to these schools, paying teacher salaries, thereby absorbing them into the public system. Since these schools were academically oriented and highly selective, other types of schools were introduced for less academically inclined students. Comprehensive Schools, providing five years of secondary education with a mixed curriculum, were established and expanded, followed by New Secondary Schools, which had a pre-vocational orientation. There were also the All-Age schools, established in the early 19th century by missionaries and private charities for children of slaves, offering instruction for children of mixed age groups, and whose scope gradually expanded to include nine years of education to rural children.

In the 1990s, the Ministry of Education, Youth and Culture decided to reduce educational stratification by upgrading a large number of All-Age schools to Primary and Junior High schools, eliminating New Secondary Schools and their curriculum as a distinctive category and merging them with Comprehensive Highs, and finally, renaming Comprehensive Highs and Traditional Highs as High schools. In 2001, there were five types of schools, down from seven earlier: (i) 363 All-Age Schools, mostly located in rural areas, offering grades 1–9; (ii) 90 Primary and Junior High Schools, upgraded from All-Age Schools, also offering Grades 1–9; (iii) 134 High Schools (comprising 59 Traditional Highs and 75 former Comprehensive Highs), offering Grades 7 to 10 or 13; (iv) 14 Technical High Schools; and (v) 3 Agricultural/Vocational Highs.

4. The first Survey of Living Conditions was conducted in 1989, which has made possible an assessment of enrollment by consumption quintile.

By 2000, gross enrollment had reached 93.5 percent in early childhood education, practically universal in primary and lower secondary education, 88 percent in upper cycle secondary education (grades 10–11), and about 14.5 percent in tertiary education. Gender parity is achieved at all levels before senior secondary education. The formal education system serves about 756,518 students at all levels, or about 30 percent of the total population. About 5 percent of the primary school students and 6 percent of secondary school students enroll in private schools.

These remarkable accomplishments reflect both a successful focus of education policy and a strong household demand for education. Government commitment is reflected in high and rising public spending—public expenditure on education rose from 3.4 percent of GDP in 1992/93 to 6.8 percent in 1997/98 and 6.1 percent in 2001/02 (average LAC public spending is about 4.5 percent of GDP). Moreover, the increase in public expenditure came during the 'lost' decade of the 1990s, when a stagnant economy witnessed many competing demands for public funding. Outside of education, training accounts for another 0.5 percent of GDP. Also, the vocational training complex for out of school youths, HEART/NTA, is financed by a 3 percent payroll tax (see also Chapter 3). In addition, household spending on education amounts to about 5.5 percent of total household spending. Of this education expenditure, about 19 percent is on extra lessons, 35 percent for lunch, 21 percent for transport.

Quality indicators. Comparing returns to education for immigrants of different countries in a single host country could provide some indication of the quality of education in the "sending" country.[5] Bratsberg and Terrell (2002) estimate country-specific immigrants' returns to education in the US labor market. Not being affected by home country labor market conditions, the rates of return provide some pointers to home country educational quality.[6] Table 5.1 regroups the Bratsberg and Terrell estimates of returns to education in the USA by country of birth of male immigrants between the ages of 15 and 64.

The mean return to education in the United States for 67 countries is about 4 percent per year for each additional year of schooling in 1980, rising to 5 percent in 1990. The returns to education of male immigrants educated in Jamaica averaged 2.5 percent per year, rising to 3.5 percent in 1990. The Jamaican male workers' returns are marginally below the returns to Trinidad and Tobago workers (2.7 percent in 1980 and 3.75 percent in 1990). The Jamaican returns are well below the median, although there is improvement between 1980 and 1990. In 1980, Jamaican workers' returns, at 63 percent of the overall mean, exceed only 5 of 66 other countries in the sample. In 1990, the return exceeds 13 of the other 66 countries, rising to 73 percent of the mean. It is reasonable to infer that the rising returns over the decade of the 1980s reflect some improvement in the quality of Jamaica's education system, notwithstanding the expansion of educational opportunity in the second half of the 20th century. However, the very large number of countries with higher returns also indicates that the quality of Jamaica's educational system has a long way to go before it catches up even with those of much poorer countries (see Table 5.1).

Another indicator of quality derives from employers' perception of school quality in 2000 (Figure 5.1).[7] While this indicator is not as robust as the previous one, since it is based on perceptions, and is also based on within-country data, and so cannot abstract from cross-country differences in judging standards, it does show a very close correspondence with the findings of Bratsberg and Terrell (2002). Employers rated highly the school quality of OECD countries, but the Central American schools obtained very low scores. The perceived school quality of Trinidad and Tobago, Uruguay and East Asia are lower than OECD's, but high relative to other countries. Jamaica is lower but

---

5. However, the average returns for each country will be affected by the distribution of occupations for the migrants of different countries, and these are unlikely to be the same across countries.

6. Their estimates of returns are negatively correlated with those reported by Psacharapoulos (1994), which they attribute to the labor supply conditions in determining education returns in home countries.

7. The employers' survey was conducted in 2000, so the rating covers the employees educated in the 1990s whereas the US censuses of 1980 and 1990 obviously do not include workers educated in the 1990s.

TABLE 5.1: RETURNS TO EDUCATION OF MALE IMMIGRANTS IN USA BY COUNTRY OF BIRTH

Country	1980 Rate of return	1980 Standard error	1980 Observations	1990 Rate of return	1990 Standard error	1990 Observations
Caribbean						
Cuba	.0302	.0009	5,262	.0330	.0009	5,480
Dominican Republic	.0122	.0019	1,324	.0210	.0014	2,102
Haití	.0119	.0017	862	.0202	.0014	1,832
Jamaica	**.0246**	**.0014**	**1,611**	**.0350**	**.0013**	**2,108**
Trinidad and Tobago	.0270	.0021	592	.0375	.0019	722
Central America						
Costa Rica	.0296	.0036	207	.0377	.0032	295
Guatemala	.0200	.0026	566	.0214	.0016	1,922
Honduras	.0254	.0034	283	.0234	.0024	701
South America						
Argentina	.0436	.0018	704	.0506	.0016	875
Brazil	.0496	.0028	246	.0417	.0019	659
Chile	.0406	.0023	352	.0438	.0021	514
Colombia	.0283	.0015	1,287	.0332	.0012	2,269
Ecuador	.0220	.0020	783	.0277	.0017	1,120
Western Europe						
France	.0531	.0017	632	.0645	.0017	623
Germany	.0509	.0009	3,314	.0634	.0011	2,149
Greece	.0300	.0014	1,963	.0429	.0021	1,454
UK	.0560	.0008	3,860	.0703	.0008	4,025
Eastern Europe						
Czechoslovakia	.0422	.0018	637	.0534	.0020	430
Hungary	.0400	.0017	753	.0482	.0021	541
USSR	.0339	.0011	1,916	.0450	.0012	1,457
Asia						
China	.0247	.0010	2,732	.0274	.0009	4,213
Japan	.0522	.0011	1,548	.0822	.0010	2,037
Korea (South)	.0333	.0010	1,774	.0449	.0008	3,448
Singapore	.0456	.0078	24	.0622	.0057	54
Thailand	.0252	.0027	235	.0341	.0021	456
India	.0382	.0009	2,082	.0476	.0007	4,500
Sri Lanka	.0497	.0048	56	.0556	.0033	141
Middle East & Africa						
Egypt	.0408	.0017	495	.0469	.0014	853
Iran	.0477	.0018	500	.0491	.0012	1,337
Iraq	.0303	.0030	241	.0431	.0025	377
Israel	.0386	.0021	457	.0562	.0017	654
Kenya	.0440	.0055	43	.0560	.0039	103
Sierra Leone	.0293	.0129	9	.0314	.0056	54
Mean (67 countries)	.0389	.0119	77,198	.0492	.0156	117,774

Source: Bratsberg and Terrell (2002), Table 1, pp. 180–181.

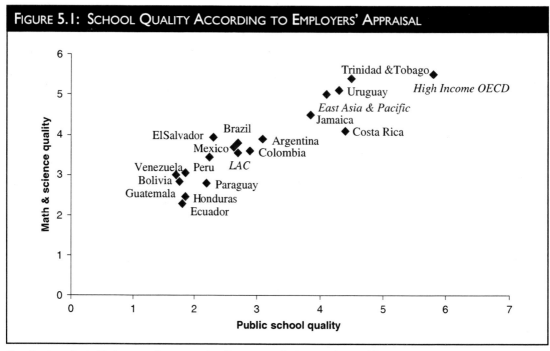

FIGURE 5.1: SCHOOL QUALITY ACCORDING TO EMPLOYERS' APPRAISAL

Key: 1 = Lags far behind most other countries; 7 = among the best in the world.
Source: Global Competitiveness Report 2001–2002, World Economic Forum.

above mid-range, which may indicate that domestic rating of Jamaica's schools is somewhat better than the international perception.

Returns to education have also been calculated within Jamaica. In keeping with the literature, private returns to education were found to be positive. An analysis of the Jamaican Labor Force Survey of 1996 found that the private returns to an additional year of primary education were 5 percent, those for secondary education 3.3 percent, those for technical and vocational training 1.1 percent, and those for tertiary education 8.4 percent (World Bank, 1999). This is below the 10 percent return worldwide observed by Psacharapoulos and Patrinos (2002). However, given the economic downturn Jamaica experienced in the second half of the 1990s, it is not surprising that economic returns to education are low. At the same time, the relatively low returns to pre-tertiary education could reflect low quality. In addition to higher quality,[8] the reasonably high returns to tertiary education indicate that the demand for higher levels of skills is still strong.

Social Returns to Education

Cross-country regressions show that education and growth are positively and significantly related in a large sample of countries. On average, a 10 percent increase in secondary enrollment is associated with a 0.17 percent change in the annual growth rate of income per capita. In the case of Jamaica, secondary enrollment increased by around 12.4 percent between the 1980s and the 1990s, and a 0.21 percent increase in growth of income per capita is attributed to this (Loayza et al, 2002).

However, these coefficients for education could be biased upward for Jamaica, which has much higher migration rates than most countries (the highest in the Bratsberg and Terrell [2002] sample). As we have seen in Chapter 2, highly educated people tend to migrate from Jamaica, with the most popular destinations being the United Kingdom (UK), Canada, USA and other Caricom

---

8. For more details on tertiary education in Jamaica, see Kim (2003) and the forthcoming World Bank report on Tertiary Education in the Caribbean.

countries. The very large scale of migration may conceivably have affected growth, by taking away potential entrepreneurs and business leaders. Thus, even if enrollment in secondary school increases, many of those enrolled are not available to the country at the precise time when they could contribute to economic growth. In other words, the effect on growth of increases in education may be lower than average in countries where the migration of educated workers is significant.

Social benefits. What is the evidence that education has yielded social benefits in Jamaica over and above the private rates of return? One obvious benefit has been the reduction in fertility.[9] The general fertility rate, the number of live births per 1000 women in the reproductive age group, declined from 100 in 1991 to 76 in 2002 (2002 ESSJ). This demographic transition has resulted in a decline in the school-age population, relieving pressure in the classroom, making possible lower student-to-teacher ratios, and freeing up resources to improve quality. Smaller families also allow parents to devote more resources and attention to their children, thereby bringing about a qualitative improvement in both family life and education attainment. These are undeniable social benefits of education.

As for the relationship between education and crime reduction, the issue is complex. On the one hand, micro-level data shows that positive school experiences appear to reduce the chances of risky/criminal behavior, even after the child has passed out of school. Sample data has been collected on youth behavior and its causes, in schools in nine CARICOM countries including Jamaica.[10] It is found that boys and girls who feel "connectedness" to a school—through a teacher or by working hard—have a less than 10 percent probability of engaging in risky behavior. For those who do not feel any connectedness, their participation in drugs was 55 percent (boys) and 30 percent (girls), violence (70 percent for both boys and girls), and so on. The positive role of the school system in reducing risky behavior is indicated by the data showing that 88 percent of the sample of students felt connected to a teacher. This connectedness was found to be reinforced by positive home and community support. The interviewed youth said that their school attendance and performance depend to a great extent on their parents' interest and monitoring. Finally, it was seen that students who perform well in school feel good about themselves and their future and do not want to jeopardize it through risky behavior that may have long-term repercussions—which provides some partial evidence that positive experiences in school can have a longer-term impact.

On the other hand, macro data shows an increase in the rate of violent crime over the last fifteen years, even as the overall enrollment rate in school has increased and illiteracy has gone down. Several factors account for this apparent inconsistency, stemming to a large extent from inequality in multiple dimensions (see also next section). The general increase in enrollment masks the inequality in access (enrollment and income are highly correlated for older children)—for example, within the poorest quintile, the percentage of 15–16 year olds not enrolled in school has stayed between 29–35 for most years between 1991–2001 (32 percent in 2001, 35 percent in 1991), and this situation creates a host of problems. Given that youth under 24 is the most vulnerable age group—this group committed 55 percent of all crimes in 1999—the substantial percentage of 15–16 year poor children that are out of school renders a large number of poor children, largely male, susceptible to engaging in crime and violence. For those out of school, there is no opportunity to receive positive and reinforcing support from the school system, as described above. Nor are the out of school youth likely to find employment and thereby be gainfully occupied—unemployment amongst 14–19 year youth was 47 percent in April 2001 (37 percent males, 65 percent females), and 28 percent amongst the 20–24 group, versus 15 percent for all age groups. Moreover, young people who did not complete secondary education (including all the 15–16 year olds who are out of school) suffer the highest rates of unemployment.

---

9. While there are many other influences on fertility, including family planning, education, especially of the mother, is a key factor in reducing fertility.

10. Data for 15695 children in school, aged 10–18, including 2635 from Jamaica. See World Bank (2002a) for more details.

Thus, it seems that receiving education in the school system influences the large majority of children in a positive way. Almost 90 percent of parents in the 2001 SLC rated their children's schools favorably. Crime begins when children start dropping out of school, which happen to be largely the poor children, owing largely to inadequate places in traditional schools after grade 9, as well as to a continuous cycle of low achievement and resultant alienation from school. The problem of crime, then, can be linked to the lack of a quality education and a positive school experience.

Inequality, Poverty and Student Achievement

While opportunities have expanded, the quality of education continues to languish. Challenges lie in low achievement (about 30–40 percent functional illiteracy at the end of primary education), high absenteeism (full attendance in school is 78 percent), especially in junior secondary education, disengagement of adolescents from educational pursuit and their tendency to drop out before completion of the cycle. The latter problem is more pervasive among boys than girls. Apart from these, there is also an issue of access at higher levels—22 percent of all students enrolled in grade 9, or about 11,000 students, cannot access grades 10 and 11 because of the lack of school places. All the above problems stem at least partly from inequality and poverty, including the family environment, as well as the historical evolution of the school system.

With increasing age, enrollment of the poor and of males suffers. Figure 5.2 shows that while enrollment ratios of the richest and poorest quintiles start out at the same levels, they diverge sharply after age 14. By the ages of 15 and 16, less than 80 percent of students from the poorest quintile remain in school, although all students from the top quintile continue with schooling. By the ages of 17 and 18, less than 30 percent of students from the poorest quintile remain in school, while even in the top quintile, less than 80 percent stay enrolled. Although males and females start out equally in enrollment in basic education, a disproportionately high number of males drop out after grade 9, so that by the time of tertiary education, females account for about 66 percent of enrollment. Thus, boys dominate the population of out of school 12–18 year olds who have completed grade 9—in 2000, males formed 61 percent of this population (2000 SLC).

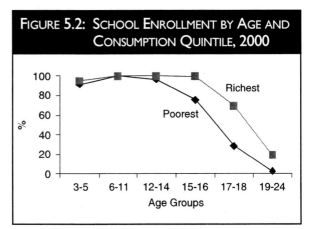

FIGURE 5.2: SCHOOL ENROLLMENT BY AGE AND CONSUMPTION QUINTILE, 2000

Source: PIOJ-STATIN 2001

Table 5.2 presents enrollment by school type and by consumption quintile. About 43 percent of students in all-age schools in 2000 were from the poorest quintile, while over half of the students in the academic, traditional high schools were from the top two quintiles. Given that all-age schools are largely in rural areas, and do not go beyond grade 9, about 60 percent of the out-of-school population lives in rural areas, which also partly explains why poverty is much higher in rural areas (Chapter 1). In tertiary education, 77 percent of students were from the top quintile, and 91 percent from the top two quintiles, but none are from the poorest quintile.[11]

The quality of schools is very uneven. About 30 to 40 percent of Grade 6 leavers read below grade level. Since placement in Grade 7 has been universal since the late 1990s, the under-achieving students tend to lag further as they move into higher grades (see also sub-section on Inequality below). This can be seen in the following:

---

11. Given the small sample size for tertiary students, the ratios tend to fluctuate. In 2001, 5 percent of tertiary students were from the poorest quintile, and 86 percent for the top two quintiles.

TABLE 5.2: ENROLLMENT BY SCHOOL TYPE IN SECONDARY AND TERTIARY EDUCATION BY CONSUMPTION QUINTILE (%), 2000

	Q1 (poorest)	Q2	Q3	Q4	Q5 (richest)	Total
All-age (Gr. 7–9)	43	30	18	6	3	100
P&JH (Gr. 7–9)	22	16	19	33	10	100
Comprehensive (Gr. 7–11)	18	24	27	18	13	100
Secondary Highs (Gr. 7–13)	13	17	20	25	26	100
Technical Highs (Gr. 7–11/13)	11	20	15	31	23	100
Voc./Agricultural (Gr. 7–11)	11	12	39	27	11	100
Adult/Night	12	0	14	24	51	100
Tertiary	0	2	7	14	77	100

Source: Jamaica Survey of Living Conditions 2000, PIOJ-STATIN 2001.

▨ In the Junior High School Certificate Examination (JHSCE, end of grade 9), the students in Primary and Junior High Schools and the former Comprehensive High Schools scored much lower on average than the Traditional High Schools (Figures 5.3 and 5.4), in mathematics and language. These outcomes have significant long-term effects—the weakness in reading impedes the students' ability to master other curricula and also to learn on their own. The weakness in mathematics impairs seriously their ability to comprehend science as well as social sciences that rely on quantitative research methods.

▨ Figure 5.5 shows that less than half of the students in the former Comprehensive High schools participate in the Caribbean Secondary Education Certification Examination of the regional Caribbean Examination Council (CXC, taken in grade 11), which is the key examination for admission in tertiary education and employment. For those who participate, the variability in pass rates across different school types is large. (Figure 5.6).

▨ The academically oriented High schools employ a higher proportion of university-educated teachers. Despite progress in recent years, the highest proportion of untrained teachers is concentrated in schools serving rural communities.

▨ Secondary school students have to pay rental fees to access textbooks, and data shows only about half the students avail of this, in spite of public financial support for the rental scheme. This affects the poor disproportionately, since the richer ones can in any case afford to buy the books. Moreover, High Schools can charge fees to the extent of 14 percent to defray operating

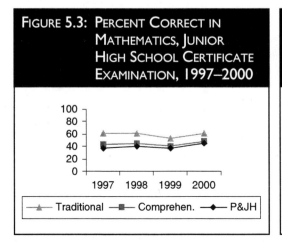

FIGURE 5.3: PERCENT CORRECT IN MATHEMATICS, JUNIOR HIGH SCHOOL CERTIFICATE EXAMINATION, 1997–2000

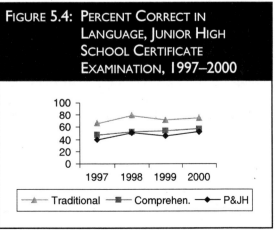

FIGURE 5.4: PERCENT CORRECT IN LANGUAGE, JUNIOR HIGH SCHOOL CERTIFICATE EXAMINATION, 1997–2000

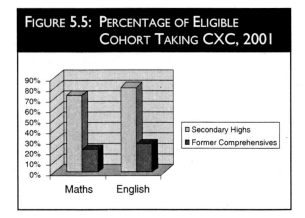

FIGURE 5.5: PERCENTAGE OF ELIGIBLE COHORT TAKING CXC, 2001

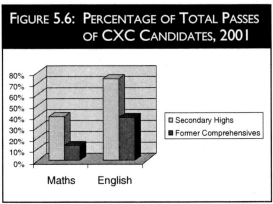

FIGURE 5.6: PERCENTAGE OF TOTAL PASSES OF CXC CANDIDATES, 2001

costs, which is used to acquire library books and instructional materials. However, since the All-Age and P&JH schools cannot charge fees, their libraries are either non-existent or poorly resourced. Without reading materials, there is little surprise that functional literacy is low in such schools. Ironically, these schools, which serve the most disadvantaged students, also have the least discretionary resources for improvement, to organize compensatory education, or to support activities that would create incentives for students to stay in school.

Poor students face multiple disadvantages. Richer children receive better quality education. Students from affluent families tend to attend private preparatory primary schools and pay for extra tutoring to prepare for the end of the primary cycle (grade 6) examination. Being better prepared, they tend to have higher test scores, which allow them to be placed in the selective, Traditional High Schools. Such tracking of students into different types of secondary schools of very uneven quality is widespread. School quality is also one among several reasons for lower attendance amongst poor students—in 2001, only 60 percent of the poorest students had full attendance (attended school for all 20 days in a reference month), compared with 87 percent of students in the richest quintile. The Kingston area had the highest attendance rate of 90 percent, while rural areas had 74 percent (2001 SLC).

Poor quality of schooling and a disadvantaged home environment are mutually reinforcing. Many students tend to come from unstable home environments, which are exacerbated by migration, with family members migrating overseas serially, with children left behind for years. Females head 43 percent of households, and almost one-fifth of children do not live with either parent.

In tertiary education, as seen above, 91 percent of students are from the top two quintiles. Poorer students also have more unstable home environments, and live in homes with a greater chance of not having a father figure (in 2001, 51 percent of poorest quintile and 37 percent of richest quintile households were female-headed).

Many fathers are in the home irregularly, have multiple mates and children with more than one mate (Blank and Monowa, 2000). The absence of a male role model has an adverse effect on the development of adolescent boys, contributing to their lower achievement and early dropout. Low academic achievement has a strong bearing on their subsequent educational aspirations, absenteeism, the risks of dropout and delinquent behavior.

Facing such severe handicaps, it is not surprising that those who do not participate in the CXC examinations or fail to pass them tend to be predominantly the poor. Table 5.3 shows that the adult population in the bottom quintile has disproportionately fewer academic qualifications—86 percent of the poorest quintile possess no academic qualification, compared with 52 percent for the richest quintile; none of the poor had a tertiary degree, while 12 percent of the richest quintile did. Looking at it another way, the richest quintile forms the vast majority of those with degrees or those with 3 or more A levels.

TABLE 5.3: HIGHEST EXAMINATION PASSED BY POPULATION 14 YEARS AND OVER NOT ENROLLED IN SCHOOL/EDUCATIONAL INSTITUTION (%), 2001

	Q1 (poorest)	Q2	Q3	Q4	Q5 (richest)
None	86.1	88.4	80.6	72.7	52.3
CXC Basic	6.8	5.2	7.9	7.5	7.1
GCE/CXC General, 1–2 subjects	2.1	1.3	3.3	3.7	3.2
GCE/CXC General, 3–4 subjects	1.9	0.9	1.4	4.1	7.9
GCE/CXC General, 5+ & 1–2 A Levels	—	0.4	1.7	1.9	4.5
GCE A Level, 3+ subjects	—	0	0.2	0.3	0.5
Degree	—	0.5	0.8	1.6	12
Other	1.3	0.2	1.1	4.7	8.9
Not Stated	1.7	3.2	3.2	3.6	3.6
Total	100	100	100	100	100

Source: Jamaica Survey of Living Conditions 2001, PIOJ-STATIN 2002.

Outcomes and Public Expenditure

Jamaica's weak CXC outcomes. A previous section showed that returns to Jamaican-educated labor in the United States were lower than for most other countries in the sample, and the last section discussed the low average achievements in primary and secondary schools. Similar results are seen in the CXC examinations (for 2001), where Jamaica is out-performed by many Caribbean countries in the CXC (Figure 5.7). Jamaica's national pass rate of under 60 percent in CXC English examinations and 30 percent in mathematics is below that of Dominica, St. Kitts, St. Lucia, Belize, Trinidad and Tobago, and St. Vincent and the Grenadines (SVG).[12]

Real expenditure has been increasing. In real terms and as a share of GDP, Jamaica's expenditure on education has increased substantially over the 1990s—from 3.4 percent of GDP in 1992/93

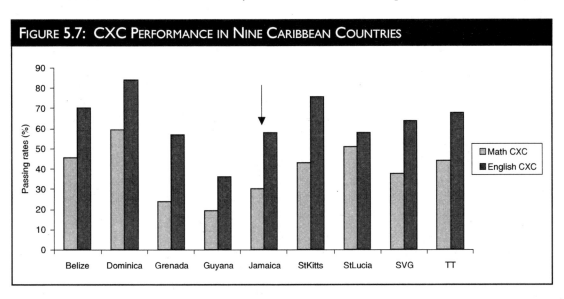

FIGURE 5.7: CXC PERFORMANCE IN NINE CARIBBEAN COUNTRIES

12. An overall judgment on the relative efficiency of the systems in Caribbean countries would also take into account the completion rates at different levels of schooling. In Jamaica, the combined survival rates (combining survival till first and last grade of secondary school) are higher than all the above countries, which means that a higher percentage of students that initially started in the primary system survive to take the CXC examinations. While this may provide some small comfort, the fact remains that the Jamaican system results in poor and skewed overall outcomes, as noted above. See World Bank (2002d).

to 6.8 percent in 1997/98 and 6.1 percent in 2001/02, and with real expenditure more than doubling over the period.

Expenditure does not guarantee outcomes. The public education expenditure to GDP ratio ". . . often bears a weak relationship to measures of output of the education system." (WDI, 2002).[13] This is also seen in the fact that Jamaica spends more as a share of GDP than 6 of the 8 other Caribbean countries in the sample above, with poorer outcomes than many countries where Governments spend less. One reason for this could be lower instructional time—Jamaica has the lowest number of classroom hours in secondary education among eight Caribbean countries, as Figure 5.8 shows, partly because crime and civil disturbances force school closures.

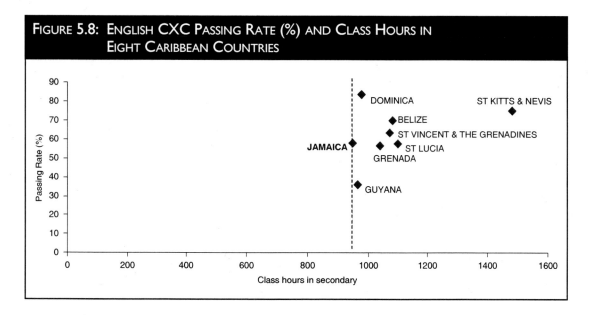

FIGURE 5.8: ENGLISH CXC PASSING RATE (%) AND CLASS HOURS IN EIGHT CARIBBEAN COUNTRIES

Distribution of public expenditure is inequitable. There are some serious problems in the distribution of public expenditure. The Lorenz curve (Figure 5.9) shows that public expenditure on early childhood, primary, and secondary education is equitably distributed amongst rich and poor students. However, tertiary education expenditure is distributed very inequitably, with the top quintile receiving 77 percent of the expenditure, which is not surprising given the enrollment patterns. Also, per student recurrent expenditure is much higher for tertiary education (US$3464 in 1999/00), compared to US$85 in early childhood, US$313 in primary, US$1925 in special education and US$533 in secondary education. As a result, overall education expenditure is regressive, with the top quintile getting 34 percent, and the bottom two quintiles getting 32 percent.

Given that the bulk of tertiary students are from the top two quintiles (91 percent in 2000), a strong case can be made for higher cost recovery in tertiary education. Currently, the government finances 55–60 percent of the budget (salary and related items) of Utech and community colleges, 70–80 percent (salary and related items, and some recurrent costs) for teachers' colleges and 80 percent of the budget of the University of the West Indies. This implies a further inequity within the category of those who have access to tertiary education, since community and teacher colleges serve students from relatively less well-to-do families. A graded increase in fees over time within the different categories of tertiary institutions will reduce inequities and generate some much-needed resources for the public exchequer.

---

13. Latin American countries on average spend a higher fraction of GDP on eduction than those in East Asian countries, with inferior outcomes. Also, changes in education spending do not have a clear relationship with changes in outcomes (mean years of education). See World Bank (2003), Chapter 4.

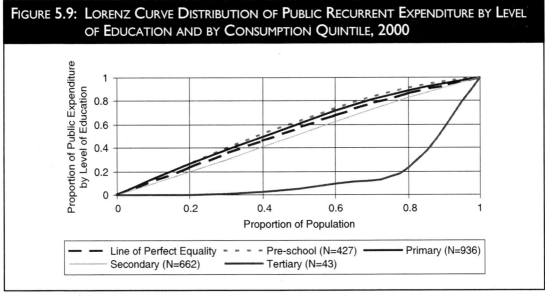

FIGURE 5.9: LORENZ CURVE DISTRIBUTION OF PUBLIC RECURRENT EXPENDITURE BY LEVEL OF EDUCATION AND BY CONSUMPTION QUINTILE, 2000

Source: Constructed from PIOJ-STATIN, 2001

Teachers' salaries are part of the general wage malaise. In 2001/02, recurrent expenditure was 98 percent of the total public allocation for education, with wages around 78 percent. As is the norm, the share of wages is much higher in the earlier stages of the education cycle. But there are several problems in the teacher wage patterns: (i) wages have increased too fast; (ii) the starting salary for a teacher is 2.6 times (with no pedagogical training) to 5 times (trained graduate) per capita GDP, while the average in the USA and Latin America is twice per capita GDP; (iii) there is severe wage compression, with the difference between the highest and lowest teacher salaries 16–18 percent, making teacher retention difficult. The implication of all this is at least at the earlier stages of the education cycle, the salaries to total expenditure ratio is too high, and have reduced the amounts left over for instructional material and maintenance.

What Has Been Done and What More Can Be Done?
The 1990s reforms. The MOEYC (Ministry of Education, Youth and Culture) embarked on a series of far-reaching education reforms in the 1990s, including:

- Services for early childhood development, from birth to six years, were integrated under MOEYC. Early Childhood Education (ECE) enrollment expanded quickly, from 75 to 91 (88 percent in the poorest quintile) percent over 1992–2001, and the goal is 100 percent enrollment.
- In primary education, continuous efforts have been made to enhance quality, provide free textbooks, improve student assessment in Grades 1, 3, 4 and 6, upgrade infrastructure of Primary, All-Age, and P&JH schools, provide pre-service training, update the curriculum of teacher in-service training, and increase the focus on literacy. Beginning in 1999, students at Grade 4 are tested to determine whether they read at grade level—automatic promotion is no longer permitted after grade 4—and to determine remedial measures.
- In secondary education, the most stratified sub-sector, MOEYC introduced a common core curriculum in Grades 7 to 9 to equalize the educational opportunity across all school types, and to balance academic and future vocational demands. Targeting five core subjects (Mathematics, Language Arts, Science, Social Studies, and Resource and Technology) and career education, it aims to develop, inter alia, effective oral and written skills, numeric and problem-solving skills, and critical and creative thinking. A new Grade 9 test was developed to

provide more valid and reliable measures of performance for diagnosis, placement and/or certification purposes. School types were reduced from seven to five through upgrading.

■ In tertiary education, cost sharing was increased to 20 percent of the economic cost while providing student loans and grants to the needy. The government has also permitted private higher education institutions as well as foreign universities to operate/offer courses in Jamaica, helping to broaden tertiary education opportunities.

The Government's *White Paper: Education the Way Upward* (February 2001) seeks to consolidate the gains of the 1990s and provide a broader vision to guide education reform in the medium term. The White Paper emphasizes quality education for all and life-long learning in an era of globalization and technological change. It seeks to:

■ Reiterate the importance of early intervention to compensate for poverty and a disadvantaged home environment, improve readiness of children in primary education, and attain 80 percent functional literacy at the end of Grade 6.
■ Provide a place in upper secondary education for every Grade 9 leaver by 2007, to increase high school students' participation and pass rates in the CXC.
■ Increase enrollment in tertiary education to 15 percent of the relevant age cohort.
■ Decentralize school management, stressing participation, performance and accountability, initiate institutional contracts, and make school performance public.
■ Protect education's share to at least 15–20 percent of the recurrent budget; offer financial assistance for book rental, fee remission and CXC examination fee subsidies for the needy to reduce inequities in cost sharing policies.

Within the overall framework suggested by the White Paper, it is suggested that some re-prioritization and modification could lead to more effective outcomes, as outlined below.

Focus on early learning and raise the functional literacy target to 100 percent. The testing of students at Grade 4 to diagnose learning problems could be advanced to lower primary education to bring all students to standard in their very first few years of school experience. In effect, the target should be for all students to read at grade level in every grade and be functionally literate and numerate by the time they graduate from primary schools. It also means enhancing the target of 80 percent functional literacy after Grade 6 to 100 percent, or else continue to run the risk of functionally less literate becoming part of the problem of youth at risk. There is no higher priority in education than this one because without strengthening the foundation, all subsequent interventions are likely to be more costly and ineffective.[14] This may need some re-orientation of public expenditure on education.

Effective early interventions entail: (a) hiring and training specialist teachers in reading and math; (b) making available high interest learning materials (including in Patois, since the majority of students speak Patois, and take time to learn English) and games in order to engage children; (c) vigorously and frequently assessing students' achievement and learning problems; (d) organizing co-curricular activities and extra tutoring to help slow learners catch-up during the week and holidays; (e) providing summer school programs for those who still need additional help; and (f) having smaller class sizes and deploying the best teachers for the lower primary grades, in keeping with the findings of education research.

International benchmarking. It is important to have some sense of how Jamaican students perform vis-à-vis students in other countries, especially those known to have good education outcomes. This can be achieved by regular participation in international comparative studies such as

---

14. Post-war success stories like Korea and Scandinavian countries, and the USA between 1850 and 1950, have all followed a pattern of bottom-up upgrading, starting with the development of basic education, followed by secondary and then tertiary education (World Bank 2003, Chapter 4).

IEA Mathematics and Science Studies and Literacy Studies, and OECD's PISA Study on knowledge of 15 year-old-students. Such studies are repeated every few years and provide an opportunity for evaluating and redesigning policy interventions.

Increase parental involvement and awareness and make school results public. Many of the bottlenecks to learning originate from the home. Greater involvement of parents in child development can provide a major boost to student achievement. Publicity campaigns, including through mass media, are needed to inform parents that: differentiated expectations for boys and girls can affect their future aspirations; building trust rather than physical punishment helps child self-discipline; story telling and reading or use of audio tapes can help children learn standard English; books are essential for learning, and parents should provide for their rental or apply for public assistance for rental; regular school attendance and doing homework will help child achievement; better educated children are better able to take care of old age parents and help their own children attain better health and education outcomes. Parenting education also means informing fathers about their critical role in their sons' development and single mothers about good practices in rearing responsible children in general. All this is not very resource-intensive but demands organized, systematic and sustained efforts. On their part, schools could make their results public, which would enable parents and the community to monitor school progress.

Encourage student involvement. On their part, schools should systematically encourage students and involve them in efforts at school improvement, encourage student self-government, provide students some discretionary funds to address issues of concern to them, and thereby also get them more engaged in the process of school-building.

Expand upper secondary education. The sharp decline in enrollment of students after age 14, especially the poor, can be attributed to the lack of school places in Grades 10 and 11, as well as poor preparation in junior secondary education. Students from All-age and P&JH schools, which offer only 3 years of junior secondary education, are more affected by the lack of supply than others. One cost-effective and quick way to provide school spaces would be to buy seats in private schools that target and achieve quality improvement, making capitation grants available to them based on their enrollment of students in Grades 10 and 11 (see also below). Private schools can also be paid to organize compensatory education to repeaters.

Improve teacher incentives and school-based management. Generally, a teaching career is not the first choice of high-achieving students. Over the years, teachers, particularly in mathematics and science, tend to leave teaching when they find opportunities in other sectors. Also, in recent times, some of the best and most promising teachers from Jamaica have been regularly recruited by New York City and the United Kingdom. Given that teachers are the most critical factor in education outcomes, motivating and retaining quality teachers becomes crucial.

Tackling this will require restructuring teacher salaries over time—not increasing them generally, since they are already high—to reduce the current compression at the top end, which is perpetuated by the practice of applying a uniform percentage increase for all scales. Smaller percentage increases for pre-trained teachers will free up resources for the top end of the scale and encourage professional upgrading of less qualified teachers.

Monetary reward is not the sole motivating factor. Currently, the Jamaican Teachers' Association provides the best teacher award on an annual basis, and allows the awardee to interact with other teachers at an international conference. This laudable effort could be extended to every school by having students and parents select the best teacher and provide appropriate recognition in the community. Colombia has implemented this scheme with much success. Another way to empower teachers and give them a sense of ownership is to permit them key roles in school-based management. Teachers could be encouraged to set targets and design strategies, based on student data, and be given discretionary funds to meet these challenges.

Increase flexibility in teacher deployment. The current practice of using students-to-teacher ratios as a basis of allocating positions (and hence public resources) to schools and of associating teachers with the schools that hire them rather than with the Ministry, has some built-in rigidities.

Once a school hires a teacher (with employment authorized by the Ministry), he/she cannot be re-deployed to another school or be retrenched from the system even when the student enrollment declines. These rigidities have led to some schools having very low student-to-teacher ratios, with others in high growth areas having unreasonably high ratios. A more flexible arrangement needs to be negotiated with the union.

Reform Education Finance. Subventions to schools are based on the number of teaching positions approved, which, in turn, are based on recommended student-to-teacher ratios for each school type. Since the ratios vary across school types, the basis for resource allocation is inherently unequal. To level the playing fields for all secondary schools (including All-Age and P&JH Schools which have Grades 7 to 9), public resources should be allocated as capitation grants based on enrollment (verifiable as average daily attendance) for all school types. In the case of All-Age and P&JH, the capitation grant for Grades 7–9 should be more equivalent to per student spending in High Schools than to primary schools. Since the average daily attendance has to be verified by periodic, unannounced inspection, this will also provide incentives for schools to encourage student attendance and keep good records.

Capitation grants have another advantage. Currently, there is little incentive for school boards not to hire the maximum number of teachers that the establishment permits. Basing allocation on enrollment allows capitation grants to be de-linked from student-to-teacher ratios and permits greater flexibility in the system. For example, the school board and teachers could decide to use part of their funds to purchase some learning material rather than hire a teacher. Allowing schools to make such decisions would increase the efficiency of resource use.

Equalizing resource allocation across school types is not enough to provide a level playing field for disadvantaged students. Special grants may be needed to support schools that, for example, have a large percentage of students reading below grade level. Compensatory education could be funded through this mechanism. Many schools need far more and better quality library resources and reading materials.

Some discretionary funds to finance co-curricular activities for students, and professional development activities for teachers, would also help schools to engage teachers and students. The Reform of Secondary Education Project II is providing an experimental school improvement grant on a three-year basis. If effective, it could be institutionalized.

Buying places from private sector schools that target and achieve quality improvement, rather than constructing new secondary schools, is likely to be a cheaper and more flexible alternative for government, and provides immediate access to students who don't have to wait for new buildings to come up. Currently, private secondary schools absorb about 5 percent of total students. However, they have excess capacity (and so usually have smaller class sizes than public schools) and struggle to cover operating costs, because the public system is free or charges only a fraction of private school fees. For each new student, a private school could be paid the equivalent of average per student recurrent spending on secondary education in the public system, which would save government the costs of capital investment as well as repair and maintenance. To take care of quality concerns, this scheme could be introduced in an incremental way, starting with those private schools that have good results, and moving on to those that achieve quality targets which can be monitored. This partnership with the private sector also gives the government the flexibility to adjust to the changing demographics of the school-age population.

In tertiary education, given its relatively high quality, the richer than average profile of those who attend, the high emigration rates, and the high private returns to education, increasing cost recovery would be desirable on both equity and efficiency grounds. For the same reasons, the student loan scheme should draw on private rather than public resources (the current scheme has not been financially self-sustaining). In this context, improving the quality of statistics on student repayment and default would help, and public disclosure of those who do not repay would mount public pressure on students to repay.

CHAPTER 6

CRIME AND ITS IMPACT ON BUSINESS IN JAMAICA[1]

Jamaica has the one of the highest rates of violent crime in the world, but a relatively low rate of property crime. In 2000, the recorded intentional homicide rate was 33 per 100,000 inhabitants, lower only than Colombia (63) and South Africa (52).[2] In terms of recorded major assaults, Jamaica experienced 215 such incidents per 100,000 (665 in South Africa, 95 in Dominica). Recorded drug offences are also among the highest in the world, at 452 per 100,000 (370 in Dominica, and highest at 987 in Norway). In contrast, property crimes are relatively low in Jamaica: recorded burglaries occur at a rate of 92 per 100,000 (1777 in the Dominica, 922 in South Africa, 134 in Mauritius), and total robberies at 89 per 100,000 (78 in Dominica, 460 in South Africa, 98 in Mauritius). In the aggregate, Jamaica experienced a relatively lower 1488 total recorded crimes per 100,000 in 2000 (10763 in Dominica, 7997 in South Africa, 3030 in Mauritius, 1289 in Costa Rica), since non-violent crimes are fewer in Jamaica, but where there is also significant under-reporting owing to low clear-up rates.

A high rate of violent crime can have many adverse repercussions:

- It has a **negative impact on the investment climate** and can deter or delay both domestic and foreign investment, and hence growth.
    - It leads to higher cost of doing business, because of the need to employ different forms of security, and diverts investment away from business expansion and productivity improvement, and may lead to a less than optimal operating strategy.
    - It leads to business losses, arising from looting, arson, theft, extortion and fraud.

---

1. The analysis on crime in this Chapter is based on a background paper prepared for this study by Harriott et al., 2003.

2. Source: website of Office on Drugs and Crime, Centre for International Crime Prevention, United Nations.

■ It leads to loss of output because of reduced hours of operation (including avoiding night shifts) or loss of workdays arising from outbreaks of violence, and avoidance of some types of economic activity.

■ It also reduces output because of the temporary (from injury) or permanent (from murder) exit of individuals from the labor force. In the latter case, the loss is not just current output, but the output in the remaining years of the individual's working life.

■ It can also cause a permanent shut-down of firms or relocation to less crime-prone countries.

■ It **erodes the development of human capital as well as social capital** and thus constrains the potential for growth. The crime situation in Jamaica seems to be an important reason for migration,[3] since the fear of crime significantly reduces the quality of life. Crime and violence have also been blamed for slowing down the rate of return of migrants back to Jamaica.[4] Also, crime forces otherwise productive individuals to occasionally exit the labor force because of violent injury to themselves or close associates, or because of social unrest in the community. Violence in some communities also causes schools to close periodically. Moreover, home and community instability is not conducive to learning and educational objectives.

■ It **diverts public resources excessively away from productive uses**[5] that have a potentially much higher impact on social development and growth, to areas such as police, justice, the medical system (for treatment of violence-related injuries and trauma). For example, between 1988/89 and 2001/02, Jamaica's budgetary expenditure for health, in nominal terms, grew 23 percent annually, whereas the budget for national security and justice grew by 62 percent. Since 1999, the budget for Justice and Correctional Services plus the Police has exceeded the budget allocation for health (PIOJ, various issues). For private citizens, it also diverts resources away from potentially useful expenditures like education, to spending on treating injury and on private security.

This report estimates that the direct cost of crime in Jamaica is at least 3.7 percent of GDP (2001 data),[6] and this does not include the impact on business. Of course, the causality also runs in reverse. Crime may result, for example, from the effect of broad socio-economic and political processes, and the outcome of distortions such as chronic unemployment and high levels of inequality.

How should the crime problem be tackled? A balanced approach is needed that addresses social factors, reduces inequality (especially inequality that is not derived from differential effort and performance), and improves educational achievement (not just enrolment), as well as ensuring effective and fair law enforcement. Many recommendations have been made in official reports in Jamaica (PERF 2001; Wolfe 1993), but these reports have not attempted to estimate costs of crime and crime control measures (these will be addressed in this chapter).

This chapter attempts to better understand the dimension and sources of the crime problem in Jamaica. A Business Victimization Survey of 400 firms was carried out for the first time in Jamaica for this report. Victimization surveys are useful because they include crimes not reported to the police, provide information on perceptions of risks from crime, and assessments of the institutional support available to cope with crime. The results of this survey, based on perceptions and experiences of crime by managers, are discussed in detail in the chapter. The recommendations in this chapter are based directly on results from the survey and econometric analysis (see Annex A). The chapter does not attempt to cover all angles of the crime problem in depth (for example, many aspects of youth violence, domestic violence, and gang- or drug-related crimes), but aims to focus on the impact of crime

---

3. See "NDM predicts brain drain," *Jamaica Gleaner*, January 6, 1999.
4. "Jamaicans staying away from home," *Jamaica Gleaner*, December 5, 1999.
5. In comparison with a more peaceful society.
6. This is a static estimate of the cost of crime during the year, and is calculated as the sum of healthcare costs, lost production days, and public security expenses.

on businesses and the economy and provide recommendations that emanate directly from this analysis and from cross-country experiences.

This chapter is organized as follows. The first section sets the context for analyzing crime by providing an overview of Jamaica's governance performance and its ranking in international governance indicators. The second section surveys the dimension of and trends in crime over the last three decades. The patterns of criminal victimization of business enterprises are discussed in the third section to appraise the direct impact of crime on economic activity. In the fourth section, the economic cost of crime is estimated, using data from the survey as well as public records and budgets. In the fifth section, the determinants of violent crime are briefly discussed based on the results of a time series econometric estimation. In the sixth section, policy recommendations are presented.

Governance in Jamaica—The International Context

Jamaica has a strong democracy, high caliber bureaucracy and good regulatory framework. Since its independence in 1962, Jamaica has been a stable democracy, led alternatively by the People's National Party (PNP), currently in power since 1989, and the Jamaica Labor Party (JLP). The thirteen parishes of Jamaica are governed by local authorities called Parish Councils. Political participation is widely exercised with a voter turnout of about two-thirds at general elections. Jamaica's tradition of democratic participation, free media, civil liberties and political rights, are substantiated by international surveys based on perceptions, where it ranks high in terms of "voice and accountability" and "political stability and lack of political violence" (see Table 6.1). The quality of the bureaucracy is rated in cross-country comparisons as high, comparable to countries such as Chile, Hong Kong and France. The public sector accounted, in April 2002, for about 10 percent of the labor force (97,285 employees, of which 32,067 were civil servants) in Jamaica.

In addition, Jamaica has a positive enabling environment for business establishment and operation. It ranks high in international comparisons of its regulatory framework—it requires 37 days to start a firm in Jamaica, comparable to 34 days in Chile. Labor regulations are not perceived to be too onerous (the labor regulation index for Jamaica is 2 on an index from 0–6, where 6 is the highest level of regulation[7]). Major steps have been taken by the Government to improve the framework for competition, such as the passage of the Fair Competition Act, the establishment of the Fair Trading Commission and the Securities Commission (to regulate the securities industry) in 1993. The financial crisis of 1996 prompted legislative initiatives, including a new Financial Institutions Act, Insurance Act, as well as amendments to the Banking Act, Securities and Unit Trust Acts and to building society regulations. Three Bills were passed by the Senate in 1999 to safeguard property right in the areas of trademark, copyright and layout designs.

However, strengths have not converted into comparable outcomes (see Figure 6.1). Public satisfaction with government policies and the government's ability to carry out its declared programs are below average in the cross-country comparisons. This public dissatisfaction could be partly explained by the perception that quality of public service provision (captured by government effectiveness) is relatively below average.

Also affecting the business environment is corruption, where Jamaica scores on average in cross-country surveys of perceptions of corruption (see Table 6.1).[8] Yet bribery and lack of transparency in government contracts are considered by Jamaicans to be important problems. Jamaica ranks poorly in perceptions of favoritism shown by government officials towards well connected firms and individuals when deciding upon policies and contracts. This is closely linked with the pressure exerted on businesses by the protection racket, and reflected in the high perceived costs imposed on businesses by organized crime (such as racketeering and extortion).

---

7. World Bank, snapshot reports, *http:/rru.worldbank.org/doingbusiness/TopicReports.*
8. Anti-corruption legislation, the Corruption Prevention Act, was passed by Parliament in 2000. This requires select government employees to file annual assets statements with a three-member Corruption Prevention Commission (further reform should aim to give the commission independent investigative powers and increased financial allocations).

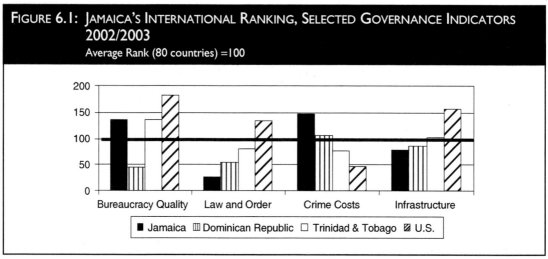

FIGURE 6.1: JAMAICA'S INTERNATIONAL RANKING, SELECTED GOVERNANCE INDICATORS 2002/2003
Average Rank (80 countries) =100

Source: See Table 6.1

In addition, very poor rule of law and crime negates the positive elements in the business environment. Jamaica's most conspicuous and severe problem is the erosion in the rule of law. Comparisons of international ratings show that Jamaica is significantly underperforming in the area of law and order relative to countries with comparable incomes per capita (see Figure 6.2). The rule of law has been shown to have a strong statistical relationship to economic growth and poverty reduction.[9] High rates of violent crime impose relatively very high costs to businesses in Jamaica (see Table 6.1).[10] Violent crime is concentrated in the inner-cities among young males, giving Jamaica the third highest homicide rate in the world, and is sourced mainly through illegal narcotics and arms trafficking.[11]

The high level of crime and violence has overloaded the judiciary with a backlog of cases, pending in high courts for over four years, in spite of the establishment of night courts to deal with minor cases. Though there are delays in the administration of justice, and legal and administrative practices are outdated and inefficient, the judicial system in Jamaica is perceived to be relatively fair and independent from political pressures (see Table 6.1).[12]

Dimension and Trends in Crime in Jamaica[13]

This section examines the basic patterns of reported crime over the last three decades (1970–2001) by analyzing the trends in crime and the geographic and economic distribution of crime in Jamaica.

---

9. It is estimated that an improvement in Jamaica's rule of law to the high level found in the Bahamas, St. Lucia, or Trinidad and Tobago in 1998 would lead to about 50% more foreign investment, 2 percentage points higher growth, and improved social indicators (World Bank 2000b).

10. For example, violence in Kingston in July 2001 is estimated to have cost Jampro more than US$100 million in foregone foreign investments. In the case of the potential sale of Union Bank in 2001 to a foreign investor, the buyer was discouraged by the riots and left the country before even starting the discussions.

11. Historically, political parties used violence and gangs to secure economic and political power and funded the arming of party supporters in local communities. When political parties withdrew from their sponsorship of gangs, the latter resorted to the drug trade and other illegal activities for resources (see Harriott 2000).

12. The reform of the judicial system has been undertaken by the government, including improving its administration and facilities, a Legal Aid Bill (to provide state-funded legal aid to the very poor), the establishment of a Justice Training Institute, and development of alternative methods of dispute resolutions. A proposal to establish a Caribbean Court of Justice as a final court of appeal is being discussed between Jamaica and other CARICOM countries.

13. Some of the survey work in this section is new in Jamaica and therefore subject to data constraints.

TABLE 6.1: INTERNATIONAL COMPARISONS OF SELECTED GOVERNANCE INDICATORS, 2002
Scale 0 (worst)—6 (best)

	Jamaica		Selected economies				Full Sample	
	% rank in sample 100 = best	Score	Dominican Republic	Trinidad & Tobago	Mauritius	U.S.	Sample Mean	Sample Size
i) Government Effectiveness and Stability								
Government Effectiveness (K. et al., 2001)[1]	43	2.6	2.7	3.7	3.9	4.9	3.0	159
Socioeconomic Conditions (ICRG, Feb 2003)[2]	45	2.5	2.8	3.0	—	3.8	2.9	140
Costs of Institutional change (GCR, 2001)[3]	52	3.9	3.3	—	4.4	5.1	3.9	75
Voice and Accountability (Kaufmann et al., 2001)[4]	73	3.9	3.5	3.7	4.5	4.5	3.0	173
Government Stability (ICRG, 2003)[5]	35	4.3	5.0	4.0	—	5.3	4.5	140
Political Stability and lack of Pol. Violence (K. et al., 2003)[6]	61	3.4	3.6	3.3	4.3	4.4	3.0	161
Bureaucracy Quality (ICRG, 2003)[7]	76	4.5	1.5	4.5	—	6.0	3.3	140
ii) Rule of Law and Business Environment								
Law and Order (ICRG, 2003)	4	1.0	2.0	3.0	—	5.0	3.7	140
Organized crime (GGR)[8]	5	2.1	3.6	3.9	5.1	4.9	4.0	80
Reliability of Police Forces (GCR)	25	2.7	2.9	3.3	3.2	5.3	3.7	80
Business Costs of Crime and Violence (GCR)[9]	9	1.9	3.0	2.9	4.2	4.7	3.8	80
Regulatory Framework (K. et al., 2001)[10]	68	3.5	3.7	4.0	3.5	4.4	3.0	168
Property Rights (GCR)[11]	51	4.2	3.2	4.2	4.6	5.4	4.0	80
Judicial Independence (GCR)[12]	55	3.8	2.8	4.5	4.2	4.9	3.6	80
Favoritism in decisions of government officials (GCR)[13]	34	2.4	2.1	2.4	2.8	3.7	2.8	80
Extent of bureaucratic red tape (GCR)[14]	38	3.9	4.0	3.7	4.0	4.2	3.9	80
Administrative burden for startups (GCR)	19	2.7	3.3	3.9	3.9	5.0	3.5	80
Hiring and Firing practices (GCR)[15]	45	2.7	3.3	3.3	2.1	4.5	3.0	80
Days to start a firm (GCR)	71	37.0	117.0	—	—	5.0	—	72
Flexibility of Wage Determination (GCR)	68	4.5	4.5	4.5	2.7	5.3	4.0	80
Infrastructure Quality (GCR)	34	2.8	3.1	3.7	3.8	5.7	3.6	80

(continued)

Scale 0 (worst)—6 (best)

	Jamaica % rank in sample 100 = best	Score	Selected economies Dominican Republic	Trinidad & Tobago	Mauritius	U.S.	Full Sample Sample Mean	Sample Size
Corruption and Irregular Payments (higher scale means less)								
Control of Corruption (K. et al., 2001)	54	2.9	2.8	3.6	3.6	4.7	3.0	160
Business costs of corruption (GCR)	48	3.9	3.2	3.9	4.1	5.1	4.1	80
Irregular Payments in Public Contracts (GCR)	25	3.0	3.6	3.1	3.1	4.8	3.6	80
Memo:								
GDP per capita, PPP $ (2001)	—	3890	6198	10018	10400	34888	—	—

1. quality of public service provision and bureaucracy, competence of civil servants, independence of civil service from political pressures and credibility of the government's commitment to policies.
2. general public satisfaction with the government's economic policies; socioeconomic factors are identified with greatest political impact for the country.
3. effect of legal or political changes over past five years on firms planning capacity.
4. extent of civil participation in political process, extent of civil liberties and political rights, including independence of media.
5. government's ability to carry out its declared program(s) and its ability to stay in office.
6. likelihood that a government in power will be destabilized or overthrown by possible constitutional and/or violent means.
7. mechanism for recruitment and training and autonomy of bureaucracy from political pressure.
8. cost imposed on businesses by organized crime such as racketeering and extortion.
9. cost imposed on business by common crime and violence (e.g. street muggings, firms being looted).
10. incidence of market unfriendly policies such as price controls or inadequate banking supervision, perceptions of burdens imposed by excess regulation in foreign trade and business development.
11. extent to which financial assets and wealth are delineated and protected by law.
12. extent to which judiciary is independent and not subject to interference by the government.
13. favoritism towards well connected firms and individuals by government officials when deciding upon policies and contracts.
14. time spent by company's senior management working with government agencies/regulations.
15. extent to which hiring and firing of workers is impeded/flexibly determined by employers.
Sources: International Country Risk Guide (ICRG) database, February 2003; Global Competitiveness Report (GCR) 2002/03, 2001/02; Governance Matters II: Updated Governance Indicators for 2000/01. (Kaufman et al.), 2002.

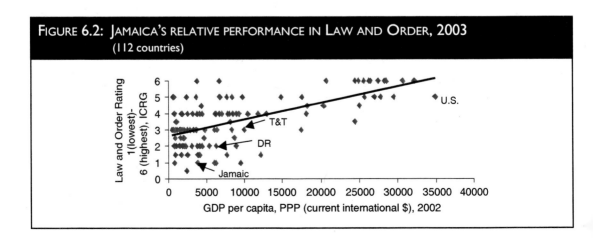

FIGURE 6.2: JAMAICA'S RELATIVE PERFORMANCE IN LAW AND ORDER, 2003
(112 countries)

Trends in Crime. The trends in violent crime over the last thirty years place Jamaica among the most violent countries in the world. The Crime Rate Indices (CRIs)[14] for Jamaica attempt to track movements in the overall crime rate for the last 30 years. There has been a relatively steady increase in the CRI over the decades (see Figure 6.3 and Annex Table A6.1), though the highest rates of violent crime were experienced in 1980 (a period of partisan political violence), followed by 1996 and 1997. The level of violent crimes and fraud were highest during the 1990s. It should be noted that under-reporting is high for certain categories of violent crime partly because the clear up or arrest rates for these types of crime is fairly low.[15]

Over the 1990s, the murder rate increased steadily and was largely driven by increasing levels of distribution and trans-shipment of drugs, leading to increased "gang wars." Between 1998 and 2000, according to police reports, drug and gang related murders accounted on average for 22 percent of total murders. Domestic violence represented about 30 percent of total murders.[16] The increasing severity of the murder problem is highlighted by comparisons with New York, a high crime city—while both Jamaica and New York experienced similar rates of murder in 1970, Jamaica's murder rate had increased to almost seven times that of New York's by 2000 (see Annex Table A6.2).

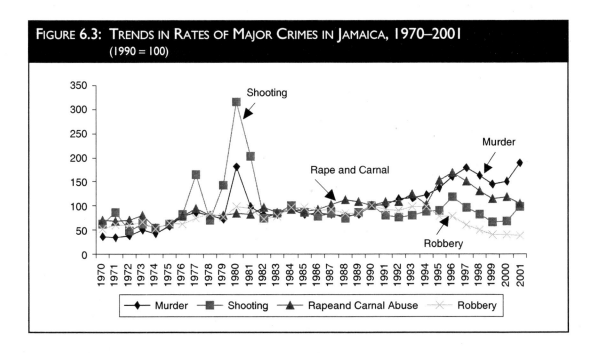

FIGURE 6.3: TRENDS IN RATES OF MAJOR CRIMES IN JAMAICA, 1970–2001
(1990 = 100)

Some types of violent crime, notably shooting (assault with a gun) and robbery, have however seen a downward trend during the 1990s. Rape and carnal abuse levels increased up to the mid 1990s (possibly due to increased levels of reporting), declining slightly since then (may have resulted from establishment of a Rape Unit in the Jamaica Constabulary Force). The fraud index shows an upward trend during the 1990s, during which there was a significant increase in the number of financial crimes associated with the rapid growth and inadequate regulation of the financial sector.

---

14. Developed for Jamaica by Francis et al. (2001). The CRI includes only violent crimes i.e. murder, shooting, robbery, and rape and carnal abuse.

15. Data for the past thirty years indicate that the percent of robberies cleared-up each year ranges from a low of 22 percent in 1991 to a high of 45 percent in 1999. The thirty-year average is 31 percent.

16. This may be an overestimate due to definitional and other difficulties.

Geographical distribution of Crime. Jamaica is divided into three counties and further into a total of thirteen parishes. Over 1984–2001, the county of Surrey (eastern Jamaica) had the highest murder rates, rising from 41 per 100,000 of population in 1984 (compared to the national average of 21 per 100,000) to 79 per 100,000 in 2001 (national average 44 per 100,000) (see Annex Table A6.3). The county of Surrey accounted on average for 61 percent of the total number of murders over 1984–2001 (while it represented an annual average of only 34 percent of Jamaica's population).

At the parish level, Kingston and St. Andrew had the highest murder rates, increasing steadily from 48 per 100,000 in 1984 to 93 per 100,000 in 2001. Kingston and St. Andrew averaged 57 percent of total murders during 1984–2001, but represented only 27 percent of Jamaica's total population. In 2001, about 51 percent of reported violent crimes occurred in the city of Kingston.[17] The second highest murder rates occurred in St. Catherine, followed by St. James and St. Thomas. These parishes all have rapidly expanding urban centers. These trends reflect the serious social problems associated with growing urbanization, including high levels of unemployment, formation of gangs, creation of slums, and an escalation of drug trafficking. Other forms of violent crimes, including shooting, robbery and rape,[18] follow similar distribution patterns.

The Profile of those involved in Crime. While violence is an endemic feature of Jamaican society, it is often concentrated among the poorest in the society, and among young males (14–24 years old), who often tend to be the victims as well as the perpetrators of violent crimes (World Bank 2001b). In 2001, males accounted for 98 percent of those arrested for major crimes (PIOJ 2002). Amongst those arrested for major crimes, 53 percent were from the 16–25 age group. Youth from inner cities are also more likely to be recruited as drug sellers because of their relatively lower opportunity costs, given that they are more likely to be school-dropouts/unemployed. Because drug sellers/dealers carry guns for self-protection and dispute resolution, the increased penetration of guns has led to greater incidences of violence among the youth.

Patterns of Criminal Victimization of Firms and Coping Strategies

The business environment is becoming more hostile and difficult. Some firms are in the grip of organized crime, but this is still an emerging problem. Crime itself and the responses to it tend to be very costly in social and economic terms and may reduce competitiveness in some sectors of the economy and retard investments or even stimulate disinvestments. International surveys rank Jamaica high in terms of the perceptions of the costs imposed on businesses by crime and violence (see Table 6.1).

In this section, the direct impact of crime on Jamaican businesses is explored. This analysis is based on the results of a detailed business victimization survey of 400 firms that was conducted in 2002 for this study, with a diverse sample in terms of size, location and sectoral origin.[19] Survey results are used to describe basic patterns of criminal victimization of Jamaican businesses and perceptions of risk, and examine their coping strategies and the degree of institutional support given to them by the criminal justice system.

The Patterns of Victimization

The criminal victimization of Jamaican firms is high. About 65 percent of all firms in the sample reported that they had experienced one or more forms of criminal victimization during 2001. Thirty-three percent of all firms were violently victimized (robbery, extortion and protection), 52 percent suffered various forms of theft, 50 percent experienced fraud, and 7 percent other forms of criminal

---

17. Includes murders, rapes, shootings and robberies.
18. While the county of Cornwall has the highest rates of rape, the county of Surrey has the highest percentage of total rapes.
19. For more details on survey methodology see Annex 6-2 and Harriott et al. 2003.

victimization. These are comparable to levels of business victimization in South Africa, which experienced similarly high levels of violent crime over an extended period. In 1999, about 68 percent of South African firms experienced theft of goods, 52 percent experienced employee theft and 56 percent burglary.[20] Violent victimization, such as robbery, was only marginally lower than in Jamaica. For some categories of property crimes (not involving the use of violence) the victimization rates were higher in some Eastern European countries (including Hungary and the Czech Republic). Some of the developed countries of Western Europe (such as the United Kingdom and France) that have traditionally had high levels of property crime also recorded greater prevalence of burglary and similar property crimes.

Some Jamaican firms experience crime on a regular basis and in multiple forms. About 27 percent of firms faced incidents of theft at least on a quarterly basis, of which 9 percent on a weekly basis. Twenty two percent experienced fraud at least on a quarterly basis. Nine percent suffered from violent victimization, and 7 percent were otherwise victimized, on a quarterly basis.

Violent victimization and Theft. Robbery, extortion, and protection are the main violent crimes that are directed at businesses. In 2001, 12 percent of firms were robbed at least once, of which 3 percent repeatedly.

Extortion and protection are probably the most serious violent crimes since, propagated by the emergence of powerful organized crime groups, they transform the environment in which businesses operate. In the case of extortion, the firm pays the extortionist in order to avoid other forms of victimization that the extortionist may threaten. In contrast, in the case of protection rackets, the person or group receiving the payment provides a real service in protecting the firm from all criminal activity, not just the potential criminality of the protector. The growth of the protection racket, especially in Kingston, is associated with police ineffectiveness and the growth of a market for protective services. Those with expertise in the use of violence and who have influence in the underworld, are well placed to provide these services. In these conditions, the criminal dons are presented with new opportunities to transform their operations into more sophisticated organized crime. Further expansion of the extortion-protection racket is likely to be accompanied by a further decline in the rate of robbery as the former is more sophisticated, less visible and less easily detectable. In 2001, about 5 percent of all surveyed firms were forced to pay extortionists, while 8 percent paid for protection.[21]

Refusal to pay extortion-protection levies is usually punished by burning down the non-compliant firm and putting it out of business, or at least expelling it from the area that is dominated by the extortionist group. In 2001, only 2 percent of the sample reported that they were victims of this crime. The non-compliant victims and other firms that were completely ruined by this form of crime would not have been detected by the survey. The survival bias in the sample therefore means that the data is likely to understate the problem.

Extortion marks a break with the historical pattern of crime in Jamaica, which has been directed at victims from a similar class background as the victimizer, usually located in the poorer communities. Upwardly directed violent crimes, in which the poor violently victimize the rich, are still relatively few, but rising.

Theft and the various traditional forms of non-violent property crimes are less threatening, but nevertheless may severely burden weak firms. This is particularly true in cases of multiple victimization involving violent and non-violent crimes (see case in Annex D).

Theft is the most prevalent crime encountered by firms, in the form of theft of cash (20 percent of firms) and theft of goods (43 percent), and appears to be positively correlated with firm size. Fraud is also quite prevalent and takes the form of the use of counterfeit money (27 percent), presentation of forged checks (18 percent), use of forged credit cards (9 percent), sale of counterfeit products (7 percent), weight and measures fraud (13 percent), solicitation of funds for charitable

---

20. Quoted in Harriott et al. (2003).
21. Underreporting is likely since managers may not admit to the paying of extortion or protection money.

organization (8 percent), and manipulation of payrolls and invoices (7 percent). The main perpetrators of some of these types of fraud are employees of these firms.

The costs of employee criminality are not restricted to the losses incurred from theft, corruption and the direct appropriation of the assets of the firm. They extend to the cost of policing the workers via more elaborate accounting systems, extensive surveillance systems, and the increased density of security guards. For societies that are well endowed with social capital, these costs to business are much lower (Figueroa, cited in Harriott et al., 2003).

Sectoral Patterns. The pattern of firm victimization may be linked to the degree and type of opportunities for crime in the sector. For example, firms operating in the financial sector are more vulnerable to employee and corporate fraud, and farms operating in the agricultural sector to theft of goods. The size of a firm may also structure opportunities for crime, as well as variation in the capability to protect assets and prevent crime.

Tourism is quite sensitive to crime, and the proportion of firms in this sector that are reportedly victimized is quite high. The main crime against hotels was theft (hotel inventories present considerable opportunities for theft), reported by about 72 percent of the firms in the sector in 2001 (see Table 6.2). About 41 percent of the firms in the sample reported that they were victims of violent fraudulent victimization (robbery, extortion, or some other method of illegally transferring their assets involving the use of direct or threatened violence). This is higher than the level reported to the police and may include the victimization of hotel guests (rather than strictly the victimization of the firm).

Crimes against visitors are relatively low. In 2000, only 0.1 percent (or 103 incidents) of all visitors to Jamaica reported being victimized.[22] Despite the high rate of violent crime in Jamaica, the low rates and prevalence of tourist victimization are explained by the relative low crime rates in tourist areas (with few exceptions).

The pattern of victimization in **agriculture** is similar to that of tourism. Theft of goods (mainly predial larceny) was the most prevalent crime, experienced by 81 percent of agricultural farms in 2001. Farms are vulnerable to crime because their expansiveness and relative openness makes it difficult and very expensive to secure them. Official police records suggest that the incidence and rate of predial larceny has been steadily declining from 18.7 incidents per 100,000 citizens in 1990 to 10.9 per 100,000 in 2001. This reflects declining opportunities for crime that accompany the progressive decline of agricultural production and fewer farms operating. But for the remaining farms, the experience of victimization is even more prevalent, as reflected in the survey.

Consistent with the structure of criminal opportunities, fraud was the most prevalent crime in the **financial services sector.** About 65 percent of the firms in the sample reported that they had been targets of fraud. Relative to the other sectors, they also reported the lowest incidence of theft (5 percent) and second lowest incidence of violent victimization.

The pattern of victimization in **manufacturing, distribution and construction** sectors is similar. Theft and fraud are equally prevalent in manufacturing (47 percent). In construction, 44 percent and 48 percent of the firms reported being victims of theft and fraud respectively in 2001. In the distributive trade, which is characterized by finished products distributed by relatively small and vulnerable firms, the prevalence of theft and fraud is greater, experienced by 53 percent and 63 percent of the firms in the sample respectively. The level of violent victimization is much lower in all three sectors.

Company size is also linked to a discernible pattern of victimization. Small firms seem to be more prone to victimization than large firms as they provide more opportunities for crime.[23] Because most entrants start out small, this acts as a barrier to entry for potential entrants, and inhibits growth. Size-

---

22. This cannot be attributed to low levels of reporting as these are higher amongst tourists than local residents. Insurance coverage is more prevalent amongst tourists, and only recoverable if the incident is reported to the police.

23. Firm size in Jamaica has fallen over the last twenty years, reflecting the decline of light manufacturing and plantation agriculture, and the parallel growth of small firms in the service sector. A firm employing fifty or more workers is officially regarded as "large."

based vulnerabilities may be accentuated by the area in which firms are located. As discussed in the previous section, there has been a general tendency for greater concentration of criminal activity in the urban areas and particularly in the Kingston Metropolitan Area.

TABLE 6.2: VICTIMIZATION BY SECTOR IN WHICH FIRM IS LOCATED AND TYPE OF CRIME
(as % of firms in the sector that are victimized)

	Theft	Fraud	Violent Crime	Total number of firms
Finance	5	65	10	20
Tourism	72	43	41	32
Manufacturing	47	47	21	53
Agriculture	81	38	41	53
Construction	44	48	28	25
Transport & Storage	43	39	12	23
Entertainment	46	46	9	33
Distributive Trade	53	63	24	79
Mining and Quarrying	—	—	—	8
Other	33	47	12	51
Total	52	50	33	377

Perceptions of Risk

The perceptions of managers of the environment in which they operate and the risks of victimization to the firm are examined below. These perceptions are a measure of their levels of confidence and investment risk that are likely to influence business decisions.

About 29 percent of managers felt that the area in which their firm was located was either very unsafe (9 percent) or unsafe (20 percent). On the other hand, 49 percent felt that their firm was located in an area that was either "very safe" (9 percent) or "somewhat safe" (40 percent). Of those firms operating in the areas perceived to be unsafe, 43 percent of their managers felt that these firms were highly likely to be violently victimized. Interestingly, the perceived risk of violent victimization (by robbery) in such firms was lower than the 66 percent risk perceived by firms in the whole sample. This finding is consistent with the pattern of fear of crime found in other studies of the general population whereby sub-populations that are most at risk are not necessarily the most fearful of victimization. Familiarity with one's environment and having a system of social support may obviate dangers and risk of victimization.

The decision making within firms may be influenced not just by the perceived risks to the firm, but also by the risks to its staff, including the managers. The fear of criminal victimization at the workplace may also be an important motivation for individual action such as the migration of skilled personnel to other firms. In the case of family firms, it may be decisive in shaping decisions about the firm itself.

Examining the perceived risks of different forms of crime shows that about 42 percent of all managers felt that they were either highly likely (11 percent) or likely (31 percent) to be murdered at the workplace. Even in the context of the high murder rate in Jamaica, this is an alarming figure. However, much of the fear may be derived from the more general crime problem in Jamaica rather than perceived dangers specifically at the place of work.[24] In terms of other forms of violent crime, 49 percent felt that an assault on them was either highly likely (13 percent) or likely (37 percent). Moreover, about 66 percent felt that they were either highly likely (25 percent) or likely (41 percent)

---

24. A 1998 survey indicated that 39 percent of the population were fearful of being murdered (see Harriott et al. 2003).

to be robbed. About 11 percent of respondents felt at risk of being a victim of extortion. About 62 percent and 33 percent felt that they were likely to be burglarized or victimized by fraud respectively. The concern with violent attacks is viewed as being closely linked to efforts to dispossess staff of their property or the property of their firms. It does not seem to be linked with work related conflicts, such as violence by aggrieved workers. Conflict resolution and mediation efforts within the workplace are therefore not likely to dissipate these fears, although such efforts may be useful is dealing with disputes between workers.

Institutional Support

Given high victimization of firms, and high levels of the fear of crime among managers, institutional support from the criminal justice system and in particular the police is vital.

Reporting is the first step in appealing for institutional support. The level of reporting may be related to the expectations of the victimized population. Reporting is high for robbery-burglary (85 percent) and fraud (60 percent) and low for extortion. Most of these reports are made to the police, since private security companies do not provide any investigative services and reporting does not seem to be motivated by attempts to recover losses from the insurance companies. For robbery-burglary, fraud, and arson, only 11 percent, 13 percent and 14 percent respectively of these cases were reported for insurance purposes (see Table 6.3). Reporting is thus based primarily on crime control expectations.

Police performance, when evaluated as the response to the last incident of crime experienced by the firm, was generally regarded as satisfactory. On this measure, 37 percent regarded the performance of the police as being good and a majority of managers from these victimized firms regarded their performance as fair (32 percent) or poor (31 percent). When the evaluation of police performance is measured in relation to the different categories of crimes that were reported by the firms in the sample in 2001, it was regarded as good in relation to the investigation of fraud, fair to poor for robbery (the most prevalent violent crime affecting firms), and poor for burglaries (the main reported property crime).[25] It may be that police responsiveness is related to its perception of the prospects for investigative success. In cases of fraud, the police are usually called after the suspect(s) is/are discovered. Robbers usually leave behind witnesses who may provide the police with leads. Burglaries, on the other hand, may be relatively difficult to deal with as there are usually fewer investigative leads. This evaluation of police performance in relation to a single specific incident of crime may be taken as a measure of their responsiveness, but cannot be equated with a general evaluation of the performance of the police.

TABLE 6.3: REPORTING AND REPORTING OUTCOMES
(% of total cases)

| | Reporting | Reporting Authority* | | | | Outcomes* | | |
		Police	Private Security	Insurance Company	Other	Recovery of items	Arrest	None
Extortion	35	80	0	0	0	0	0	50
Fraud	60	87	9	13	6	17	40	43
Robbery	85	96	10	11	2	19	22	66
Arson	—	85	0	14	14	—	—	100
Other	60	85	4	0	13	17	30	59

*These categories are not mutually exclusive.

25. A significant proportion of firms were very dissatisfied with police performance. About 42 percent of the firms that had reported incidents of burglary in 2001 regarded the performance of the police as "poor." The respective figures for robbery and fraud are 32 percent and 24 percent.

As the assessment of police performance becomes more general, the impressions of the victims and the general public tend to become less favorable (see Box 6.1 and Annexes C and D). In contrast, the evaluations of the manager-respondents in this survey seem to be more favorable than other evaluations of the general public, and this could be partly due to the perceived increased police responsiveness to the needs of the economic elite and those of their firms. Nevertheless, an area of police work that attracts criticism is the quality of their investigations in cases that are put before the courts.

The courts are seen as not adequately giving the institutional support that is needed to deal effectively with both criminal and civil cases. The process is seen as being too long and time consuming. Many firms and individuals are therefore forced to find other ways of coping with some types of crime and business related conflicts.

Coping Strategies

In response to the crime problem and limited institutional support, most firms have adopted a variety of coping strategies. The main elements of these strategies are target hardening (making the firm less vulnerable to crime), adjusting the organization of business activity to reduce opportunities for crime, and in some cases striking an accommodation with criminal networks.

Target hardening measures include installing special fencing, grill works, alarm systems and other such protective measures designed to make illicit entry more difficult. Criminal threats from within are countered by upgrading internal security and accounting systems. Security guards are used as part of the internal surveillance system as well as for dealing with external threats. In response to the demand for this service, over the last twenty years, the private security business has rapidly expanded. However, its role is a very limited one, and which does not diminish the dependence on the police force. There remains a hope that the police may still be able to effectively control the crime problem. Many managers and their representative organizations are quite willing to enter into new relationships and partnerships with the police that may involve sharing the cost of new crime control initiatives. As yet, however, there have been no practical outcomes.

In areas where crime networks are most powerful and institutional support weak, new adaptations have taken place and an accommodation has been struck with "dons" of organized crime who offer protection services. As indicated in the cases below, these processes may be significantly altering the business environment in some sectors, especially in construction, where in some areas of the country it is difficult to operate without striking an accommodation with the dons and/or cultivating protective political links. Extrapolating this trend, only companies in some relationship with criminals would survive in the construction sector or be able to undertake some types of projects. Organized crime has always exhibited very strong monopolizing tendencies. More generally, without more effective institutional support, more firms may resort to criminal adaptations and corruption such as defrauding their clients and tax evasion as a method of coping.

Other adjustments involve more directly changing the organization of business activity. A significant proportion of firms, have opted for closing before dark (36 percent). This practice could be particularly damaging in the manufacturing sector, where second shift production is abandoned and productive capacity remains idle for much of the day. The fear of criminal victimization may also be altering employment practices. Residents of stigmatized inner city communities constantly complain that they are excluded from employment opportunities because they are seen as high risk employees. It may be argued that there is a higher risk involved in employing someone from a high crime/violence prone area as such persons may be coerced into facilitating robberies or other crimes. This "rational" discrimination may in turn further compound the crime problem in two ways. First, by reinforcing the exclusion of sections of the urban poor who already live in crime prone areas, and in so doing facilitating the justification for crime as a "survival" strategy. Second, the excluded are likely to resort to the services of the crime dons in order to force firms to employ them, further compounding the crime problem (see Box 6.1).

Firm Response in Jamaica

Protective measures. To deal with the threat of crime, most firms undertake protective measures (see Table 6.4). (See also Table 6.7 and sub-section below on business practices and prospects, where firms cite the increased cost of security as the most frequent impact of high crime). These include the installation of metal grills on buildings (58 percent of firms), special fencing, and hiring unarmed security guards (49 percent). Just over 30 percent of companies either hire armed security guards or install electronic alarm systems. Many companies (between 33 and 40 percent, depending on the industry) also close before dark and/or have taken steps to improve/upgrade their accounting and record-keeping systems to reduce employee crime and fraud. Again, the method of security employed depends on company size. Whereas small firms tend to install metal grills and fence the premises, large firms use fences and security guards. Seventy-five percent of very large companies (those with annual revenue of J$100 million or more) hire unarmed guards, while 63 percent hire armed guards. Almost 60 percent of large companies use armed guards. For small companies, the costs of hiring security are relatively high, and the need for this type of protection is also lower. Only 30 percent of micro-enterprises (those with annual revenue of less than J$5 million) hire guards. Sectorally, it is firms in banking/finance that most tend to use multiple preventive measures to combat crime, with 90 percent hiring armed guards, 85 percent installing alarm systems, internal security, and upgrading accounting.

Reduced working hours. One of the effects of crime on business is that it forces reduced hours of operation. As noted above, about 36 percent of the firms listed closing before dark as one of the measures to protect themselves against crime. One in five firms reported that they would increase their hours of operation if their location experienced reduced levels of crime over an extended period. Many firms demonstrated willingness to operate longer hours if their place of operation was perceived as safer—43 percent of firms in distributive trades, 30 percent in banking/financial services and 24 percent in entertainment. Firms reported that, on average, they would be willing to remain open an additional 3.6 hours per day if they were located in a safer area. The potential loss of output and efficiency arising from the very significant curtailment of working hours could be large.

The Economic Costs of Crime

The Approach

The beginning of this chapter outlined the different ways in which crime can negatively affect society and the economy. This section attempts to estimate some of these costs to the Jamaican economy, for both the public and the private sector. The focus is on the impact on business, since it is key for competitiveness and long-term growth prospects.

The estimate of the cost of crime presented in this chapter is a lower bound one, partly due to the longer-term impact that violent crimes such as extortion have in structuring the business environment in some sub-sectors. Box 6.1 above narrates how a construction company was forced to place incompetent workers as skilled staff on its payroll, resulting in poor construction, the need to rebuild within a short period of time, and in highly inflated costs.

Another general issue relates to the value of stolen goods. It can be argued that stolen goods are not lost to society as a whole, and so should not be counted as a cost. Only the difference between the value for the original owner and the value for the criminals (which will be smaller, since goods and assets have specificity of use) should be counted as the cost to society. On the other hand, criminals spend so much time on illegal activity, which is a social loss, and in equilibrium the value of goods should be equal to the opportunity cost of the criminals' time, so all property losses should be considered social losses (see Fajnzylber et al. 2000). It is this approach that is followed here.

While not analyzed in detail in this Chapter, the increasing influence of the drug trade and its linkage with violence needs to be mentioned. Drug related activities have been shown to induce crime and lead to increased homicides (for Latin America, see Fajnzylber et al. 2000), arising from

TABLE 6.4: DISTRIBUTION OF RESPONDENTS BY SELECTED MEASURES TAKEN TO PROTECT FIRMS AGAINST CRIME & NATURE OF ORGANIZATION

(% of firms)

	Banking/ Financial services	Tourism	Manufacturing & processing	Agriculture	Construction	Mining & quarrying	Transport & storage	Enter- tainment	Distributive Trade	Science & technology	Commu- nications	Other	Total
Closing before dark	60	9	34	32	40	38	15	18	57	25	62	35	36
Installing grill	50	47	72	38	52	38	39	58	80	75	54	71	58
Special fencing of premises	55	75	64	59	40	38	39	39	46	50	8	29	49
Installing electronic alarm system(s)	85	31	23	12	32	25	31	5	53	25	23	21	31
Hiring unarmed security guard(s)	60	91	45	44	48	25	39	42	46	25	39	50	49
Hiring armed security guard(s)	90	38	21	25	28	50	19	27	30	25	31	29	31
Hiring community protection	5	3	11	7	16	13	4	12	11	—	8	3	9
Internal security system	85	38	32	27	24	50	42	24	47	—	54	21	37
Upgrading accounting/record system	85	69	55	41	48	38	39	18	58	3	62	35	50

BOX 6.1: CONSTRUCTION FIRM IN KINGSTON METROPOLITAN AREA

Background

This is the case of a family owned construction firm, which is located in the Kingston Metropolitan Area. It was established in 1970 and is mainly involved in the development of infrastructure and civil engineering works, including the construction of roads and housing. Its clients are usually government and private developers. It is a medium size company that employs 30 permanent workers and, on average, 400 temporary workers. Its revenue is approximately J$200 million annually.

Crime Problem

The firm is challenged by a wide variety of crime problems such as the theft of construction materials, robbery of its payroll, fraud, and protection racketeering.

More complicated is the problem of extortion which the company has experienced in a variety of forms. One form is that of so-called area leaders (usually the local party leader and/or criminal "don") and community residents demanding to be put on the company's payroll as a condition for permitting the construction project to proceed. This is simply a levy or tax that is imposed on the firm for doing work in *their* area. In some instances, this problem is resolved by insisting that those making the demand at least appear to do some work. On the settlement of this problem, the negotiations then move to another stage. Most of these persons are usually unskilled with little or no experience of work. Yet they then demand, often with success, that they be employed as skilled workers at a salary that is commensurate with this category of work. The result is usually poor quality work, which in the case of roads and other infrastructure works is usually counterproductive as these edifices tend to collapse under conditions of intensive use or flooding. The cycle is completed with reconstruction taking place in a manner similar to the initial project. At times, these defective works have to be destroyed and reconstructed thereby further escalating the cost of construction. Refusal to comply with these corrupt practices may lead to the disruption of the project. These practices are not restricted to Kingston. May Pen, Montego Bay and other parts of Jamaica are also known for this type of activity. The company may, at times, reject these demands, and in some instances may accommodate them.

Accommodation may also involve allowing area leaders and criminal dons to determine who (from their communities) will be employed on these projects. The local don may then extort payments from persons that he has advised or instructed the firm to employ. These payments are usually a percentage of the weekly salary of the workers. By settling the matter in this way, the firm avoids disruptions to their project either as work stoppages or as constant demands for employment by community members. Where powerful organized crime networks are involved, even regular employees of the firm and other skilled workers who reside outside of the jurisdiction of the don, may also be required to pay a percentage of their salaries in return for permission to work in the area.

On some work sites, party political competitiveness may result in violence. For example, on a recent project in a relatively safe section of Kingston, politically induced gang warfare erupted on the work site. The Company was contracted to construct several buildings on the campus of a tertiary institution. The temporary employees were drawn from the surrounding communities which have different party affiliations. At one time point, these workers were drawn from seven different communities. Workers from one area could not work on sites where residents from an opposing area were working. These employment monopolizing tendencies resulted in gang warfare. In this context, a work related dispute between workers and a subcontractor employed by the firm resulted in the death of the latter.

The firm has also had to contend with other kinds of crimes. Payroll fraud is not uncommon. At times, supervisors attempt to extract overpayment for work done, or there may be fictitious names on the payroll. This is less detectable in construction where there is a large temporary staff that may change frequently over the life of the project.

(continued)

BOX 6.1: CONSTRUCTION FIRM IN KINGSTON METROPOLITAN AREA (CONTINUED)

In order to reduce its vulnerability to robbery, the firm would pay its employees by checks. Recently however, the banks have refused to offer this service to the company as they claim that the construction workers tend to disrupt business activity at the banks and are disorderly, refuse to conform to simple procedures such as joining the lines in the bank, and are rude to other customers and to the staff. In some cases, conflicts between workers on the work sites are renewed in the banks. The result of this is that the company is forced to handle the payroll as cash and to bear the additional costs of contracting a security company to provide protection for the cash.

Impact of Crime
These conditions affect the operations of the firms in various ways:

—Control of the workforce by criminal "dons" leads to poor quality work, an unreliable workforce and the inability to meet deadlines.

—Intensive criminal activity has at times led to the company discontinuing some contracts and consequently losing income. For example, in the case of a government contract to build/repair two schools, despite the security "provisions," there were significant losses due to theft and no reliable estimate of what the cost or time needed for completion would be. The military had to be used to complete the project. Even then, the army took 2 years and 9 months to complete a project that would normally take 9 months, and the fixtures had to be installed 6 times due to theft.

—Increased cost of projects. On average, about 10 percent of the budget for each project is the anticipated cost of theft of materials. These costs are borne by clients, but are usually hidden from them.

—Increased security costs. Private security at its main office costs approximately 0.5% of its annual revenue and this is a relative minor part of the security costs of the company. Much greater costs are incurred on the work sites.

—The working hours of some employees are restricted by crime and violence in the areas where projects are located as well as in those areas where they reside. This impairs the work of the company, as some projects require an extended workday. Some skilled workers may even refuse to work in violence prone areas.

Institutional Support
The firm regards the police as being fairly responsive to calls for assistance in cases of employer–employee and employee-employee violence. More generally, however, they are not able to meet the policing needs of the firm. The experience of the firm is that police units have a poor record in recovering stolen items and are unable to give preventive support.

The company has no experience with the criminal court as problems are usually dealt with informally. The proprietor believes that it is pointless taking formal independent action against offenders who criminally victimize the firm as lawyer fees are usually higher than the cost of the materials or cash that are stolen. The firm however relies on the courts to settle civil/business disputes and these are often quite lengthy.

Survival Techniques
Some innovative adaptations to the social environment seem to be occurring. In the case of this firm, they have attempted the following:

—As noted above, the budgets of projects are inflated to compensate for theft and may also be inflated as theft under the pretext of compensation for theft. This has the effect of passing on the costs of crime to the client.

—The company employs formal and informal security services and relies heavily on private security.

—It has found a way to strike an accommodation with area leaders and dons and uses them to control the labor force. This is a tension filled relationship that involves elements of extortion directed at the firm, as well as partnerships, with criminal coercion directed at the labor force.

Despite the problems discussed above, the company has no intention of closing its operations. This is a company that will find innovative ways of adapting to its environment and surviving.

Source: Harriott et al. 2003

turf-wars between different networks of producers and distributors. Some of the money from the drug trade is spent in Jamaica on home construction, the establishment of legitimate businesses, importation of goods for distribution, and various services, leading to higher levels of employment and income for other people in apparently legitimate businesses. However, such illegitimate economic activities can hardly form the basis for long-term growth. While these activities contribute to the economy, they are also giving greater impetus to violent crime, which, as will be seen below, imposes a major cost on society.[26] The police estimates that drug-related killings now account for more than 20 percent of murders annually. Some of the killings labeled as 'reprisal' are probably also rooted in the drug trade. As the importance of illegal activities in overall economic activity expands, there will likely be more conflicts as the large sums of money and the lack of formal contracts encourage defection from verbal agreements.

The illegal economic activities of transnational networks rooted in some Latin American countries have generated considerable problems for legitimate business. For example, drug trafficking may contaminate legitimate exports leading to security measures that slow down the processing time of perishable products. The consequent delays in delivery and other problems will tend to increase the cost of conducting business internationally. The increases in costs imposed on legitimate traders might over time drive some out of business (see also Chapter 7).

Measuring the Impact of Crime on Economic Activity

The economic impact of crime is estimated by aggregating the following: (a) medical expenses incurred on crime-related injuries, by both Government and individuals;[27] (b) loss of output arising from death and injury; (c) cost of security provision by public and private entities based on the premise that even though such output is part of the economy's productive activity, it does not produce directly beneficial goods, and involves high opportunity costs; (d) direct business losses of firms arising from crime, such as extortion, fraud, theft and looting; and (e) other costs, such as likely shutdown of firms, and impact on investment and expansion intentions. The data sources for this exercise include government budgets and public records, and various official reports (SLC, ESSJ). Private costs are more difficult to measure, especially those incurred by business. The business victimization survey, discussed earlier, was conducted to assess these private costs. Table 6.5 provides an indicative summary of the quantitative impact of crime, which will be amplified in the following sections.

The Costs of Crime on the Public Sector, Individuals and Business

(a) Health Care Costs

Injury costs—health care. Given limited resources, violence strains the public health system and diverts medical services away from children and the aged. Intentional injuries in Accident and Emergency (A&E) departments of public hospitals accounted for 43 percent (34,037 cases) of the total caseload in 2001, with 98 percent due to deliberate injury to another person. This yields a total public health cost of interpersonal violence of J$996 million in 2001,[28] and amounts to nearly 14 percent of the net recurrent expenditure of the Ministry of Health for 2000/01.

---

26. In Belmont, Westmoreland, it is suspected that the drug trade (transshipment of drugs from South America) has fueled unprecedented economic activity, including construction of new homes and purchase of new motor vehicles. At the same time, an otherwise quiet fishing village has had a rapid increase in murders.

27. Since human life is valuable in itself and is (even in purely instrumental terms) worth more than its contribution to the economy, this method only produces a lower bound estimate of what crime costs the economy.

28. It is assumed that the total cost to the public health system of intentionally inflicted injuries is proportional to the share of such injuries in total A&E admissions. The cost of 33,356 (98 percent of 34,037) cases of intentional injuries valued at 1996 cost was J$541 million (equal to three times the cost of treating victims in 1996, since there were three times more victims in 2001 than 1996). Inflated by consumer prices yields the 2001 figure of J$996 million.

TABLE 6.5: ANNUAL IMPACT OF CRIME, SUMMARY

Expenditure	Cost
I. Healthcare costs + Lost Production	3.7% of GDP
II. Private Expenditure on Security	
Average	2% of revenue
Micro firms (<J$5 million annual revenue)	17% of revenue
Medium firm (J$10–20 million annual revenue)	7.6% of revenue
Very large firms (>J$100 million annual revenue)	0.7% of revenue
III. Direct Costs	
Extortion, Fraud, Robbery/Burglary, Arson	
Micro firms (<J$5 mn) and firms with revenue J$20–50 mn.	9% of revenue
Firms with revenue J$10–20 mn. and >J$50mn.	2% of revenue
Losses from Looting (experienced by 70 out of 400 firms in sample)	
57% of firms	< J$100,000
19% of firms	J$100,000–500,000
4% of firms	J$1 mn.–5 mn.
Average losses from work days lost from temporary closures	
2001	1 million
2000	J$400,000 (range: J$44,000–2 mn)
IV. Other costs	
Closure of firms	2.5% of GDP

In addition, the cost of treatment to private citizens is estimated at about J$255 million in 2001: (i) annual costs of hospital stay for 15,884 victims of violence in 2001, at an average cost of stay of J$5068 per year, estimated at J$81 million;[29] (ii) costs of hospital stay for patients at the University Hospital of West Indies, assuming it costs 7.5 as much as the Kingston Public Hospital, estimated at J$159 million in 2001; (iii) annual costs of hospital visits and medication borne by the private citizen estimated at J$17 million. This is estimated on the basis that patients visit the hospital twice each year (SLC), at an average cost of J$199 per visit, and purchase medicine at an average cost of J$454 (an underestimate since we assume that each patient purchases medication only once).

(b) Loss of Output from Injury and Mortality
Injury. In addition to treatment, hospital stay and medication, victims of violence exit the workforce for the period of their recovery. The average length of hospital stay for accident and injury patients is 8.3 days.[30] Also, the average victim of injury is out of the workforce for an additional two weeks for recovery. Using the average weekly wage of J$8423 (calculated as the average wage of a murder victim, weighted by the distribution of victims in different occupation groups), the average lost output due to injury is estimated to be J$337 million.

Mortality. Mortality costs are measured by the loss of output that individuals would have contributed to the economy in that year. Wages are used to proxy the contribution of labor to output. Using the occupational distribution of murder victims from a random sample of murder cases over the past three years, and estimates of the average wages of various occupation groups, an average weekly wage is estimated at J$8423. Assuming a monthly murder rate of 81 per month,[31] the estimated annual output loss of murder victims is about J$194 million in 2001.

---

29. Average cost of hospital stay from PIOJ-STATIN (1998), inflated by consumer price index for 2001 figure.
30. Source: Ministry of Health.
31. The annual average murder rate over 1997–2001 was 973 (or 81 murders per month). This does not exclude the one percent of murder victims who are not in the labor force.

Table 6.6 shows that the mortality and injury costs together yield an estimate of annual loss of about J$0.5 billion or 0.2 percent of GDP.[32]

(c) Cost of Provision of Security in the Government and Business Sectors

Public Expenditure on Security Services. Total expenditure on security services (defense, justice and correctional services, and police) was J$10.5 billion in 2000/01. About 56 percent of this expenditure was allocated for police services. To put it in context, the total expenditure on security amounted to 57 percent of the budget for education and 146 percent of the budget for health. Unlike the case of health expenditure, it is not possible to ascribe the portion of security expenditure that is a direct response to crime and violence, but note that most of government expenditure on the police and courts serves to deal with criminal cases (of all the cases filed in Resident Magistrate courts in 2001, only 10 percent were civil cases).[33]

Private expenditure on security. The business victimization survey finds that in 2001, private security expenditure by firms was on average J$1 million, or about 2 percent of annual revenue of the average firm, but with wide variations by size of establishment. For micro enterprises (annual revenue less than J$5 million), average annual private security expenditure was J$281,820, or an average of 17 percent of annual revenue. Medium-sized firms (J$10–20 million in annual revenue) spent an average 7.6 percent of annual revenue on private security, while very large firms (annual revenue above J$100 million), spent an average of J$1.8 million or 0.7 percent of revenue. There are also "informal security" costs in the form of protection-extortion, which were on average $791,159 for the 5 percent of firms in the survey who admitted to paying.[34]

In addition to the above, the cost of installing new security devices such as grills or other physical changes to the premises was on average J$137,871 annually, and was undertaken by 95 (24 percent of sample) firms in 2001. Fifty-eight firms installed electronic alarm systems in 2001 at an average cost of J$214,806. Seven percent of the firms surveyed also installed other protective devices at an average cost of J$329,276. Installation expenses range from 0.3–0.7 percent of average revenue.

(d) Direct Business Losses from Crime—Extortion, Fraud, Theft, Arson, Looting

The annual cost of crime in four specific categories (extortion, fraud, robbery/burglary, and arson) and any "other" cost due to crime were surveyed. All categories of crime combined caused 116 firms of the 400 surveyed firms to suffer losses amounting on average to J$665,011 in 2001. In most cases (81), losses were due to robbery and/or burglary, at an average cost of $538,522. Seventy-one firms suffered losses as a result of 'other' types of crime, at an average cost of J$258,477. Nearly 10 percent of firms reported losses as a result of fraud. Though there were only a few cases, the most expensive crime was arson, for which the average firm lost over J$1 million. Combined direct costs of crime as a percentage of revenue are highest, at about 9 percent, among micro firms and firms in the 20–50 mil-

---

32. It should be emphasized that this figure is an understatement of the true cost of interpersonal violence. First, it ignores the value of property damaged or destroyed during the violence. Second, it ignores pain and psychological stress suffered by victims and their families. Third, in addition to the output lost as a result of a killed worker, society incurs a cost in producing another worker with similar skill. Finally, the long-term consequences are often far greater than the immediate impact, whereas here our analysis is not dynamic. A more elaborate study would also consider the loss of potential future earnings of murder victims and earnings lost through injury-related disability.

33. While some public expenditure on security is inevitable, the concern is with the excess expenditure as a result of the high level of crime. To the extent that even the most peaceful societies incur expenditure on security provision (indeed, there is a deterrent aspect to good and effective justice and policing), there is an upward bias in assuming that all of the expenditure on security arises from crime. However, this should be viewed in the context of the underestimation of the overall costs of crime in other parts of the analysis (see, for example, footnote 34).

34. The low rates of response regarding payment for protection reflect an unwillingness to admit to entering into agreements with criminals. It must be noted, however, that the average payout is as high as 80 percent of the cost of hiring formal security services.

lion dollar annual revenue group.[35] In all other categories, average losses are no more than 2 percent of average revenue. Average losses due to crime, as a proportion of revenue, are highest in manufacturing and processing (5.7 percent) and distribution (2.5 percent), "other sectors not specified" (2 percent), and lowest in the banking/financial services sector (0.06 percent).

In addition to the above is the cost of looting. Twenty-four percent of the firms reported being looted over 1997–2001, with 70 (18 percent) experiencing the last incident of looting in 2001. Agricultural firms are most affected, accounting for about 30 percent of firms looted over 1997–2001, the majority being micro firms. More generally, more than 40 percent of firms that have suffered from looting are micro enterprises. Incidences of looting are concentrated in the KMA, Montego Bay and St. Ann, which together account for 63 percent of the looting over 1997–2001. Of the 70 firms looted in 2001, 57 percent had losses of less than J$100,000, 19 percent between J$100,000 and J$500,000 and 4 percent between J$1 million and J$5 million.

(e) Costs of Lost Work Days Arising from Firm Closure

Violence resulted in an average loss of three work days per firm in 2000 and 2001, affecting 19 percent (13 percent) of sampled firms in 2001 (2000). More than 75 percent of affected firms were located in the Kingston Metropolitan Area (KMA), across all sectors of the economy. Firms in banking/financial services and entertainment experienced the highest rate of closure (4 days) in 2000. In 2001, manufacturing (4 days), distributive trade (3.6 days) and entertainment (3.5 days) were the most severely affected. Companies in distributive trade were particularly affected—in both 2000 and 2001, they accounted for 30 percent of closures due to violence,[36] while representing only 20 percent of the sample (this may partly be due to violent outbreaks often involving roadblocks in Jamaica). The closures in manufacturing, distributive trade and entertainment reduced the annual operational time of the companies by 1–2 percent.

In the KMA, average losses of firms **that were forced to close** in 2000 were J$400,000, ranging from an average loss of J$44,000 in the entertainment industry to losses of $2 million in mining and quarrying. In 2001, average losses in the KMA rose to over $1 million, coinciding with the large increase in murders and shootings in 2001. About 85 percent of firms claimed that losses arise not just from foregone output, but also because workers are paid even for lost hours of work.

(f) The Overall Costs of Crime

The total cost of violent crime is estimated at J$12.4 billion or 3.7 percent of GDP in 2001 (see Table 6.6). Per capita, this represents a loss of J$4725. This is a lower-bound estimate of the cost to society—not only does it not include the costs suffered by business, which have been detailed above, but it also does not include an estimate of the more dynamic and long-term effects, such as the impact on investment and productivity. For example, an IADB study (IADB 1999) found that the social costs of crime, including the value of stolen properties, in the Latin American region were over 14 percent of the region's GDP. Excluding the value of stolen goods,

TABLE 6.6: THE ANNUAL ECONOMIC COST OF CRIME, 2001
(J$ million)

I. Health Costs	1.3 bn (0.4% of GDP)
Public Health System	995.7
Private Citizens	254.5
II. Lost Production	0.5 bn (0.2% of GDP)
Mortality	194.1
Injury due to Crime	337.2
III. Public Expenditure on Security	10.5bn (3.1% of GDP)
Total I + II +III	**12.4 bn (3.7% of GDP)**
IV. Private Expenditure on Security	2% of revenue

35. Manufacturing and Processing, Agriculture, Distribution and Entertainment make up 70–73 percent of these two categories.

36. This may be an underestimate since informal distribution services, which probably account for a large part of informal sector activity in Jamaica, are not captured.

social costs were 4.9 percent of Latin America's GDP. Of this, 1.9 percent of Latin America's GDP accounted for potential lives lost and other heath-related costs, 1.6 percent for expenditures on police and judiciary, and 1.4 percent for the cost of private security.

Impact of Crime on Business Practice and Prospects—Survey Results

Jamaica is a highly open economy, with firms in exporting and import-competing sectors subject to intense competition, especially given the appreciation of the exchange rate in the 1990s. In such sectors, domestic firms are unlikely to be able to pass on the costs of crime in the form of higher prices. Here, it is more likely that crime cuts into profits, reducing opportunities for investment and expansion. In the tourism industry, for example, revenue that could be used for expansion has to be diverted to promotion in order to keep visitors interested in Jamaica. In other cases, crime could threaten firm survival.

While firms in non-tradable sectors such as construction may be able to pass on some of their crime-related costs to their clients, they sometimes have to abandon projects when crime costs become excessive. In the worst-case scenario, they might have to shut down or, where possible, relocate outside of Jamaica.

Higher security costs. In answering the question about the impact of crime on business practice, 51 percent of the respondents said that increased costs of security were at least somewhat significant (see Table 6.7). Larger firms are more likely to report that crimes lead to higher costs of security, with 53 percent with 50 or more employees citing significant or highly significant increases in security costs. The corresponding figure for firms with 20–49 employees was 38 percent.

Crime has a less significant impact on firms that are less than 5 years old, with only 21 percent reporting at least a significant increase in security costs.[37] Younger firms are likely to be in service industries such as computers and communications, and entertainment. The corresponding figure for firms in existence for 15–24 years was 43 percent, and 39 percent for those in existence for more than 25 years. These firms are mostly in the traditional sectors, such as manufacturing and processing and agriculture,[38] which are more prone to crime. These are also the sectors that are more likely to face tougher international competition and therefore less able to pass on security costs in prices.

The effect of crime on security cost is felt most severely in tourism, distribution, manufacturing and processing, and entertainment. Crime has had a significant or highly significant effect on security cost on 52 percent of firms in tourism, 53 percent in distribution, and 37 percent in manufacturing, processing and mining. Firms in the tourism industry have been able to counteract some of the more severe effects of crime on visitor arrival by aggressive advertising in the tourism market, but have also had to spend more on security provision. The distributive trade has been severely affected by crime owing to its vulnerability to theft, arising from storing and transporting large inventories of stocks. Manufacturing and distribution together contribute 35 percent of GDP, and tourism contributes about 10 percent of GDP and has strong sectoral linkages. Crime, by significantly increasing the cost of production, must be seen as an important factor in reducing profits and constraining expansion in these key sectors, hence an important constraint to the growth of the economy.

Investment plans. In analyzing the relationship between crime and investment, 39 percent of firms indicated that crime has affected their plans for business expansion, with 24 percent reporting the effect as being either significant or highly significant. At the same time, 37 percent of firms stated that crime has had a negative impact on their plans to invest in productivity improvement

---

37. However, the smaller *increase* in security costs reported by younger firms could be partly explained by younger firms starting out with higher security costs than older firms owing to higher crime levels in more recent years.

38. Manufacturing and processing, distribution, and agriculture comprise 60 percent of the firms in the 15–24 and 54 percent of the firms in the 25 and over age groups.

TABLE 6.7: IMPACT OF CRIME ON BUSINESS PRACTICE (%)

	Highly Significant (1)	Significant (2)	Somewhat Significant (3)	Significant (1+2+3)	Insignificant	No Impact	Total Number of Respondents
Increased cost of security	18	17	16	51	11	38	300
Increased cost of services purchased	4	4	10	18	17	64	291
Negative impact on worker productivity	4	4	14	22	23	55	290
Negative impact on plans for business expansion	14	10	15	39	17	44	304
Negative impact on investments to improve productivity	10	10	17	37	16	47	301
Other	5	3	5	13	14	73	79

(Table 6.7). One-third of the firms in the distributive trade noted that crime has had a highly negative impact on their plans for expansion, and one-quarter of such firms reported that crime has negatively affected their plans for investment in worker productivity. Overall, the industries most likely to delay expansion plans because of crime are distribution (50 percent), agriculture (48 percent), and transportation and storage (47 percent). These same three industries, along with tourism, are those in which crime has most significantly reduced plans for improvement in worker productivity. Larger firms, measured by employment, are more likely to blame crime for lack of investment in expansion and worker productivity.

Firms' view of prospects. Most firms (75 percent) felt that even with the current high crime environment, they would remain in operation in the next three years. Six percent of firms said that if the current level of crime continues, they did not expect to remain in business in the next three years, while 19 percent were uncertain about their prospects. The largest proportion of firms that expect to close operations in Jamaica (either relocate outside of Jamaica or close operations permanently) if the crime situation did not improve in the next three years were in the distributive trade (18 percent of firms). This was followed by tourism (15 percent), entertainment (14 percent), agriculture (11 percent) and manufacturing and processing (10 percent). In all cases (except tourism), firms were more likely to close permanently than to relocate outside of Jamaica.

If all the firms that foresee a closure of operations do actually shut down, GDP could decline by about 7.5 percent over the next three years, or about 2.5 percent per year.[39]

Policy Options

Measures to control crime, regardless of how modest, require additional resources from a country already suffering from a fiscal crisis. Based on the results of the business victimization survey, while managers wish to see an improvement in public safety and a sharp reduction in crime, they are unwilling to support increased taxes. Data from the survey indicates that only 12 percent of managers were supportive of increased corporate taxes to fund crime control and 67 percent were opposed (21 percent were undecided). This may be explained in part by a low level of trust in government (see Table 6.1, government effectiveness) and the problem of corruption. However, managers are willing to provide financial support for specific collective solutions that directly affect them and over which there is some direct accountability.

---

39. Calculated as a weighted average of each sector's contribution to GDP.

The econometric analysis (Annex A) shows that the determinants of violent crimes in Jamaica are similar to those encountered in other countries (for Latin America see Fajnzylber et al., 2000): (i) negative incentives, or deterrence i.e. more imprisonment, more crimes cleared up, and tougher sentencing are all significantly and negatively associated with some of the violent crimes considered, and (ii) positive incentives i.e. higher per capita income, higher share of labor income in GDP, and lower youth unemployment (for rape, marginally) are also associated with lower crime rates (except murder). Policies to reduce crime should consider both dimensions of the problem—to increase both the direct costs of committing crime (the expected punishment) and its opportunity cost (the loss of income in the labor market).

An effective crime strategy would need to address the reform of the police and judiciary to make them more effective, and other measures to generally promote pro-poor growth (which is the subject of this report), including improving education outcomes, creating job programs for urban unemployment, and promoting investment in rural areas. The strategy could focus on police accountability and police/community relations, and investment in the police (increase probability of capture), in the judicial system (probability of conviction), and in prisons (probability of punishment), while not compromising on human rights. A good example of a multi-pronged strategy in a high crime urban center is Cali, Colombia, where a program targeted six strategic areas: improvements in monitoring of crime, improvements in the police and judiciary, community enhancements, promotion of equity (education, public services and housing), youth programs and other special policies (for example, prohibition of bearing arms on certain days, "semi-dry law"). As a result, homicides were reduced by 600 per year between 1994 and 1998 (see Annex E).

The policy options can be grouped under four themes:

Identify and measure the crime problem.

- **Strengthen official data collection on crime** so that data availability is both frequent and reliable in order to detect crime trends and identify groups most at risk.[40] The official data on the incidence of major crimes is inadequate, as evidenced by under-reporting of certain crimes by the public. Furthermore, while regional crime data is available, comparable regional economic data is not available, making a geographical understanding of crime-causes difficult.
- **Conduct frequent general and specialized victimization surveys** on the dimensions and impact of crime, and use these to inform policy, improve policing methods, inform public discussions on crime control, and as instruments for holding the criminal justice system and government accountable.

Improve law enforcement for crime deterrence.

- **Upgrade investigative capacity of the police** to improve cleared-up rates for violent crimes, and thereby deter crime (in 2001, only 42 percent of reported murders were cleared [PIOJ 2002]). Some effort is already being made to improve the training of police investigators and to extend and improve the application of the forensic sciences and criminalistic techniques to the investigative process (under Jamaica Constabulary Force's Crime Management Project). As the main concern of the population is with the murder rate, special measures are needed to improve the investigation and adjudication of these cases. A special fast tracking mechanism could be considered to allow for speedy disposal of these cases without depriving accused persons of rights associated with due process.
- **Accelerate the introduction of special commercial courts** to deal with dissatisfaction with the adjudication of commercial disputes and cases brought before the civil courts. This would accelerate the processing of cases and facilitate greater specialization in this field among lawyers and judges. In turn, this may result in greater confidence in the judicial system and its ability to ensure speedy and fair outcomes. A slight variation of this model

---

40. Also see Fajnzylber et al. (2000).

works effectively in Colombia, where there are special judges dedicated to handling debt collection cases.

Improve social prevention to address the root causes of crime.

- **Improve the quality of the school experience,** especially for poor students. A significant fraction of the poor, and more so males, tend to drop out of school, end up poorly educated and unemployed, and become susceptible to delinquent behavior. To address this, the disparities between different school types need to be reduced, and special efforts directed to schools that have large numbers of students reading below grade level (see Chapter 5). Also, school programs should be enhanced to include teaching of social and conflict resolution skills to students (also see National Committee on Crime and Violence 2002).

- **Form effective partnerships between the police, business and local communities,** particularly given scarce police resources. This would involve setting of common goals and sharing information.[41] In Sao Paulo, Brazil, a project was carried out to reduce violence through community policing and community cooperation with the police, as a result of which homicide rates fell by 12 percent (see Annex F). Recommendations have also been made to use reformed gang leaders to help combat crime and violence (Government of Jamaica 2002).

- **Build social capital** such as greater trust and lower tolerance to crime and violence, especially through interventions in the home, school and the workplace. An example of the development of citizen culture is in Bogota, Colombia, where a multiple action plan focused on improving law, culture and morale (amongst other outcomes, homicide rates declined by 30 percent)(see Annex G).

Apply focused interventions.

- **Target high crime urban areas,** especially the Kingston Metropolitan Area, to reduce the impact of crime on the business community. The Report of the West Kingston Commission of Enquiry (2002) highlights the need for a 'national development program' for the inner-city communities specifically aimed at housing, social amenities and business facilitation. A positive urban regeneration initiative is the Business Improvement District (BID) program following the December 2002 recommendations of the Kingston Redevelopment Committee. The BID aims to provide incentives (investment, growth, improved housing) and deterrents (using modern crime prevention technology such as close-circuit television).

- **Target youth at risk** with specific youth development programs in addition to the schooling focus mentioned above. To control youth violence, the Jamaica Constabulary Force has set up almost 340 Youth Clubs (with membership of over 12,000), and a program to target inner city youth for skills training. An example of a focused intervention to reduce youth violence is in Boston, USA, where the total crime rate declined by 29 percent (violent crimes by 16 percent) through preventive and controlling measures involving local authority and the local community (see Annex H).

---

41. To tackle rising crime, the government of Jamaica initiated reforms in the security forces following the Hirst and Wolfe enquiries in the early 1990s. For example, an Office of Professional Responsibility and a Police Public Complaints Authority were established in 1994 to deal with complaints of police excesses. Also, Community Consultative Committees (CCCs) were established, but they were not effective due to insufficient community involvement. However, the continuing distrust between the police and inner city community residents may require reviving the CCCs, or finding alternative mechanisms to fight crime and violence which involve Jamaica's active civil society. In January 2002, the government of Jamaica announced an anti-crime plan, which includes new legislation, the modernization of the police force (improved equipment and increase in number of officers), anti-terrorist collaboration between police and military, and greater surveillance of the coastal borders to prevent the smuggling of drugs and guns. Also, an agreement has been reached between the police force and private security companies to cooperate on sharing information related to crime.

CHAPTER 7

IMPROVING JAMAICA'S INTERNATIONAL COMPETITIVENESS

Despite a largely favorable external demand scenario, Jamaica's exports have declined in U.S. dollar terms and its current account has deteriorated since 1996, owing to an exchange rate that appreciated over 1992–1998, rising wages that exceeded growth of productivity, and costs of rising crime. A prime example of this deterioration is the decline in the apparel industry after 1995. To improve growth, Jamaica has to increase the growth rate of its exports, since it is a very open economy, and the domestic market is small. Thus far, its most successful exports have been based on exploitation of natural resources, in particular tourism and bauxite.

Jamaica faces by and large a favorable scenario in the demand for its goods and services in external markets. Services including tourism are increasing their share in world trade (arising from a greater than one income elasticity), and Jamaica's GDP is increasingly dominated by services, producing a broad congruence between production and growth of export demand. In other areas including manufactures, Jamaica's small size may work in its favor, since it has such a miniscule share in world markets that even a large increase in its share would only make it a niche player. Also, even though the phase-out of the MFA in 2005 and the erosion of ACP preferences likely to occur in 2007 are likely to affect exports of sugar, bananas, and apparel, these together constitute a relatively small 11.3 percent of GNFS exports. In any case, Jamaica often does not fulfill its quota even in preferred commodities, demonstrating that its competitiveness problems are largely domestic.

Thus, the onus is on Jamaica to improve its exports by tackling domestic issues and policy constraints. While tariff reform has largely been accomplished, the imposition of stamp duties since the early 1990s has increased prices of key consumables and put upward pressure on wages. Also, while the exchange rate that appreciated between 1992–1998 has seen significant depreciation since 2002, it is important to ensure that these gains in exchange rate competitiveness are preserved, implying continued flexibility in exchange rate policy as well as limited increases in wages. The lower pass-through of the nominal exchange rate on prices will also encourage continuation of a flexible approach to exchange rate policy. Other issues that need to be addressed in order to improve Jamaica's competitiveness include:

- The increase in wages that outstripped inflation and productivity gains for many years, implying that the wage-based REER is even less competitive than the one based on CPI.
- The high incidence of crime and its impact on costs, national image and security.
- The difficulty of accessing credit for small companies/start-ups, which inhibits one of the potential engines of export growth.
- The customs problems in accessing inputs, particularly packaging and bottling inputs.
- The high cost and inadequate coverage of infrastructure and utilities, particularly water and roads, and the unreliability of power supply.

Evolution of Trade in Jamaica 1980–2001

Over the two decades 1980–2001, Jamaica's average annual compound growth of merchandise exports has been a meager 2 percent. Within this, there have been long periods during which exports declined, between 1980–1987, and most recently since 1996. Imports grew 5.3 annually over 1980–2001, and the growth has been less erratic than exports. Services trade has grown more consistently than merchandise, and since 1992, services exports have exceeded those of merchandise (see Table 1 and Annex Table A7.1). Historically, Jamaica has produced and exported a few primary commodities and imported a wide range of products, including food, consumer goods and capital goods. Annex Table A7.1 shows the Structure of Exports and Imports over 1980–2001.

TABLE 7.1: EXPORT AND IMPORT GROWTH IN JAMAICA (US$ million)						Growth, compounded (%)	
	1980	1990	1995	2000	2001	1980–01	1995–01
Exports—goods	962.7	1156.8	1796	1562.8	1454.4	2.0	−3.5
Exports—GNFS	1408.1	2313.2	3393.9	3588.5	3355.1	4.2	−0.2
Imports—goods	1038.1	1624.8	2625.3	3004.3	3072.6	5.3	2.7
Imports—GNFS	1413.5	2395.5	3729.1	4446.4	4591.9	5.8	3.5
Major Exports:							
Manufacturing (excl. free-zone)	133.8	174.7	410.3	271.9	192.2	1.7	−11.9
Apparels (incl. free-zone)	—	220.5	553.0	390.2	290.5	—	−10.2
Bauxite and Alumina	735.7	728.3	704.2	729.8	736.4	0.0	0.7
Tourism	240.6	740.0	1068.8	1332.6	1232.2	8.1	2.4

Source: Bank of Jamaica; Statistical Institute of Jamaica

Structure of Merchandise Exports. Traditionally merchandise exports were dominated by sugar and bananas. In the 1960s bauxite exports began to rise sharply, reaching 76 percent of merchandise exports in 1980, as bauxite mining capacity rose. The growth of bauxite exports also shifted trade towards the United States. However, the share of bauxite has since fallen, erratically, to about 50 percent of exports. Apparel exports based on export processing zones, grew rapidly in the 1980s—from a negligible level in the early 1980s, the share of apparel in merchandise exports grew to 40 percent in 1993. However, apparel exports have declined in both absolute and relative terms since the mid-1990s, and only accounted for 20 percent of exports in 2001. In dollar terms, wearing apparel exports fell by about 46 percent during 1995–2001 in the face of intense competition from Costa Rica, Haiti and the Dominican Republic (see Box 7.3 on La Moda). Apparel exports were also responsible for the initial increase in the share of manufactures in merchandise exports, which rose from 6.5 in 1970 to over 25 percent in 1993, but declined to 22 percent in 2001. Overall, the structure of Jamaica's exports continues to be dominated by primary products and unskilled labor-intensive manufactured products.

Tourism and the Services sector. The services sector, especially tourism, has been playing an increasing role in foreign exchange earnings and the economy (see, for example, Annex Table A7.2). The share of services in the exports of goods and non-factor services increased from 33 percent (of which tourism 17 percent) in 1980 to 57 percent (tourism 37 percent) in 2001. The shift in Jamaica mirrors the changes in world trade, where services trade has been growing much faster than trade in goods, rising from a share of 19 percent of world exports of goods and non-factor services in 1980 to almost 28 percent in 2001. Apart from tourism, the largest category of Jamaican service exports is transport services (consisting mainly of passenger fares from national airlines and port charges), where growth of inflows has been over 10 percent annually over 1996–2000. Inflows from insurance and financial services doubled over 1996–2000, and those from other business services (including migrant personal incomes, fees for various types of professional services, free-zone rents and utility payments) more than trebled.

Given Jamaica's emphasis on higher education, it could be argued that exports of services such as call centers, data processing, etc., should have been higher. Nonetheless, it is true that one outcome of relatively high quality higher education and training can be seen in the buoyant figures for remittances (over 1980 to 2001, net private transfer receipts increased 10 percent annually, arising from migration of skilled workers).

Structure of Imports. The Jamaican economy is highly import-dependent, with goods and services imports averaging 66 percent of GDP over 1990–2000. Like services exports, services imports have also grown, though not as much. Between 1980 and 1993, the share of (non-factor) services in total imports almost doubled from 22 percent to 40 percent, but declined thereafter and has stayed largely around the 30 percent level since then.

Within merchandise imports, fuel, food and manufactures form the major categories. After the second oil price shock in 1979, fuel imports increased to 38 percent of merchandise imports in 1980. With oil prices declining in the 1980s and much of the 1990s, this share declined to a low of 10 percent in 1998 and stood at 13 percent in 2001. Food imports have been in the range of 6–16 percent of merchandise imports in most years. Manufactured goods imports fell in the 1970s owing to the imposition of quantitative restrictions (QRs), but these recovered in the 1980s after most QRs were eliminated by 1985, and had gone up to over 67 percent of merchandise imports in 2001, from 40 percent in 1980.

Direction of Trade. The direction of Jamaica's trade is largely driven by location, and political and economic ties that drive trade preferences in some cases. About 39 percent of its merchandise exports in 2000 (28 percent in 1990) were directed to the USA, and another 38 percent to the EU and Norway (42 percent in 1990). In terms of the major service export, tourism, the concentration is even higher—over 70 percent of visitors originate from North America, with 30 percent from the Northeast, including New York. Reducing the volatility of foreign exchange earnings may require greater diversification, especially in tourism, where a higher share of European visitors could help to mitigate the effect of regional shocks such as September 11. Merchandise imports are sourced from North America (47 percent in 2001), Caricom countries (13 percent), the EU and Latin American countries (10 percent each).

Trade Policy Reforms

Stop-go reforms until 1987. During the years of Jamaica's rapid growth, 1952–72, restrictions on imports were relatively low, although QRs began rising in the 1960s. In the 1970s, QRs were levied on a wide range of goods, and high tariffs were imposed on other goods. This policy reflected an era of "democratic socialism" and a very weak BOP situation. According to King (2001), ". . . 1980 represented a historical nadir for the closure of the Jamaican economy." In the 1980s, QRs were gradually eased—in 1984 for most raw material and capital goods and in 1985 for most consumer goods.

After an intervening period (1985–1987) of across the board tariff increases, the Government in 1987 began a four-year trade reform program. Duties were reduced and simplified, increasing transparency and reducing the scope for discretion.

Acceleration in trade reforms from 1991 onward, along with opening of the capital account.
In 1991, Jamaica introduced capital account convertibility. Also, starting in 1991, it intensified trade
reforms, in several respects. All QRs and licensing requirements for both exports and imports were
eliminated in 1991. The public import monopoly of the Jamaica Commodity Trading Corporation
was also ended in 1991. In terms of tariff reform, Jamaica led the process of reforming Caricom's
Common External Tariff (CET), through agreements reached in 1992 (see Figure 7.1). In 1997,
Jamaica further reduced its own tariffs significantly, bringing the average (un-weighted) tariff down
to 10.9 percent, including a maximum of 30 percent for industrial goods and 40 percent for agricultural ones. Applied rates were an average of 20 percent for agriculture, 10.3 percent for industry, and
4.3 percent for mining. Uruguay Round bound rates were 50 percent for industrial products and
100 percent for agricultural products. Since 1997, the average tariff level has fallen by two percentage
points, to the 2002 average of 8.9 percent. The tariff range for products specified in the CET sched-
ule is 5–20 percent, with capital goods in the range of 0–5 percent.

Another positive development was the move in 2002 from reference prices to actual prices as a
basis for customs tariff valuation. This change significantly increased transparency in the custom
valuation process and is expected to reduce the base price of imports and also reduce distortions.

Reversing the cut in protection somewhat has been the imposition of higher additional stamp
duties (ASDs). While customs tariffs are not large except on selected commodities, since the early
1990s Jamaica has levied additional stamp duties on the duty-paid value of imports.[1] These duties
protect local production and are applied on agricultural products, beverages, tobacco and aluminum
products.

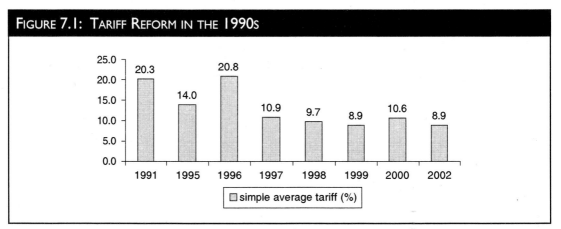

FIGURE 7.1: TARIFF REFORM IN THE 1990S

Source: IMF, WTO

The protection on a range of agricultural products affects the average Jamaican consumer by
putting upward pressure on their prices. In turn, this puts pressure on wage levels and could be one
reason why dollar wages have been increasing more than Jamaica's immediate competitors (see King
2001 and later in this chapter). Protection for some agricultural products, including poultry, meat
and dairy products includes stamp duties (as of 1997) on agricultural products range from 65 to
90 percent. In 2001, the ASD on beef was raised from 32 to 80 percent.

Moreover, in 2002, the tariff on a number of products—meat, poultry, tomatoes, cabbage,
carrots—was raised from a modal rate of 40 percent to 100 percent (the bound rate under the
Uruguay round), and the ASD on these increased from 32 to 80 percent. This meant that the

---

1. Additional Stamp Duties on Customs Warrants Inward (see WTO 1998). For example, if the invoice
price of the good is 100, and the tariff is 100, the duty paid value of goods is 200. The ASD will be levied on
the base of 200. Thus, an ASD of 80 percent will mean a total customs tariff of 260 percent.

effective total duty on these products increased from 84.8 percent to 260 percent! Even allowing for 25 percent lower base prices as a result of the move to actual price valuations in 2002, the effective duty would be 85 percentage points more than in the case where the duty was 84.8 percent.[2] This increased duty would in turn allow domestic producers an "umbrella" under which they could raise prices, at the expense of consumers.

Has Jamaica Reaped the Full Gains From Trade?

Jamaica is a very open economy, with merchandise trade to GDP ratios around 60 percent, and GNFS trade to GDP at 113 percent currently. The share of trade has risen substantially over the last quarter century—GNFS trade to GDP has risen over 45 percentage points between the decades of the 1960s and 1990s. Recent work by Dollar and Kraay (2001b) categorizes Jamaica as a "globalizer," meaning that it is in the top one-third of a group of 72 developing countries in terms of the increase in trade relative to GDP between 1975–79 and 1995–97.

International evidence suggests that increased integration would normally be associated with significant growth and development. For example, the Dollar and Kraay study show that the weighted average growth rate per capita of globalizing countries rose from 3.5 percent to 5 percent between the 1980s and 1990s, while that of the non-globalizing ones rose from 0.8 percent to only 1.4 percent. This result arises from the fact that traded products are generally produced more efficiently than non-traded products. Hence, a reallocation of resources implied by an increasing share of trade in GDP would result in a transfer to more efficient sectors, and consequently improve growth.

Although Jamaica was a globalizer, its external opening only began in the latter half of the 1980s. Growth picked up in the latter half of the 1980s, but thereafter the positive impact of the further trade reforms and the other structural reforms appears to be have been more than offset by other factors, resulting in disappointing GDP growth. In particular, the banking crisis, terms of trade shocks, deteriorating external conditions and a cyclical reversion from the high growth of the late 1980s all contributed to the poor performance in the 1990s (Chapter 2; Loayza et al, 2002). Typically, banking crises bias the flow of resources to larger and better-known companies, away from start-ups and smaller companies, preventing structural change in trade patterns and realization of the full gains from trade.[3] Yet, another factor in the slow growth of the 1990s may have been a loss of competitiveness.

The Decline in Competitiveness in the 1990s

World market share fell. Table 7.2 shows that Jamaica's share of world merchandise exports fell steadily from 0.036 percent in 1994 (and similar figures in the early 1990s) to 0.024 percent in 2001, a fall of one-third. This was accompanied by an even larger proportionate decline in the share of exports in GDP (in nominal terms), from 32 percent to 19 percent. If GDP growth was disappointing in the latter half of the 1990s, export growth was even more so. After doubling between the mid-1980s and end-1980s, merchandise exports have fallen since 1995. Manufacturing employment has declined since 1997 and manufacturing exports since 1995. Agricultural output and exports peaked in 1996, and have generally declined since then. Even the growth in tourist receipts slowed down in the second half of the 1990s.

The appreciation of the real exchange rate over 1992–1998 is one factor in this uninspiring export performance. The real exchange rate (REER) is often itself considered as an indicator of competitiveness. The REER (CPI-based), which had appreciated between 1985–89, also appreciated

---

2. Assuming a base price of 100, the total price of the good with customs duties will be 184.8 in the initial case with 40 percent CET and 32 percent ASD. With the new CET of 100 percent and ASD of 80 percent, the new price would be 360. If we assume instead that the base price is 75 (owing to the use of actual prices), then the total price would be 270, which is 46 percent or 85 percent points higher than the price of 184.8.

3. King (2001) writes that the banking crisis has inhibited the structural transformation of production and exports that would normally have been expected upon opening of the trade and payments regime in the 1990s.

over 1992–1998. After January 2002, and especially between late 2002 and May 2003, the Jamaican dollar has depreciated, significantly reversing much of the earlier appreciation. Over 1992–2001, the wage-based REER had appreciated even more than the CPI-based REER, reflecting the high wage increases over 1992–1998 (see Chapter 2). Because these wage increases exceeded productivity increases, firms' profits were adversely affected.[4]

The real exchange rate and exports. Figure 7.2 shows the very close linkage between Jamaica's share in world merchandise exports and the REER, with the correlation coefficient being–0.6. Similarly, the share of Jamaica's G&S exports (also true for merchandise exports) in its GDP and the REER have a correlation coefficient of –0.8.[5] (Figure 7.3).

	Merchandise Exports (US$ billion)		Share in World Merchandise	Exports/ GDP	Imports/ GDP	Trade/ GDP	REER[a]
Year	Jamaica	World	Exports (%)	(%)	(%)	(%)	1990=100
1985	0.57	1872.0	0.030	27.1	47.8	74.9	96.91
1986	0.59	2046.4	0.029	21.4	30.4	51.8	104.13
1987	0.73	2401.4	0.030	22.1	32.8	54.8	102.77
1988	0.90	2742.0	0.033	23.5	32.8	56.2	104.98
1989	1.03	2981.5	0.035	23.4	36.8	60.1	112.35
1990	1.19	3395.3	0.035	25.9	36.9	62.8	100.00
1991	1.20	3489.1	0.034	28.9	38.4	67.4	90.15
1992	1.12	3730.2	0.030	30.2	41.7	71.9	78.07
1993	1.11	3877.3	0.028	23.3	40.5	63.8	88.19
1994	1.55	4262.4	0.036	32.4	43.9	76.3	86.61
1995	1.80	5094.2	0.035	31.6	46.1	77.7	92.37
1996	1.72	5339.4	0.032	26.9	42.5	69.4	109.87
1997	1.70	5529.0	0.031	23.3	38.9	62.2	126.93
1998	1.61	5441.0	0.030	21.6	36.7	58.2	134.22
1999	1.50	5626.4	0.027	19.9	35.7	55.6	132.96
2000	1.56	6353.6	0.024	20.2	39.0	59.1	130.59
2001	1.45	6129.9	0.024	18.7	39.5	58.2	131.76

TABLE 7.2: MERCHANDISE TRADE AND EXCHANGE RATES IN JAMAICA'S ECONOMY

a. Real Effective Exchange Rate, based on IMF's Information Notice System (INS) methodology
Source: IFS Yearbook 1997, IFS January 2002, IMF; IMF

Similar results are obtained from econometric analysis—over 1980–2000, the GNFS exports to GDP ratio in Jamaica is significantly and negatively related to the REER, and positively to US GDP.[6] These results are consistent with worldwide experience on misaligned exchange rates as discussed in Box 7.1.

4. An update on the labor-cost based REER is not available.
5. Appreciation in and of itself tends to decrease the share of exports in GDP, since exports and GDP have to be quoted in a common currency.
6. The equation for exports of goods and non-factor services is:
$\log(X/GDP) = -3.0 - 1.04*\log(REER) + 1.2*\log(US/GDP)$
t statistics: (–1.0) (–7.6)   (1.7) $R^2 = 0.80$

The equation for non-factor services alone is very similar.

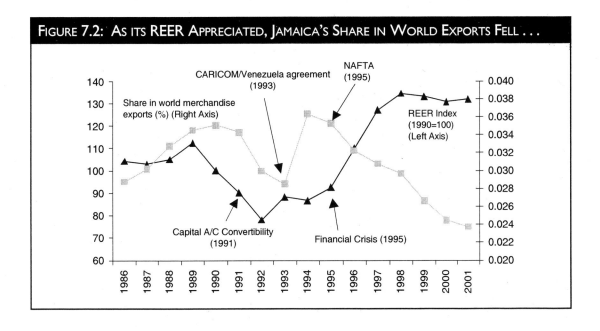

FIGURE 7.2: As its REER Appreciated, Jamaica's Share in World Exports Fell . . .

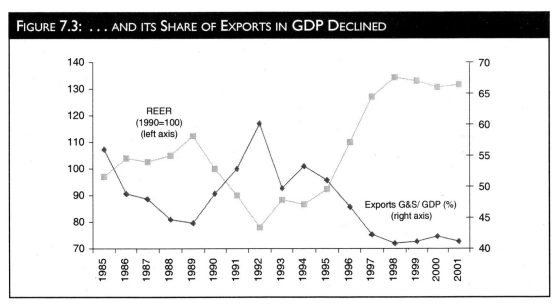

FIGURE 7.3: . . . and its Share of Exports in GDP Declined

Source: International Financial Statistics, IMF.

The appreciation of the exchange rate has also created added pressure on import- competing industries. As noted above, protection of imports was reduced substantially from the late 1980s to the mid-1990s. Normally, tariff reductions are accompanied by a depreciation of the exchange rate, which helps to compensate for the tariff decline, but in Jamaica's case the relationship was often the reverse—for example, after 1992, when tariffs were reduced as agreed under the CET, the ER was appreciating! This would increase the competitive effect on the domestic sector doubly, and may go some way to explain the decline in the domestic manufacturing sector, and also explain the political pressure from the domestic producers of poultry, meat, eggs, and such, to increase protection.

BOX 7.1: THE IMPACT OF AN APPRECIATED EXCHANGE RATE

An appreciated exchange rate (ER) means that prices of the tradables sector will be lower than in non-trad-ables, non-tradables will be more profitable, and resources tend to flow into the production of non-tradables, that is, for the home market. Imports will be high, and export production will tend to be unprofitable. (See, for example, Dornbusch and Kuenzler 1993). Also, if imports arising from an appreciated ER have displaced domes-tic production of tradables, then this process is not easy to reverse, since there are substantial costs associated with shutting down production as well as starting production afresh. Overvalued ERs also affect growth through reduced productivity, since it is the export and import-competing sectors where productivity advances are often most rapid. Moreover, the defense of an overvalued currency through tight monetary policy can lead to recession.

In a 24 country study, Cottani et al. (1990, reference in Shatz and Tarr 2002) found that ER misalignment was strongly related to low per capita GDP growth, and to low productivity; capital did not go to companies or sectors that could make the best use of it, and misalignment was also related to slow export growth and slow agricultural growth. Other such studies are discussed in Shatz and Tarr (2002). Loayza, et al. (2002), also find a negative relationship between overvaluation and growth, holding other standard macro-economic variables constant.

Without underplaying the role of other factors, such as productivity, crime, and high cost utili-ties discussed below, this discussion suggests that with a more competitive real exchange rate, Jamaica probably could have increased its share of exports in GDP as well as in world trade. The issue, of course, is how policies can affect the real exchange rate. One set of policies is of course the monetary-fiscal mix—a tighter fiscal, looser monetary mix tends to yield a more depreciated real exchange rate. Another policy instrument is the nominal exchange rate (see Box 7.2 below on the issue of the inflationary impact of ER depreciation). Changes in the nominal exchange rate tend to have an effect on prices (the pass through), which reduces the impact of a nominal depreciation on the real exchange rate. Of course, the degree and time pattern of pass-through depend on mone-tary policy and the macroeconomic situation. Recent evidence suggests that in Jamaica the "pass through" of exchange rate depreciation into prices has decreased substantially, following years of slow growth.

Starting in 2002, the nominal and the real exchange rate have begun to depreciate (a process which accelerated in April and May 2003 owing to concerns about the macroeconomic situation), which should help improve the competitiveness of Jamaica's tradable goods and services. As men-tioned above, the challenge will be to ensure that recent and possible future potential gains in exchange rate competitiveness are preserved, which implies continued flexibility in monetary policy and avoidance of wage increases in US dollar terms. Of course, any depreciation that occurs will need to be managed and sound macroeconomic fundamentals maintained, lest concerns about debt sustainability (see Chapter 3) and current account sustainability translate into a large, destabi-lizing change in the exchange rate.

Jamaica's Business Environment for Exports

Cross-country Comparisons

Although firms, not countries, compete in world markets, countries' governments can influence the competitiveness of firms by promoting education, investing in infrastructure and providing a sound legal and institutional framework. In recent years increasing attention is being paid to comparing the competitiveness of countries along these lines. The Global Competitiveness Report prepared annually by the World Economic Forum presents two approaches to assessing the competitiveness

---

BOX 7.2: THE PASS THROUGH FROM THE EXCHANGE RATE TO PRICES

While the evidence on the export response to the real exchange rate appears quite solid, the Jamaican authorities have been reluctant to allow large nominal depreciations of the exchange rate for fear of inflation. In the past, some major episodes of inflation have been linked to depreciation of the Jamaican dollar.

There is reason to believe that the pass-through effect of the exchange rate on inflation has reduced in the 1990s. A recent study by McFarlane (2002) shows that six months after an initial shock to the ER, the pass-through to inflation had gone down from 80 percent over 1990–95 to 45 percent over 1996–2000. Our analysis comes up with very similar results, and finds that the coefficient of the nominal exchange rate has reduced significantly between 1960–79 and 1980–2000, from 0.53 to 0.42.[7] Indeed, the experience between 1997 and 2002 shows that nominal annual depreciations of less than about 10 percent do not seem to engender inflationary expectations. More recently, between January 2002 and July 2003, the nominal effective exchange rate depreciated 24 percent, consumer prices rose 15 percent, and real depreciation of 18 percent was achieved (IMF data for exchange rates). Earlier, in 1993, 1995 and 1996, single-digit ER depreciation was associated with annual inflation of between 20 percent and 26 percent.[8]

Several factors could explain the reduced pass-through: a) Owing to years of low or negative growth, there is now a large gap between actual and potential output, and this would dampen inflationary impulses. b) In a study of 71 countries, low inflation was found to be associated with lower pass-through, owing to the role of expectations and price inertia.[9] Going by this, low inflation in Jamaica since 1997 would have helped. c) World inflation is trending downward, including that for low and middle income countries, and the forecasts for 2003–15 (GEP 2003) project the lowest average annual inflation rates since 1970, and this would benefit Jamaica, given its highly open economy. d) Customs tariffs have been declining steadily, with the simple average going down from about 25 percent in the 1980s to the low level of 9 percent in 2002. The low tariffs and open economy mean that domestic manufacturers and retailers have little room for maneuver in setting prices, since there is the real and potential threat of competition from imports and from new retailers in case existing retailers decide to increase or keep high profit margins.

The related and implicit question here is the fear of inflation spinning out of control with depreciation. In order to remain within the low pass-through regime, monetary policy will need to stay at a level where inflationary expectations are not engendered.

---

of a country. The Growth Competitiveness Index (GCI)[10] represents an estimate of prospects of growth for the coming five years. The second, the Current Competitiveness Index (CCI),[11] uses micro indicators to measure the "set of institutions, market structure and economic policies supportive of high current levels of prosperity" referring mainly to an economy's effective utilization of its stock of resources. Both indices use available statistical data as well as the results of an executive opinion survey conducted in the countries covered on the business environment, and ranks countries relative to each other, with the best country rated 1. Table 7.3 gives the results for Jamaica in comparison with neighboring countries also covered by the report.

---

7. The equation simply regresses inflation against the percent change in the J$/US $ exchange rate and a constant term. More sophisticated analysis comes up with very similar results.

8. Of course, this simplifies the inflationary phenomenon, and neglects the impact of other factors on inflation.

9. See Choudhri et al. (2001).

10. The GCI is comprised of three sub-indices: level of technology, quality of public institutions and macro economic conditions.

11. The CCI is an aggregate measure of micro competitiveness, taking into account company operations and quality of the business environment.

TABLE 7.3: COMPETITIVENESS RANKINGS FOR JAMAICA AND NEIGHBORING COUNTRIES, 2001
(75 countries)

	Jamaica	Trinidad and Tobago	Dominican Republic	Costa Rica
Growth Competitiveness index (GCI)	52	38	50	35
Technology index	43	52	44	32
Public institutions index	43	36	54	37
Macro economic environment index	71	25	46	42
Current Competitiveness index (CCI)	40	34	59	50
Company operations ranking	31	27	59	34
Business environment ranking	44	37	58	52

Source: WEF, Global Competitiveness Report, 2001.

Jamaica ranks low on the GCI compared to its regional competitors, especially because of poor macro economic conditions, including poor past growth performance. It scores higher on the CCI and the ranking of company operations. The business environment ranking is modest, however (see also Chapter 6 for general governance comparisons).

Competitiveness Problems According to Firm Surveys

Analyses focused on Jamaica indicate some specific competitiveness issues. A survey of several sectors conducted in 2001 for this report shows mixed results in terms of their meeting international best practices of efficiency and productivity—in tourism, hotels met international best practices (not surprising given their links to international firms), but in agro-processing companies, there is substantial deviation from international best practices. The survey points to some oft-recurring themes external to the firms that detract from their international competitiveness, and these echoed the findings of a 1995–96 survey of 100 Jamaican exporting firms (Harris 1997).[12]

Exchange rate. Companies surveyed generally favored an exchange rate that was stable and competitive. Stability here is not the same as constancy of the exchange rate, but implies a low level of volatility and movement in accordance with fundamentals.[13] In terms of competitiveness of the ER, several companies in the hotel and agro-processing sectors indicated that in the mid-1990s high local cost increases and a constant nominal exchange rate had reduced their profitability, as they were not able to pass on cost increases to final customers (recall the significant real appreciation between 1994 and 1998). Also, the depreciation of the euro vis-à-vis the dollar in the late 1990s hurt the competitiveness of Jamaica's products and services in the European market.

Quality and costs of workers. The main problem here appears to be the wage costs.[14] The survey indicates that there is generally no problem in attracting workers, except for those with specialized skills. Companies are generally satisfied with the commitment and work attitudes of their workers, and with the workers trained at HEART academies, especially in the IT and hotel sectors. In manufacturing, companies prefer workers with previous experience in manufacturing, which may pose a problem if manufacturing contracts further.

---

12. Since the Harris (1997) survey includes 100 firms, and since Jamaica does not have too many large exporting firms, it is no surprise that 50 percent of the Harris-sample firms have less than 100 employees. The 2001 survey, on the other hand, was focused on key sectors and has a larger proportion of bigger firms.

13. The negative impact of exchange rate volatility on exports is also confirmed in Harris (1997). He also finds low export growth to be correlated with high variance of the exchange rate in a cross-section analysis of CARICOM countries.

14. In Harris (1997), labor costs ranked 7th in terms of the obstacles to increasing exports, which was higher than when the firms started export business. Labor costs may have ranked even higher as an obstacle had the survey been done in the late 1990s.

Wage costs have increased substantially, exceeding productivity increases every year between 1992 and 1998, except 1994 (Chapter 2; IMF, p. 25, 2002 Selected Issues). Between 1994–98, wages rose an average of 19 percent in US dollar terms every year. Over these years, unit labor costs rose faster than the GDP deflator, implying a decline in the profitability of domestic production. Although wage increases have been marginally lower than GDP inflation recently, the level of the wage-based REER (and the CPI- based REER) remains substantially higher than in the mid 1990s. The behavior of wages also demonstrates the lack of flexibility in the labor market (see Chapter 2).

Labor relations from the companies' viewpoint are generally better with non-unionized workers, since it facilitates the introduction of more flexible conditions. Changes in ownership in some firms (for example, in the agro-processing industry) in the past few years have been used to forge new relations with employees. In addition, some firms have decided to bear the high cost of redundancy in an effort to negotiate new relations with a new set of employees or even old employees willing to agree to the new terms. Productivity-based compensation is being introduced in some firms. Some firms complained about regulations regarding worker layoffs, but these are not generally shared.

Finance. The larger companies financed a considerable part of their investments from their own cash flows, which in some cases had been augmented by disposal of assets. Moreover, larger companies have easy access to subsidized credit lines (Development Bank of Jamaica, ExIm Bank) and offshore finance. However, smaller companies, as well as potential entrants into exports, have difficulties in accessing credit. Banks consider them too risky for channeling subsidized DBJ funds, and charge higher interest rates and subject them to stricter capital requirements. These considerations would have become even more important after the financial crisis of 1995. In the Harris (1997) survey, the cost of finance ranked as the highest obstacle to increasing exports, and the requirement for collateral ranked in fifth place. For small and medium companies, the costs of capital could be reduced if banks could make better judgments about their credit risk including that of new borrowers. Establishment of credit registries can help in this process (see Chapter 4).

Access to inputs. Companies in the agro-processing sector often had difficulties accessing raw materials in the right quantities and in a timely fashion. Packaging is a particularly thorny issue. With the closure of the local glass factory, most bottles (a major cost factor in beverage industries, particularly rum) have to be imported. In other beverage industries, bottles have been replaced by plastics materials, particularly PET bottles. These are produced locally, often by the users, though the environmental effects of plastic bottles still need to be addressed. For industries producing sauces, bottles are still used and have to be imported. Also, most other packaging material is being imported. Delays due to slow customs procedures increase the cost of imported materials and require that larger inventories be kept. The hotel industry is increasingly using local foods and other inputs, though local quality and timely delivery can pose problems. These problems have continued to persist since the Harris (1997) survey, where the cost of imported inputs ranked fourth in terms of the obstacles to exports, and the supply of local raw materials was in sixth place. Thus, as in many countries, the customs procedures need to be streamlined so imports can flow easily into exportables.

The costs of utilities, including energy, water and telecommunications, are considered high and their reliability low. The Harris (1997) survey ranked the cost of energy as the second biggest obstacle to increasing exports. In our 2001 survey, it was seen that several companies are investing in energy and water-saving technologies and at the same time in stand-by electricity production to ensure access in case of interruption in public supply. High utility costs are one of the many factors that have contributed to the decision of some companies to relocate production capacity abroad, even if this is a marketing disadvantage as in the case of rum (rum bottled in Jamaica has a better image in markets). While telecommunications have improved significantly in recent years, and there is an expectation that the recently privatized power company will be able to improve reliability of power supply, inadequacy in water supply continues to be an impediment to investment and growth (see Box 7.3).

Crime. The need to strengthen security as a result of increasing crime is a major issue for most companies (see Chapter 6 for details). In the agro-processing industry, increasing costs are being incurred to ensure that export shipments are not contaminated with drugs. For export shipments, security costs are sometimes estimated as high as 5 percent of sales. High and increasing crime and extortion have necessitated the use of security companies in and around plants. Crime also limits the possibility and raises the costs of multiple shift operations, by increasing the costs of transporting night-shift workers and requiring higher night pay differentials. It may even limit operations to a single shift. These cost-of-crime issues are particularly important for industries such as call centers, information technology, and textile producers, where multiple shifts are the norm internationally. Crime can also raise the costs of distribution by making access to crime-prone areas more difficult. For the tourism industry, crime adversely affects the number of visitors and requires more expenditure on marketing and promotion, and on provision of security.

BOX 7.3: INADEQUATE INFRASTRUCTURE LIMITS INVESTMENTS, COMPETITIVENESS AND GROWTH

Jamaica has made notable progress in some areas of infrastructure but there is much more that needs to be done. Inadequate or unreliable infrastructure is still a drag on investments, competitiveness and growth. The two areas that have seen marked progress are telecommunications and ports. In telecommunications, privatization and liberalization since 2000 have served to encourage significant private sector investment, resulting in improvements in coverage and access. The penetration of mobile phones is very high, at almost 50 per 100 people, while that for fixed line services, at 18 per 100 people, exceeds what may be expected based on GDP (PPP). In addition, tariff rates have fallen, and the reliability of service has improved, but lags most developed countries.

The continuous implementation of a strategic development plan for the Island's sea ports has helped to keep the ports functioning relatively efficiently, and the Ports Authority of Jamaica is widely regarded as one of the better performing publicly-owned infrastructure providers. The two major airports have fared less well, as their facilities are below international standards despite the importance of tourism to Jamaica. Recent private participation in the operation of the Sangster's International Airport (the airport with the largest tourist throughput) is expected to raise and maintain the service level to an internationally acceptable standard. The viability of Air Jamaica, which is the largest user of the airport, will continue to pose a problem to the sector (as also to the fiscal position of the Government, see Chapter 3).

Unreliability of power supply may be the most significant electricity-related constraint to growth. Electricity costs are higher than in many countries, but while there is scope for some efficiency gains, Jamaica's dependence on imported oil for fuel (natural in a small island economy) renders some of the higher costs inevitable. It has been suggested that replacement of the old steam system with modern diesel plants could lower fuel consumption by up to 40 percent, but this has not been established. Grid coverage is fairly extensive for domestic supply (87 percent of households), but rural coverage is more limited. In April 2001, the Jamaica Public Service Company, with a monopoly over transmission, distribution and most of generation, was privatized. Since then, JPS has increased generating capacity, but only improved reliability marginally, an area on which it expects to focus in the immediate future.

The water and sewerage infrastructure in Jamaica is inadequate, inefficiently operated (unaccounted for water is 65 percent, high by international standards) and unevenly distributed. Repeated and unplanned injections of funds in the sector have been a serious drag on the fiscal budget. Significant investments in several sectors including tourism, manufacturing and real estate may have been jeopardized due to the National Water Commission's inability to provide water for the proposed developments. Current tariff levels, though high, are inadequate to cover operating costs, much less to provide for the significant investment required to expand and improve the service. Very large investments are now needed to meet existing demand—one estimate puts the investment requirement at over US$1.5 billion for potable water and sewerage systems.

(continued)

BOX 7.3: INADEQUATE INFRASTRUCTURE LIMITS INVESTMENTS, COMPETITIVENESS AND GROWTH (CONTINUED)

Although Jamaica has an extensive network of roads, most roads, particularly rural roads, are inadequately maintained and in poor condition. The resultant high cost of transport of goods and persons adversely affects the competitiveness of several sectors, particularly agriculture, tourism and manufacturing. In an attempt to improve road infrastructure, the government has invited private participation through Build-Own-Operate (BOO) concessions to operate toll roads on some of the major thoroughfares.

In summary, where there have been marked improvements in two critical areas of infrastructure i.e. telecommunications and ports, the major benefits from these improvements are being constrained by significant weaknesses in other areas of infrastructure, especially water and roads.

Source: Ehrhardt et al. 2003.

Overview. In sum, the firm survey suggests that not only has the real exchange rate led to a loss of competitiveness, but that competitiveness has been reduced by rising labor costs (in excess of productivity improvements), finance costs (for smaller firms), access to inputs, and crime. Many of these problems were also an issue in the Harris 1995–96 survey. It is no surprise that Jamaica's export performance has suffered in the 1990s, and it has come to rely more and more on its natural resource based advantages, primarily tourism and bauxite-alumina.

The Role of FDI

Export performance has been found to be positively and consistently related to FDI in a large number of studies, especially in high-technology products in developing countries.[15] In the case of Jamaica, FDI has been largely attracted to telecommunications, bauxite mining and tourism, and, more recently, power, with the privatization of the power company.

FDI in telecom, especially in mobile telephony in recent years, is geared to exploiting Jamaica's domestic market. By helping to improve the quality of electronic communications, such FDI has improved the export environment in general, and so has been a positive influence on exports.[16]

Apart from telecom, FDI has been occurring in two of Jamaica's biggest export earners (as also the largest sectors in the domestic economy), tourism and bauxite. There is little doubt that such investment in bauxite and tourism has helped increase exports in these sectors, and this is not only because of the improved technology and practices that accompany FDI. In the case of bauxite, much of the exports are intra-firm trade, which explains much of manufactured exports worldwide. In tourism, improved links with markets arising from overseas investors' knowledge and contacts also helps increase the number of tourists. FDI in tourism has been mainly at the upper end of the market.

Recent FDI inflows are mainly confined to the above sectors (see Annex Table A7.3), although recent success in domestic investments in mega retail stores focused on consumption goods appear to have spurred some FDI in this area. The pattern of FDI corroborates the view that Jamaica's competitive strengths appear to lie in resource-based industries (telecom is an infrastructure sector and is a different case). Attracting significant FDI into other sectors, especially in manufacturing and other services, will require the same improvements as are needed for improving exports in general. In other words, FDI is likely to occur in other sectors in a big way only if they are seen to be potentially competitive. Non-competitive sectors cannot simply be made competitive through FDI, even if such investment could be attracted through very large sops and incentives.

---

15. See Lall (2002) for a recent reference.

16. Already, in the 1995–96 Harris survey, exporting firms found telecommunications to be less of a constraint than when they started export business. See also Box 7-3.

The Performance of Tourism

Tourism is critical to Jamaica's growth and employment, and has been one of the few sectors that has been growing in the 1990s. The GDP in the hotels, restaurants and clubs sector has grown 2.6 percent annually over 1991–2001, and its share in GDP has gone up from 8 to 10 percent over this period. Tourist receipts (in U.S. dollars) grew by 5 percent annually. Direct employment in tourism is estimated at about 85,000 people or about 9 percent of the labor force (of which about 30,000 in accommodations). Tourism also stimulates activity in other sectors such as food, manufacturing, construction, trade and transport.[17] Tourist receipts constitute 37 percent of total exports of G&S.

Americans dominate Jamaica's hotel (stopover) tourist market, with 65 percent of such arrivals coming from the USA in 2000. Moreover, this share increased over 1991–2000 owing to buoyant economic activity in the United States and the increased relative cost to European visitors. The number of European visitors rose by 20 percent over the period, while the number of Canadian arrivals did not change.

Can tourism continue to provide the impetus to GDP that it has in the past? In the more recent period, even not including the events of September 11, tourism growth seems to have leveled off. For example, tourism receipts (in U.S. dollars) grew 8.8 percent annually over 1991–95, but fell to 5.1 percent annually over 1996–2000. In terms of world tourism expenditure, Jamaica had a share of 0.39 percent in 1983, but this dropped off in the later part of the 1980s to around its 2000 level of 0.28 percent. Figure 7.4 shows the relationship between Jamaica's share of the Caribbean, a more directly relevant market, and the REER. It shows that its most recent decline in share in the 1990s in the Caribbean market coincides with the appreciation of the REER over 1992–1998. The declining share even after 1998 could at least in part be due to the exchange rate continuing to be uncompetitive (given its large appreciation earlier). Moreover, in the second half of the 1990s, Jamaica has lost market share to the more popular destinations in the region, such as the Dominican Republic, Cancun and Aruba. Tourist receipts in the Dominican Republic grew 13 percent annually over 1995–2000. It may seem that Jamaica may have to work very hard to even maintain its share of the Caribbean tourism market, let alone increase it, and its tourism sector may be unable to provide the same growth impetus that it has in the past.

A hopeful sign is the continued investment in Jamaican hotels by the private sector and especially the foreign private sector. Over the past two-three years, 1300 new beds have been added to the hotel capacity, including two major foreign-owned hotels, the Ritz-Carlton in Montego Bay (430 rooms) and the RIU hotel in Negril (450 rooms). Another 1300 rooms are under construction. These 2600 rooms constitute an addition of over 12 percent to the total rooms available for tourists in 1995.

On the "micro" side, the hotel sector in Jamaica appears to meet best international practices in terms of productivity and efficiency, especially the mixed hotels and the all- inclusives, but on the macro side, Jamaican tourism seems to have suffered a loss in its competitiveness (market share) after 1993. It is possible that after 9/11, Jamaica will benefit from a tendency of American tourists to stay closer to home, but Americans may also wish to remain in the U.S., and Jamaica's ability to attract those who are willing to go abroad will depend on the competitiveness of Jamaica, compared to other Caribbean and Mexican destinations.

The Jamaican tourist industry continues to trade on its endowments, namely, "sun, sand, and beaches." These, along with proximity to the United States, music and entertainment continue to give the Jamaican tourism product a degree of uniqueness, allowing it to continue to attract substantial numbers of tourists. However, our 2001 survey indicates that the hotel business suffers from being a part of a high cost economy, with the upward pressure on wages in the 1990s. The real exchange rate appreciation appears to have hurt, particularly with respect to the European mar-

---

17. One estimate by the World Travel and Tourism Council in 2001 shows that such related activities employ about 170,000 workers and generate about 20 percent of Jamaica's GDP.

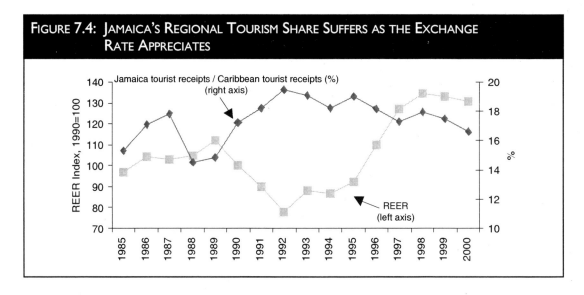

FIGURE 7.4: JAMAICA'S REGIONAL TOURISM SHARE SUFFERS AS THE EXCHANGE
RATE APPRECIATES

ket in the latter part of the 1990s (Jamaica has lost share of European visitors with respect to most Caribbean countries). In Jamaica it is often argued that the exchange rate makes little difference to the industry, since prices are in US dollars, but local expenditures on wages, food, crafts, etc., amount to 65 percent of tourist expenditure, at least in the first round. An appreciated currency will mean fewer Jamaican dollars for local purchases. Lower costs in U.S. dollar terms would allow Jamaican hotels to quote lower prices in U.S. dollars and attract more visitors. Crime and harassment of tourists outside hotels affects the image of the industry, and means both higher security costs and a need for more promotion expenditure to attract the same number of visitors.[18] Crime also affects the attractiveness of Jamaica as a cruise stopover, which would provide some benefits outside the isolated hotel enclave. The underdevelopment of the road infrastructure inhibits traveling within the country and the spillover outside hotel enclaves. For smaller properties with less than 100 rooms, access to capital is difficult, banks view these hotels as not very viable, and in fact this sector is declining. If these factors are reversed, then the profitability and competitiveness of the tourism industry will improve, and translate into an increase in its growth.

Another issue related to the hotel sector is its contribution not only to employment, but to tax revenue. Although there have been attempts by the Caribbean countries to present a united front, and limit incentives to external investors in the hotel sector, it appears that competition for the investors has led to numerous special arrangements. These arrangements, in turn, reduce the taxes that Jamaica is able to obtain (see Chapter 3). Although new agreements to limit tax incentives may be signed, it remains true that unattractive destinations will tend to offer concessions. Conversely, if Jamaica can improve its competitiveness, as described above, it will not have to compete as much in terms of tax concessions.

Decline in the Apparel Sector Reflects the Decline in Competitiveness

Jamaica developed competitive advantages in the Wearing Apparel sector during the 1980s, permitting this industry to exhibit high growth. From a level of US$167 million in 1988, exports grew to over US$533 million in 1995, and employment, to some 35,000. Jamaica became the fifth largest supplier of the United States Market.

Favorable location, low labor costs, and strong Government incentives initially allowed Jamaica to take advantage of opportunities provided under the US Caribbean Basin Economic Recovery (CBI) Act, attracting major investments from Far-Eastern exporters.

---

18. See Alleyne and Boxill (2000), quoted in Annex 6-1.

The United States is the main market for exports of wearing apparel from Jamaica. Other export markets are CARICOM and Europe. Exports to the United States are primarily 807 or cut, make, and trim (CMT) manufactures. In the 807 operation, firms assemble garments from imported pre-cut fabrics on contract for specific clients in the USA; US import duties are paid only on the value added component of the product. In CMT operations, fabrics are cut by the garment producer and subject to strict quality control by overseas clients. Jamaican owned firms and some US owned firms are usually involved in 807 operations, generally established in Jamaican customs territory. CMT firms are mainly of Asian ownership and located in the free-zones. Exports to Europe largely originate from companies in the free zones. The main export products include: jackets, denim trousers, gym-wear, cotton shirts, women's dresses, skirts, blouses, underwear, knitted wear and T-shirts. Major competitors in the export market include Mexico, Guatemala, Honduras and Haiti.

The North American Free Trade Area (NAFTA) agreement, the emergence of new low wage competitors in Central America, and rising labor cost in Jamaica, together with negative developments in the market combined to erode Jamaica's competitive position, resulting in a decline of the industry in the latter 1990s (for example, see Box 7.3 on the La Moda garment company). Some 47 companies closed and/or relocated operations between 1996 and 2000, although during 1999, six plants became operational, including an expansion, with a total capital investment of approximately US$2.5 million. Plant closures have reduced employment in the Apparel industry by 10,000 over the past five years, and by 2000, exports of garments had declined to US$360.5 million, and US$289 million by 2001 (2001 ESSJ, Table 10-7). The one saving grace in this is that exports from the free-zones have declined far less than through the normal customs route—falling from US$283 million in 1995 to US$214 million in 2000, while customs exports fell from US$270 million to US$77 million.

The 807 apparel exports have been competing on the basis of price (production cost), and the adjustment of exchange rates during the 1980s were helpful in improving competitiveness. However, the lower labor costs in Guatemala, Haiti and Honduras as well as the advantages enjoyed by Mexico under NAFTA, will be difficult to challenge. There is renewed interest in production of high fashion garments, capable of competing on the basis of quality and brand recognition, particularly among local manufacturers, and the Jamaican Government has introduced programs designed to assist this effort. To help the apparel industry compete, the Government's Special Assistance program provides concessionary financing, as does the Development Bank of Jamaica, and Exim Bank.

La Moda's experience reflects the general problems facing the apparel industry—an appreciated exchange rate, high wages, high crime-related costs and high energy costs (see Box 7.3). Moreover, the bar for being competitive keeps rising, with firms constantly striving to improve productivity. La Moda's experience shows that Jamaican firms may have lagged in this respect too. Apart from this, trade union activity in free-zones also affects cost competitiveness negatively. At the same time, Government has had to intervene when firms abuse local labor codes, e.g. attempts to evade legal provisions regarding payment of workers when companies close down.

Impending Issues in the International Trade Agenda

Jamaica's exports (like the rest of the Caribbean) benefit from preferential trading arrangements in the EU, United States, and Canada. The most significant products enjoying preferences are bananas, sugar and apparel. While preferred exports are only 11.3 percent of GNFS exports, they are far more important in terms of their share of total employment and output. For example, employment in sugar is 38,200, constituting 4 percent of the employed workforce.

These preferences will be diluted very significantly in future years, in the context of ongoing discussions on the FTAA, and the EU-ACP protocol, as well as the abolition of MFA quotas. The challenge for Jamaica is how to adjust and restructure its domestic sectors in the face of this impending erosion of preferential market access. Given substantial employment in, combined with a general lack of competitiveness of, the above sectors, restructuring and enhancing efficiency will be vital to preserving even a part of such employment.

BOX 7.4: THE DECLINE OF THE LA MODA GARMENT COMPANY

Background. La Moda is an 807 garment contractor in Kingston which works on a contract basis for a Sara Lee subsidiary in the United States. Fully local-owned, the company has been in operation since 1986. At the time of its establishment, Sara Lee supplied some of the equipment. It employs 350 workers on a one shift basis, having grown slowly from an operation which initially employed 25 workers. Materials are supplied in cut form by the contracting company, and sewing is done in La Moda for an assembly fee. Products are low profit margin garments such as t-shirts. Over the past few years, the orders have been declining and the company is on the verge of closing down.

Benchmarking. La Moda meets international best practices in terms of productivity and product quality. The contracting company regularly measures productivity and product quality. The results are disseminated among the supplying companies. For many years, La Moda was on the top of the list of suppliers in the region. Presently, the contracting company has nine contractors in El Salvador, Honduras, Haiti, and the United States. However, over the past few years, companies, especially in El Salvador, have improved their productivity. As a result, La Moda is now ranked fourth in terms of performance, following companies in El Salvador. It is, however, still considered a "low maintenance" company by the contracting companies, needing less regular checks than other companies in the region.

Competitiveness Factors. At the micro level, La Moda has been able to motivate workers, which has resulted in acceptable levels of productivity and low absenteeism (2 percent as compared to an industry average of 6 percent in Jamaica). However, at the macro level there is a problem—La Moda cannot compete with suppliers from lower wage countries in the region. It has been forced to reduce the contract rate from 10 US cents per minute to 8.5 US cents; even at this price it does not break even. Competitors in Haiti, Honduras and El Salvador supply at a contract price of 7 US cents per minute. Labor costs in Haiti are one-third of La Moda's average of about US$1.5 per hour. Another major cost is security, particularly to prevent contamination of containers by drugs. Security costs are estimated at 6 percent of sales. Also, energy costs are considered relatively high. In general, cost increases including wages since the mid-90s have been higher than the nominal exchange rate depreciation. Cost factors and low productivity have been the main reason for foreign owned garment companies shifting from Jamaica to Mexico and to Haiti.

Another problem faced by the company has been the restrictions imposed by standards. As a full-time contractor, the company must meet strict certification requirements, such as the World Wide Responsible Apparel Program (WRAP), which sets standards for labor conditions. Such certification requirements make it difficult to compete with companies that are full-package producers (i.e. producers buying and cutting their own materials), which are not subject to these standards.

Competition in Markets. The introduction of the enhanced CBI has not significantly improved Jamaica's competitive position. Foreign investors from Asia prefer to go to Haiti or the Central American countries, which also benefit from the enhanced CBI. La Moda has been actively looking for other buyers, but has not succeeded. Buyers are reportedly not interested in Jamaica. An option for La Moda would be to make the transition to a full package (cut make and trim) producer and move into higher quality products. It has made efforts in this direction, distributing samples of products to potential buyers, but there was no interest. It is especially difficult to undercut Asian producers. Also, moving into full package production requires considerable investments in cutting equipment and computers, as well as engaging higher quality staff. This is considered too risky given the lack of interest from buyers. The company has taken to close the factory once current orders have been met.

Conclusion. A 1997 study by Kurt Salmon Associates had already suggested that Jamaica's competitiveness in apparel production was declining, concluding that Jamaica had become one of the higher cost options for apparel sourcing in the Caribbean Rim. One way out, that of moving to higher quality products, would require significant investment and intensive marketing efforts.

Access to the U.S. and Canadian markets. In the USA, Jamaica currently benefits from the Caribbean Basin Trade Partnership Act (CBTPA) or enhanced Caribbean Basin Initiative (CBI), which provides NAFTA parity for most exports. In addition, Jamaican garment exports made strong gains through duty concessions (not zero tariffs) under article 807, for goods made from US materials. However, with Mexico enjoying free trade access to the USA under NAFTA since 1995, there was an erosion in the benefit from article 807. With the enhanced CBI becoming effective in 2000, parity with Mexico was largely restored. The enhanced CBI covers textiles and garments and provides for free trade status, though under strict rules of origin and other eligibility criteria.[19] The enhanced CBI will expire in 2005 with the establishment of the FTAA. Moreover, increased competition is also likely from Asian countries with the impending abolition of MFA apparel and textile quotas in 2005.

Jamaican sugar exports to the USA also benefit from a duty-free quota of 1,584 metric tons. It also benefits from duty-free access to the US market for rum exported to Canada and blended and bottled for re-export to the United States.

Under CARIBCAN, in force since 1986, Jamaica enjoys duty free access to the Canadian market, conditional on local content of 60 percent and under strict rules of origin (excluding textiles, clothing and footwear). This agreement is subject to a WTO waiver until 31 December 2006. Discussions with Canada to develop a more mature trade and economic agreement, to culminate in an FTA, began in March 2001.

Access to the EU market. Jamaica has preferred access to the EU market under the Lome agreements with ACP countries, which have provided duty-free access for most products, but this access will end in 2008. Also, various commodity protocols for ACP countries provide a preferred quota for sugar, rum and bananas at prices exceeding world prices.[20] Less reliance on preferred access (as happened in the last decade[21]) will help Jamaica prepare for the erosion of preferences. By 2008, these privileges will have been phased out as per the Cotonou Agreement between the EU and ACP countries. Negotiations on more WTO compatible agreements between ACP countries and the EU are scheduled to start soon.[22]

Improving the Framework for Exports and Development

Increasing exports is imperative for Jamaica's growth. This means that Jamaica has to tackle those issues that have made exports uncompetitive, prevented restructuring of the export industry, and by and large not allowed new and dynamic sectors and firms to emerge, one of the mainstays of export growth.

In general, improving the exporting framework means providing a supporting environment in terms of prices/exchange rates, adequate infrastructure and credit, and minimizing the detrimental effects of crime. None of this is specific to exports in particular. Improvement in any of these parameters would create conditions for higher exports as well as growth. Action on the following fronts will help to increase exports, trade and also help to increase the impact of trade on growth:

---

19. The CBTPA provides unlimited duty-free access to CBI apparel produced from US fabric. It also contains a special quota allocation for the duty-free shipment of a limited amount of CBI apparel produced from CBI fabric and US yarn. Meeting these criteria poses a significant challenge.

20. For example, for raw sugar the world market price was 42 percent of the EU price in 2001.

21. In 2000, the products enjoying preferred access under the commodity protocols accounted for 30 percent of Jamaica's exports to the EU, as compared to 55 percent in 1991.

22. Apart from the above, Jamaica also has one-way free trade agreements with Venezuela (since 1993) and Colombia (since 1995). The agreement with Venezuela provides either immediate duty-free export to Venezuela or phased reductions for selected product groups (fresh produce, confectionery, cosmetics, wooden furniture, processed foods, medicaments and spices). Both agreements foresee a gradual replacement of tariff preferences with reciprocal liberalization. Jamaica also has a Trade and Cooperation Agreement with Cuba, which includes duty free access into Cuba for specified products. The agreement also covers protection of investment, protocols for implementing which are under preparation.

- Ensuring that policies allow the recent gains and future potential gains in exchange rate competitiveness to be preserved, by continuing a flexible exchange rate policy and avoiding polices that would push up wages in US dollars. At the same time, maintenance of credible macroeconomic policies will be required in order to prevent the possibility of an excessive correction in the exchange rate.
- Eliminating the stamp duties that are levied on selected imports, especially food, so as to reduce the price increases that accompany exchange rate depreciation.
- Reducing crime, which is a major cost for exporters (Chapter 6).
- Improving the credit climate for small companies and start-ups (Chapter 3).
- Reducing the cost and providing better coverage of water and sewerage services, improving roads, especially rural roads, and improving the reliability of power supply, and ensuring that all these are fully financed by user charges.
- Improving access to imported inputs by making customs procedures more efficient.

ANNEXES

IDENTIFYING THE DETERMINANTS OF CRIME

The determinants of violent crimes in Jamaica identified in the analysis below are similar to those encountered in other countries (for Latin America see Fajnzylber et al., 2000): (i) negative incentives, or deterrence—that is, more imprisonment—more crimes cleared up, and tougher sentencing are all significantly and negatively associated with some of the violent crimes considered, and (ii) positive incentives (higher per capita income, higher share of labor income in GDP, and lower youth unemployment) are also associated with lower crime rates (except murder). Policies to reduce crime should consider both dimensions of the problem— to increase both the direct costs of committing crime (the expected punishment) and its opportunity cost (the loss of income in the labor market).

Previous econometric analyses of crime in Jamaica. Much econometric work on the determinants of crime has followed the classic paper of Becker (1968), such as Cerro et al. (2000) on Argentina, Fajnzylber et al. (1998) on Latin America and Meera et al. (1995) on Malaysia.

Work on Jamaica has involved different levels of econometric sophistication. Using multiple regression analysis, Ellis (1991) has examined "crime-correlates," and analyzed the relationship between the total number of crimes and unemployment (+), the GDP (−), the food price index (−), the number of police (+), the arrest rate (−) and the age cohort 14–24 years (+), with the signs indicating direction of influence. Boxill and Alleyne (2000) used multivariate analysis to study the impact of crime on tourist arrivals. Their findings suggest that crime has a negative impact on tourist arrivals but this impact was relatively small, with advertising and promotion expenditure being mitigating factors. This finding is important from the perspective of the cost implications of crime. Costs are incurred on two counts: (i) crime reduces the number of tourist arrivals to Jamaica and (ii) crime induces more expenditure to offset the negative effects of crime.

In a recent paper Francis and Campbell (2001) examined econometrically the determinants of violent crime in Jamaica over 1970–1999. Violent crime was measured by an index of crime rates consisting of the major violent crime categories of murder, rape and carnal abuse, shooting, and robbery. Using an adaptation of the Engle-Granger error-correction model and following Pudney et al. (2000), it was found that:

- Short run increases in GDP per head had a highly significant negative or deterrent effect on the crime rate with an absolute elasticity of approximately 1.6.
- The share of employee compensation in the GDP had a significantly positive short run effect on crime.
- The size of the police force had a significant short term deterrent effect.
- The imprisonment rate, measured by an index of imprisonment for violent crime, had highly significant short and long run deterrent effects, interpreted as incapacitation effects, with absolute elasticities of 0.35 and 0.42 respectively.
- Male youth unemployment increased crime but was statistically significant only in the long run with a relatively small (0.29) long run elasticity.

Supply functions for violent crime. This analysis builds on the previous work by Francis and Cambell, by updating the dataset to 2000 and by extending the set to include a measure of the gross secondary school enrollment rate (Hariott et al. 2003).[1]

The estimation considers a simultaneous equation system of major violent offenses i.e. murder, rape and carnal abuse, shooting and robbery. The rationale of using a simultaneous equation approach is that some of the explanatory variables such as the size of the police force could themselves be determined by the levels of crime.

The variables along with their expected signs are described below:

- For each of the four separate equations the dependent variables are the murder rate, the rape and carnal abuse rate, the robbery rate, and the shooting rate. All dependent variables are expressed as number of recorded offenses per 100,000 people in Jamaica.
- GDP (1995$) per head is expected to influence crime as higher income tends to eliminate the need to engage in criminal activity. However, the impact of this variable is ambiguous as the literature points to the increasing opportunity of say robbery arising from the availability of more goods and services.
- Unemployment rates among 14–24 year old males is expected to increase crime. Both the victims and perpetrators of violent crimes tend to be young males, and are usually unemployed or in the lowest occupational stratum of the labor force (see Chapter 5). The argument that a person will weigh the relative returns from legal and illegal activities in contemplating criminal behavior for economic gain appears to be even more forceful in the context of high and chronic unemployment where legitimate opportunities for gain are virtually non-existent. Unemployment can have opposing effects, where economic hardship from unemployment might motivate crime, but there is the opposite "opportunity effect" (risk of acquiring criminal record) which deters some types of crime. In order to capture the different effects of unemployment on the various types of violent crime, separate equations are developed for the crimes in which unemployment appears as an explanatory factor.
- The share of employee compensation in GDP is expected to have a deterrent effect on crime, the notion being that higher income shares for labor are consistent with more income equality. A long enough time series on the Gini coefficient is not available.
- The size of the police force as measured by the number of police officers per 100,000 persons is expected to be a deterrent factor at least in the long run. This could possibly exhibit a positive effect on the crime rate through the registration effect, which implies that more police officers can encourage or induce an increase in recorded offenses and consequently higher crime rates. The issue of the likely endogeneity of the size of police force variable is tackled by including a separate equation in the system to explain this variable.

---

1. While completion rates are a better measure of educational attainment, this data is only available periodically at censuses of population.

- The imprisonment rate for each specific type of violent crime is used as an explanatory variable for the particular crime. Imprisonment through the incapacitation effect is expected to lead to lower crime rates.
- The cleared-up rate for each specific type of violent crime is used as an explanatory variable for the particular crime. It is expected that the cleared-up rate will have a deterrent effect as it proxies the chance of being arrested for the particular crime.
- A length of sentence variable measured by the median length of sentence in months per prisoner is expected to have a deterrent effect on crime. It is possible that the opposite effect can be found as the length of sentence can lead to higher crime rates if prisoners are not rehabilitated and tend to become repeat or habitual offenders.
- The gross secondary school enrollment rate as measured by the number of students, irrespective of age, enrolled at the secondary level, divided by the number of persons in the age group 10 years to 19 years, is expected to have a deterrent effect on violent crime, as opposed to crimes such as embezzlement and fraud. A better educated population is better able to assess the consequences of criminal behavior and is expected to decide against such activity.[2] It is also likely that more educated individuals have better opportunities for legitimate employment.
- An index of the overall crime rate computed as a weighted average of indices of the four categories of major violent crime (murder, rape and carnal abuse, shooting and robbery) is included in the simultaneous equation system as an explanatory variable for the police force variable and the security expenditure variable. It is theorized that the size of the police force and security expenditure are endogenous to the system and as such are explained *inter alia*, by lagged values of the crime rate. The index is constructed by first expressing the several crime rates as indices with a 1990 base. The four indices for each year are converted to a single index for each year by applying weights: murder: 50, rape and carnal abuse: 20, shooting: 20 and robbery: 10.
- An index of the overall cleared-up rate computed as a weighted average of indices of the four categories of major violent crime i.e. murder, rape and carnal abuse, shooting and robbery is included as an explanatory variable for the police force variable and the security expenditure variable. The index is constructed in a way to the overall crime rate index, discussed above, with an identical weighting system.

Following Meera et at. (1995) and Campbell (2002) supply functions are estimated for each of the four categories of violent crime in the context of a simultaneous equation system. The equations of the system are:

(1) $\ln \text{Murder Rate}_t = \beta_0 + \beta_1 \ln \text{Murder Imprisonment Rate}_t + \beta_2 \ln \text{Murder Clear-Up Rate}$
$+ \beta_3 \ln \text{Youth Unemployment Rate}_t + \beta_4 \text{ Size of Police Force}$
$\text{per 100 persons}_t + \beta_5 \ln \text{Labor Share}_t + \beta_6 \ln \text{GDP per head}_t$
$+ \beta_7 \ln \text{SEcurity Expenditure per head}_t + \beta_8 \ln \text{Length of Sentence}_t$
$+ \beta_9 \ln \text{Secondary Enrollment Rate}_t + \varepsilon_t$

(2) $\ln \text{Rape Rate}_t = \alpha_0 + \alpha_1 \ln \text{Rape Imprisonment Rate}_t + \alpha_2 \ln \text{Murder Clear-Up Rate}_t$
$\alpha_3 \ln \text{Youth Unemployment Rate}_t + \text{KK as for equation (1)K} + u_t$

---

2. Secondary school enrollment has unexpected positive and significant effects on violent crimes (see Table below). This may be because higher levels of education increase crime 'productivity' at higher rates than legal activities. Second, the higher the educational level, the higher the levels of reported crime. Third, the equation may simply be capturing an upward trend in both crime and enrollment.

(3) In Robbery Rate$_t$ = γ_0 + γ_1 In Robbery Imprisonment Rate$_t$ + γ_2 In Robbery Clear-Up Rate$_t$ + γ_3 In Youth Unemployment Rate$_t$ + K as for equation (1)K + v_t

(4) In Shooting Rate$_t$ = λ_0 + λ_1 In Shooting Imprisonment Rate$_t$ + λ_2 In Shooting Clear-Up Rate + λ_3 In Youth Unemployment Rate$_t$ + K as for equation (1)K + η_t

(5) In Security Expenditure per head$_t$ = ω_0 + ω_1 In Crime Rate Index$_{t-1}$ + ω_2 In GDP per head$_{t-1}$ + ω_3 In Size of Police Force per $100,000_{t-1}$ + ω_4 In Cleared-Up Rate$_{t-1}$ + w_t

(6) In Size of Police Force per $100,000$ persons = ϕ_0 + ϕ_1 In Crime Rate Index$_{t-1}$ + ϕ_2 In Security Expenditure per $100,000$ persons$_{t-1}$ + ϕ_3 In GDP per head$_{t-1}$ + ϕ_4 In Cleared-Up Rate$_{t-1}$ + r_t

The data analyzed over the period 1970–2000 are from the Planning Institute of Jamaica (PIOJ) and Statistical Institute of Jamaica (STATIN).

The variables in the model were examined for non-stationarity using the Augmented Dickey Fuller test and were all found to be I(1). The Johansen Co-integration test showed that each equation in the simultaneous equation system was co-integrated, with each equation having at least two cointegrating equations. The results of the application of two-stage least squares (2SLS) to the key equations of the interest are summarized in the table below. In the application of 2SLS, all the exogenous and lagged endogenous variables in the entire model are used as instruments.

The findings with regard to the estimated equations are summarized in the tables below.

Source: Harriott et al., 2003.

RESULTS:
TWO-STAGE LEAST SQUARES REGRESSION FOR THE JAMAICAN CRIME SYSTEM, 1970–2000[a]

Crime Rates	CRIMP	CLEAR	YUNE	SOPF	LAB	GDP	SECURE	LOS	SERATIO	R² & Adj. R²
Murder	-0.31012 (.0002)	-0.84675 (.0001)	.226747 (.3644)	.843075 (.0254)	.337811 (.4933)	.606454 (.2331)	.79178 (.0043)	.091387 (.7558)	.590576 (.012)	.936459 (.907866)
Rape & Carnal Abuse	-.01576 (.2015)	.010867 (.9313)	.464247 (.1278)	-.02062 (.9672)	-1.33471 (.0022)	.619881 (.3017)	.63923 (.0982)	.061107 (.8496)	.67554 (.0074)	.802732 (.713961)
Robbery	-.13482 (.1914)	-.71946 (.0001)	-.1489 (.6916)	-.24024 (.5814)	-1.02941 (.0458)	-1.45471 (.0498)	-.36891 (.321)	-.041985 (.2866)	.410854 (.2467)	.69817 (.562347)
Shooting	-.0165 (.6464)	-1.15888 (.0000)	.312285 (.2227)	1.327423 (.0008)	-.75974 (.0934)	.820717 (.162)	-.37507 (.1879)	-.66884 (.0399)	.876738 (.005)	.914059 (.875385)

Notes: a) Figures in the parentheses are the probability values for the t-statistic.
Crimp=Imprisonment Index, Clear=Cleared-Up Rate, Yune=Youth Unemployment, SOPF=Size of Police Force, Lab=Share of employee compensation in GDP, GDP=Gross Domestic Product, and Secure=Security Expenditure, Seratio=Secondary School Enrollment Ratio. Los=Median Length of Sentence, Secure=Security Expenditure, Los=Median Length of Sentence, Seratio=Secondary School Enrollment Ratio.

Variables	Murder +	Murder −	Rape and Carnal Abuse +	Rape and Carnal Abuse −	Robbery +	Robbery −	Shooting +	Shooting −
Imprisonment Rate		✓		✓		✓		✗
Cleared-up Rate		✓	✗			✓		✓
Youth Unemployment	✗		✓			✗	✗	
Size of Police Force	✓			✗		✗	✓	
Labor Share	✗		✓			✓		✓
Gross Domestic Product	✗		✗			✓	✓	
Security Expenditure	✓		✓			✗		✓
Median Length of Sentence	✗		✗			✗		✓
School Enrollment Ratio	✓		✓		✗		✓	

Note: +, − represents the sign of the coefficient; ✓, ✗ represents statistically significant or insignificant coefficients respectively

METHODOLOGY FOR BUSINESS VICTIMIZATION SURVEY

The business victimization survey consists of 92 items some of which were taken from the United Nations Interregional Crime Research Institute business victimization questionnaire. The survey was administered in face-to-face interviews to a sample of 400 Jamaican firms. A quota sample was designed and used in this survey. The justification for this design was based on the following:

- No up-to date sampling frame of establishments currently exists.
- The sampling frame of enumeration districts (ED's) is designed primarily for household surveys. Whereas the ED's could be modified and used for a survey of establishments, this process would be costly and time consuming.
- A random sample of establishments would be time consuming, in view of the factors mentioned earlier.

Quota samples are widely and successfully used in Jamaica. The advantages of this design include (i) selected establishments distributed throughout the island, (ii) relatively inexpensive, (iii) relatively easy to locate the establishments, and (iv) non-responses easy to deal with. The disadvantages include (i) establishments not randomly selected, hence an element of personal bias in the selection, and (ii) the estimation of population parameters, for example, averages, could not be tested for precision by the calculation of sampling errors.

The island was stratified into two geographical regions, East and West. Eastern Jamaica includes the parish of Kingston and St. Andrew, St. Thomas, Portland, St. Mary, St. Ann, St. Catherine, and Western Jamaica includes the parishes of Clarendon, Manchester, St. Elizabeth, Westmoreland, Hanover, St. James and Trelawny.

Two hundred and fifty (or 62.5 per cent) of the establishments were selected from eastern Jamaica. The rationale for this is that the Kingston Metropolitan Region (KMR), which includes

Kingston, Urban St. Andrew and Portmore is located in this area, and most of the establishments in Jamaica are located there.

Establishments in each area or stratum were further stratified into 12 economic activities: Bank/Financial Services, Tourism, Manufacturing and Processing, Agriculture, Construction, Mining and Quarrying, Transport and Storage, Entertainment, Distributive Trade, Science and Technology, Communications and Other. Within each economic activity, establishments were further stratified by size—"small" defined as firms with 1–19 permanent employees; "medium" as firms with 20–49 permanent employees; and large, 50 or more permanent employees.

Establishments within each sub-stratum were then selected by a non-random process primarily because the population of establishments within the sub-stratum was not known. Every effort was made to ensure that the establishments that were selected were fairly evenly distributed over the geographical area of each stratum.

The sample includes only existing firms. Those firms which have been completely ruined by crime are excluded. This survival bias exhibited by the sample means that the survey data may tend to underestimate the extent of criminal victimization (see Harriott et al, 2003, for distribution of the sample by area, economic activity and size).

Source: Harriott et al., 2003.

CASE OF SERVICE STATION NEAR MONTEGO BAY

Background

This company is a service station located on the outskirts of the city of Montego Bay which is considered to be the "tourism capital" of Jamaica. The present operator has been managing it for the last three years. Although the area is not a business district, there are other businesses in the vicinity of this firm, a few of which have recently been robbed. The company employs 14 persons. It is the second largest service station in Montego Bay and the third largest in the Western region of the island. The proprietor, is a Jamaican who has recently resettled.

Crime Problem

The service station does not have a particularly problematic history of being a target for criminals. A past proprietor was however shot for reasons unknown to the present one. In recent times, the firm has suffered from a number of criminal attacks. In the first quarter of 2002, the service station was robbed in successive months. The losses were approximately $30,000 in cash, and $500,000 in cash and phone cards, respectively. At the time of this survey (mid-2002), there were also two incidents of burglary. Both were allegedly done by drug addicts. In the first incident, the company lost about $6,000, and in the second, it lost $10,000.

According to the proprietor, crime has had the following impact on the company:

- It inflates the cost of the product as goods and services are priced to recover losses that are incurred.
- Wages are depressed as losses due to crime reduce the ability to pay higher wages.
- Opening hours are reduced.
- Insurance costs are high and are expected to increase as the number of incidents of criminal victimization of the company continue to increase.
- Loss of valuable workers. The members of his staff are very fearful of violent criminality and after the second robbery, one member of the staff resigned.

Survival Techniques

The major adjustments to the crime problem that have been made by this company involve considerable target hardening by the employment of private security personnel and the installation of burglar bars and other similar measures. Security guards are employed for seven days per week. This costs approximately $621,000 per year and the maintenance of a panic button system costs an additional $54,000 per year. Grills, panic buttons and other physical changes have been put in place. Installation of these security systems cost $100,000.

Interestingly, the proprietor has resorted to questionable self-help measures. The drug addicts who burglarized the firm were found and threatened with violence. This measure was celebrated as a successful way of dealing with the problem. The robbers were a more difficult proposition. The resort to self-help reflects a low level of confidence in the police service and anticipates a poor and ineffective response on their part.

Institutional Support

The police are seen as indirect contributors to the crime problem. He details his experiences as follows:

- The first incident of robbery was reported to the police. In response, no apparent investigative work was done by the responsible police officers. Neither fingerprints nor statements were taken.
- The second incident was similarly reported to the police. On their way to the crime scene, the police were confronted by the perpetrators. A shoot out ensued and the criminals escaped. After this, the police visited the business and asked a few questions. The police promised to return for a "proper statement" but this was not done until after the proprietor was interviewed on a talk show and the police superintendent in charge of the region was subsequently called to account by the press. Three days later, the perpetrators were killed in a police shoot-out and the victims of the robbery called to identify the bodies. Since then, eight members of the "Toyota gang," which had allegedly robbed the firm, have been killed and six are in jail.

The experiences with the courts have been similarly negative. The most recent experience of this firm is in attempting to bring charges against a worker who defrauded the company of what may be regarded as a significant sum for a firm of this size. The clerk of the court was assessed to be incompetent. As a result of this, the case was unduly lengthy and after seven months, it was closed.

The proprietor expects the crime problem, and indeed *his* crime problem, to get worse. New forms of crime, especially extortion, are anticipated, with criminals in Montego Bay replicating the methods of their counterparts in Kingston. The proprietor protects himself by spending less time at his business place and avoids staying there late in the evenings or weekends. However, he does not intend to close his company.

Source: Harriott et al., 2003.

CASE OF FURNITURE MANUFACTURING FIRM IN KINGSTON METROPOLITAN AREA

Background

This company is a family owned firm that manufactures furniture. The company operates under an international license and supplies its products to the various retail outlets in Jamaica and other CARICOM countries as well as sells directly to consumers. Its operations are centered in the Kingston Metropolitan Area, with its manufacturing plant located in the high crime industrial belt and an outlet is located in relatively low crime dormitory city of Portmore. By Jamaican standards it is a fairly well established medium to large company. It has been in operation for 38 years, and at the time of writing, it employed 58 persons. Its sales revenue for 2001 was $135 million. It may be considered one of the less vulnerable companies in the manufacturing sector.

Crime Problem

It is confronted with a wide range of crime problems, including robbery, burglary, employee theft, and extortion by criminal gangs that operate in the area in which its manufacturing plant is located. The firm has been robbed twice in consecutive years, the last instance being in 2001. Losses incurred were $1 million and $1.1 million respectively. There has been a history of burglaries and employee theft of component parts for its products, which are later assembled in the neighboring community and sold on the black market. Moreover, the manufacturing plant is located within close proximity to two relatively large squatter communities. Residents from one of these communities treat the plant as a source of free electricity. The company is forced to pay the bill. To do otherwise is to run the risk of retaliation—that may take violent unpredictable forms. This situation has persisted over a period of 5–6 years.

The economic impact of crime on the company includes the following:

- It is forced to restrict its opening times and manufacturing operations. The manager estimates that were the area crime free, the company would extend its operations by 40 hours per week.

- The company pays an additional 30 percent in insurance premiums because of the risks associated with its present location and past experiences with criminal victimization.
- Its utility bills are extraordinarily high.
- The high cost of security. Maintenance of private security costs approximately 2.9 percent of the sales of the company.
- Some potential customers refuse to visit the premises.

Institutional Support

Support from the institutions of the state including law enforcement has not been good and has not prevented or even reduced the problems of the company. Despite the best intentions of the police, the problems have remained. They have proven to be ineffective. Indeed, some police officers have sought to exploit the predicament of the company by demanding that it pay them to investigate some of the incidents of crime that were reported by the company.

The experience with the courts has been similar. Cases take very long for the process of adjudication to be completed. The company has been involved in one such case (as a victim of fraud) since 2001 and it is still before the court.

Survival Techniques

In response to its crime problem, the company has been forced to adopt a number of costly internal and external security measures. The importance of security to the company is reflected in the fact that its Chief Executive Officer now has direct responsibility for its security system. It contracts a private security company which provides it with armed guards, and in addition, has installed alarms, security cameras, "panic buttons" and sensor alarms.

The company recognizes the need for collective measures. It has taken the initiative, via its representative organization, the Jamaica Manufacturers Association, to propose a collective solution to the crime control problem in the industrial belt that would involve all the companies that operate in the Kingston industrial belt cooperating and engaging in a partnership with the government/police, and would entail joint funding of a dedicated police unit.

This company is determined to remain in its existing business and to try to solve the problems presented by crime. It is particularly eager to try to find lawful collective solutions.

Source: Harriott et al., 2003.

PROGRAM DESEPAZ, DESARROLLO, SEGURIDAD Y PAZ (DEVELOPMENT, SECURITY AND PEACE) IN CALI, COLOMBIA

Background

From 1983 to 1993, the annual homicide rate in Cali increased by 366 percent, from 23 to 90 per 100,000 habitants. Homicides and motor vehicular deaths were the primary causes of deaths in the city. Added to the significant rise in the crime and violence rate was the public perception of violence and insecurity as the most serious problem in the city; so serious that running mayor Rodrigo Guerrero put violence reduction and improvement of public safety as the central issue of his political campaign. On election, DESEPAZ was created, an acronym for the Spanish words desarrollo (development), seguridad (public safety), and paz (peace).

Objectives

- Strengthen democratic institutions
- Empower the Community
- Assess and address priority needs
- Promote peaceful conflict resolution through a communication strategy resolution

Activities and Achievements

Six strategic areas were targeted by the program.

- *Monitoring.* A series of epidemiological studies and opinion polls were conducted in order to fully investigate and study violence, thus facilitating the implementation of strategic solutions.
- *Institutional improvements.* Police forces were improved by ensuring secondary education for all police officers and the precincts were refurbished; Legal services were also ameliorated by creating 10 Mediation Centers, 20 Legal Aid Offices, creating and improving the Family Violence Intake Centers, developing the concept of houses of peace (which would include all these legal services). The judicial system was computerized.

- *Community enhancements.* Several programs aimed at citizens' education for peace were created: the Community council for governance, where secretaries of the office and the Mayor of the City of Cali met with all the community representatives to talk about the problems that these communities were facing, discuss plans of actions, and revise the accomplishments of previous projects; the Children Friends of Peace, a campaign in which children were asked to bring their gun toys in return for passes to amusement parks; Teaching tolerance and community coexistence between citizens through televised commercials which were broadly accepted and had a positive impact on the public.
- *Promoting equity.* The city ameliorated the education programs, the public services, and housing in the at-risk zones.
- *Youth programs.* The city implemented the PARCES program: PARticipación, Convivencia, Education, Superación (Participation, Coexistence, Education and Overcoming) which attracted 1400 youths and offered them psychological orientation, support for recreational activities and support in job searches. The mayorship of Cali also created the Youth Houses, which are recreational areas for youngsters; the Intercommunal Olympic games; and the Program "Entering Generation," which is a Youth Organization of Small Businesses.
- *Special Policies.* The implementation of the "semi-dry law," aimed at prohibiting the sale of alcohol after 1:00 a.m. on weekdays and 2:00 a.m. on weekends and holidays; the prohibition of bearing arms on special days; and the traffic accidents prevention program.

Outcomes, Impacts

- Between 1994 and 1998, the number of homicides in Cali reduced by 600 per year.
- Unemployment reached 7 percent in 1994 but increased the following years.
- Since 1993, DESEPAZ has been publishing weekly data.

Source: "A Resource Guide for Municipalities: Community Based Crime and Violence Prevention in Urban Latin America," forthcoming, World Bank.

POLICE AND COMMUNITY COOPERATION FOR REDUCTION OF VIOLENCE IN DIADEMA, SAO PAULO, BRAZIL

Background
This project was carried out by the Fernand Braudel Institute of World Economics, which is associated with the Fundaçao Armando Alvares Penteado in Sao Paolo, Brazil.

Objective
Develop a model program of how to reduce violence in Brazil's high-risk urban areas through community policing and community cooperation.

Activities and Achievements
- Pulled together support between diverse political actors
- Launched monthly town meetings in partnership with the Mayor, the City Council, Military and Civil Police Chiefs, business, religious and community leaders
- Developed contacts and in-depth knowledge on violence reduction approaches, which are transferable to other Brazilian cities
- Founded partnerships between the different city community authorities and community residents

Outcomes, Impacts
- A 12 percent decrease in homicide rates; 11 percent decrease in car thefts
- Increased public awareness on the problem of violence; initiated dialogue and effective police initiatives
- Founding of a Social Defense Coordinating office and a Municipal Public Safety Council to study and implement various approaches to violence prevention
- Introduced a Municipal law regulating the functioning of bars after 11:00 p.m.
- Implementation of a task force to work with parents, students and teachers in the area of violence prevention in the city; a pilot project targeting school violence

- Provision of a computerized criminal mapping system
- Creation of an anonymous telephone system for criminal activity report. In 2001, 65 of the 352 anonymous calls resulted in real arrests
- More police and community cooperation
- Increase in dialogue from other cities' officials, cities facing problems with violence such as Sao José, dos Campos and Campinas.

Source: "A Resource Guide for Municipalities: Community Based Crime and Violence Prevention in Urban Latin America," forthcoming, World Bank.

CITIZEN CULTURE IN BOGOTÁ (CULTURA CIUDADANA EN A LA ALCADÍA DE BOGOTÁ), BOGOTÁ, COLOMBIA

Background

Between 1995 and 1997, the City of Bogota invested approximately US$130 million (3.7 percent of the city's budget) in a multiple action plan on citizen education supported by the several local agencies. This program stemmed from the hypothesis of the possible separation between three systems regulating conduct: law, culture (at the collective level), and morale (individual conduct).

Objectives

Encouraging self-regulation of collective and individual conducts, thus diminishing the breach between individuals and the law.

Activities and Achievements

- Created a monthly newsletter with actual information on delinquent activities.
- Implemented the "dry law" (ley zanahoria) prohibiting the sale of alcoholic beverages after 1:00 a.m.
- Launched the voluntary disarmament program in coordination with religious groups/churches.
- Increased the number of Family Violence Intake Centers (Comisaría de Familia) from 6 to 13.
- Reinforced, with the help of the police, security fronts by grouping neighbors.
- Professionalized the police by specializing 4,750 police officers
- Restricted illegal substances.
- Sensitized the public on rules of community living through Citizen or Community days.

Outcomes, Impacts

■ The homicide rate decreased from 72 to 51 per one hundred thousand inhabitants.
■ One year after the implementation of the program, homicide cases related to alcohol intoxication were reduced by 9.5 percent and by 26.7 percent after two years.
■ The disarmament campaign gave apparent results, common homicides decreased by 23 percent to 30 percent the first three months of the campaign.
■ The number of youths injured by drugs during holiday seasons decreased by one third.

Source: "A Resource Guide for Municipalities: Community Based Crime and Violence Prevention in Urban Latin America," forthcoming, World Bank.

FOCUS ON YOUTH: THE MODEL OF THE CITY OF BOSTON, MASSACHUSETTS, USA

Background
In the early 1990's, a total of 152 homicides per year were committed in the City of Boston, an increase from an average below 100 in prior years. Reports showed that approximately 75 percent of these homicides were linked to gangs in a city where nearly 40 different neighborhood gangs were indexed (a gang population of 4,000).

Objectives
Reduce teen/youth violence at the municipal level through preventive and controlling measures involving local authority and the local community. This program was selected by the National Crime Prevention Council (NCPC), in the USA, as one of six leading American cities with the highest crime reduction in ten years.

Activities and Achievements
- Launch of the Cease Fire Operation through gun control and gang control policies: sanctions strengthened for repeated offenders; police patrolled regularly to check that offenders on probation were in compliance with their probation orders. The police reinforced the control of arms trafficking.
- Creation of a coalition between the police and social workers to come up with effective measures to prevent and control gang violence illustrated by the Youth Service Providers Network (YSPN), partnership between the police and the Boys and Girls Clubs.
- Implementation of the Strategic Planning & Community Mobilization Project (SP&CMP) aimed at improving the relationship between citizens and the police, increasing the citizens' confidence in the police.
- Promotion of peaceful means for resolving conflicts amongst youths.

Outcomes, Impacts
- The total crime rate declined by 29 percent, or from 5,302 to 3,768 cases.
- The property crime rate decreased by 31 percent, or from 4,613 to 3,187 cases.
- The rate for violent crimes was lowered by 16 percent, or from 689 cases to 580.

Source: "A Resource Guide for Municipalities: Community Based Crime and Violence Prevention in Urban Latin America," forthcoming, World Bank.

ANNEX TABLES

ANNEX TABLE A1.1: JAMAICA—CONSUMER PRICE INFLATION, (% CHANGE IN CPI, END YEAR), 1990–2002

	1990	1991	1992	1993	1994	1995	1996	1997	1998	1999	2000	2001	2002
ALL GROUPS	29.8	80.2	40.2	30.1	26.8	25.6	15.8	9.2	7.9	6.8	6.1	8.8	7.3
FOOD AND DRINK	29.0	84.3	40.3	31.8	27.2	27.6	12.1	8.9	4.0	3.9	4.4	6.8	7.8
Meals Away from Home	28.1	65.9	51.1	39.8	26.3	37.8	17.1	10.7	8.0	3.4	5.6	3.1	4.1
Meat, Poultry and Fish	38.3	92.2	38.4	29.4	16.1	26.6	9.0	5.6	4.4	1.8	2.7	4.9	4.6
Dairy Products, Oils and Fats	33.1	159.5	38.1	26.4	28.4	18.3	13.1	3.3	1.6	2.0	4.2	5.3	3.3
Baked Products, Cereal and Breakfast Drink	29.2	96.7	48.1	18.2	32.8	33.3	13.4	1.1	3.9	1.2	5.9	2.0	8.7
Starchy Foods	8.3	49.8	39.4	36.5	40.0	32.5	9.3	28.6	0.7	7.3	8.9	17.6	10.3
Vegetables and Fruit	34.8	35.5	41.0	63.1	18.8	24.0	7.2	19.1	2.6	8.6	-0.1	14.1	25.7
Other Foods and Beverages	15.0	68.3	22.8	25.0	62.8	18.6	17.9	6.4	5.7	9.6	4.6	6.3	2.8
FUELS AND OTHER HOUSEHOLD SUPPLIES	42.8	94.1	30.8	18.6	18.7	37.1	20.6	7.3	9.7	2.9	7.6	10.7	2.2
Household Supplies	31.3	126.1	33.3	14.1	17.1	11.0	20.9	6.4	3.7	2.0	2.6	2.7	3.5
Fuels	64.5	45.7	25.3	29.7	22.3	91.2	20.3	8.3	16.8	3.9	12.8	18.1	1.2
HOUSING AND OTHER HOUSING EXPENSES	38.5	64.7	32.4	20.9	32.6	17.4	13.8	10.2	9.6	24.4	17.5	*4.2	15.2
Rental	13.5	12.2	21.7	8.7	31.0	33.5	31.8	25.7	24.6	9.1	18.5	29.4	6.8
Other Housing Expenses	45.7	77.2	34.4	22.9	32.8	15.1	10.9	7.2	6.2	28.5	17.3	*-1.5	17.8
HOUSEHOLD FURNISHINGS AND FURNITURE	19.5	70.9	34.8	30.3	13.8	30.5	12.9	8.1	3.9	3.5	8.9	4.8	5.4
Furniture	22.8	68.1	38.1	26.9	12.7	33.3	8.3	4.0	8.1	6.8	6.0	10.0	10.8
Furnishings	18.4	73.2	32.5	31.7	14.4	29.1	14.7	9.6	2.4	2.2	10.1	2.8	3.2
HEALTHCARE & PERSONAL EXPENSES	29.4	87.3	41.9	32.0	21.2	18.0	21.8	8.8	7.4	7.6	6.7	5.5	5.0
PERSONAL CLOTHING FOOTWEAR AND ACCESSORIES	23.6	75.0	73.0	24.9	16.6	24.0	22.8	10.6	3.7	5.6	4.5	3.4	3.9
Clothing Materials	12.1	86.6	57.2	21.0	5.6	17.5	21.9	6.7	8.4	5.8	0.6	1.4	5.6
Readymade Clothing and Accessories	26.4	85.2	77.2	23.7	13.6	22.3	27.6	9.3	2.9	3.6	3.2	2.8	1.8
Footwear	24.0	67.6	71.5	26.7	20.4	26.1	15.0	10.5	2.4	5.7	7.1	4.1	4.6
Making-up and Repairs	20.6	34.9	67.8	31.9	36.8	32.7	26.7	23.0	9.2	15.5	5.5	5.4	10.2
TRANSPORTATION	26.3	62.0	20.6	34.0	36.4	15.0	28.5	2.1	25.8	4.3	3.9	26.6	2.2
MISCELLANEOUS EXPENSES	29.0	72.5	50.1	36.8	35.6	21.8	25.7	15.9	23.3	16.2	6.3	15.7	8.2

Source: STATIN, Government of Jamaica.

ANNEX TABLE A2.1: JAMAICA—MAIN AGGREGATES OF GROSS DOMESTIC PRODUCT, 1990–2001
($ million)

	1990	1991	1992	1993	1994	1995	1996	1997	1998	1999	2000	2001
GDP in producer's values, constant 1986 prices	18,942	19,100	19,417	19,799	19,975	20,181	19,968	19,624	19,559	19,472	19,602	19,940
GDP in producer's values, current prices	32,990	49,750	81,175	110,881	148,020	185,630	220,417	240,563	254,086	274,333	307,039	334,699
GDP at purchaser's values, current prices	32,990	50,062	84,913	118,342	158,365	200,027	237,382	258,026	273,429	294,076	329,171	358,036
GNP at current prices	29,868	44,982	78,070	113,653	150,413	191,452	232,530	253,371	263,583	281,533	315,111	335,526
National Income at current prices	27,342	41,240	71,557	104,765	139,204	176,816	213,630	235,284	244,385	260,073	290,487	308,728
National Disposable Income at current prices	28,457	42,971	77,186	112,367	153,914	194,459	235,122	256,544	265,686	282,693	321,706	344,297
Compensation of Employees at current prices	13,875	20,300	33,255	49,838	64,952	90,411	112,769	124,992	134,198	144,700	160,351	172,867
Private Final Consumption Expenditure, current prices	21,408	32,758	53,880	79,953	108,150	139,785	162,340	174,685	181,900	196,641	223,341	245,990
Government Final Consumption Expenditure, current prices	4,301	5,772	7,587	13,876	16,469	22,635	32,476	40,134	46,752	48,633	53,570	55,710
Net National Savings at current prices	2,748	4,441	15,719	18,537	29,295	32,040	40,306	41,725	37,034	37,418	44,796	42,597
Per capita GDP at factor cost, constant 1986 prices	7,996	7,997	8,052	8,132	8,122	8,111	7,938	7,725	7,629	7,542	7,548	7,642
Per capita GDP at market prices, current prices	13,926	20,960	35,215	48,604	64,392	80,394	94,368	101,565	106,654	113,908	126,755	137,215
Memo:												
Mean Population ('000)	2,369	2,389	2,411	2,435	2,459	2,488	2,516	2,541	2,564	2,582	2,597	2,609

Source: Statistical Institute of Jamaica.

ANNEX TABLE A2.2: JAMAICA—GROSS DOMESTIC PRODUCT BY INDUSTRIAL SECTORS, 1990–2001
(current J$ million)

	1990	1991	1992	1993	1994	1995	1996	1997	1998	1999	2000	2001
Agriculture, Forestry & Fishing	2,346	3,583	6,632	9,092	13,251	17,039	18,854	19,551	20,633	20,552	21,327	22,888
Mining & Quarrying	2,831	4,821	6,852	6,356	9,435	11,712	11,345	12,003	11,242	12,013	13,827	14,820
Manufacturing	6,131	8,861	14,960	19,229	25,461	30,094	34,353	35,938	36,285	39,043	43,212	46,554
Electricity & Water	809	1,527	2,826	3,757	4,632	6,289	7,029	7,362	8,105	10,246	12,877	14,125
Construction & Installation	3,587	5,565	9,382	12,341	15,555	21,187	23,598	25,517	26,236	27,667	30,963	34,763
Distributive Trade	6,476	9,270	17,235	23,966	32,965	41,084	50,422	53,798	56,542	59,694	66,984	71,590
Transport, Storage & Communication	2,623	4,163	5,746	10,431	13,919	15,940	20,125	22,977	26,233	29,415	32,206	37,809
Financing & Insurance Services	2,573	3,548	6,336	7,264	12,936	15,719	19,853	17,593	17,794	22,030	25,019	21,577
Real Estate & Business Services	2,006	2,550	3,730	5,092	7,259	9,734	12,609	14,631	16,038	17,677	19,330	21,563
Producers of Government Services	2,581	3,475	4,779	9,882	10,614	15,116	23,064	27,410	31,059	34,045	37,104	40,296
Miscellaneous Services	2,832	4,525	7,319	8,620	11,894	13,495	15,884	17,529	18,629	20,768	23,017	23,862
Household & Private Non-Profit Institutions	229	274	451	559	819	1,084	1,341	1,484	1,404	1,657	2,010	2,100
LESS Imputed Bank Service Charge	2,034	2,411	5,071	5,709	10,719	12,861	18,061	15,231	16,114	20,475	20,835	17,249
TOTAL GDP at producer's values	**32,990**	**49,750**	**81,175**	**110,881**	**148,020**	**185,630**	**220,417**	**240,563**	**254,086**	**274,333**	**307,039**	**334,699**
PLUS Value Added Tax*	—	312	3,738	7,461	10,345	14,397	16,965	17,463	19,344	19,743	22,132	23,337
TOTAL GDP at purchaser's prices	**32,990**	**50,062**	**84,913**	**118,342**	**158,365**	**200,027**	**237,382**	**258,026**	**273,429**	**294,076**	**329,171**	**358,036**

*In 1991, a system of Value Added Tax (GCT) was introduced which replaced the majority of the taxes on commodities. GCT, unlike the former taxes, does not form part of Producers' Prices.

Source: Statistical Institute of Jamaica.

ANNEX TABLE A2.3: JAMAICA—GROSS DOMESTIC PRODUCT BY INDUSTRIAL SECTORS, 1990–2001
(constant J$ million at 1986 prices)

	1990	1991	1992	1993	1994	1995	1996	1997	1998	1999	2000	2001
Agriculture, Forestry & Fishing	1,290	1,303	1,451	1,590	1,694	1,736	1,798	1,551	1,529	1,549	1,380	1,451
Mining & Quarrying	1,521	1,607	1,566	1,571	1,680	1,565	1,683	1,738	1,795	1,774	1,746	1,811
Manufacturing	3,722	3,466	3,506	3,471	3,470	3,439	3,300	3,218	3,077	3,055	3,083	3,101
Electricity & Water	733	747	776	802	798	826	867	915	973	1,020	1,054	1,066
Construction & Installation	1,707	1,718	1,725	1,717	1,609	1,725	1,632	1,567	1,476	1,455	1,458	1,487
Distributive Trade	3,419	3,458	3,666	3,776	3,799	3,959	4,016	4,053	3,990	3,971	4,024	4,030
Transport, Storage & Communication	1,641	1,708	1,801	1,969	2,068	2,271	2,477	2,618	2,765	3,003	3,242	3,445
Financing & Insurance Services	1,659	1,967	2,122	1,999	2,945	2,901	2,760	2,244	2,207	2,606	2,892	2,910
Real Estate & Business Services	1,412	1,495	1,586	1,651	1,756	1,834	1,867	1,787	1,765	1,751	1,755	1,774
Producers of Government Services	1,247	1,237	1,231	1,227	1,203	1,212	1,210	1,223	1,229	1,231	1,229	1,237
Miscellaneous Services	1,837	1,809	1,843	1,947	1,948	2,004	2,047	2,098	2,138	2,184	2,289	2,247
Household & Private Non-Profit Institutions	121	124	108	98	107	112	107	96	90	88	87	87
LESS Imputed Bank Service Charge	1,366	1,540	1,965	2,019	3,100	3,404	3,794	3,484	3,475	4,215	4,636	4,706
Total GDP at Constant Prices	**18,942**	**19,100**	**19,417**	**19,799**	**19,975**	**20,181**	**19,968**	**19,624**	**19,559**	**19,472**	**19,602**	**19,940**

Source: Statistical Institute of Jamaica.

ANNEX TABLE A2.4: JAMAICA—GROSS DOMESTIC PRODUCT BY INDUSTRIAL SECTORS, 1990–2001
(% growth over previous year, constant J$)

	1990	1991	1992	1993	1994	1995	1996	1997	1998	1999	2000	2001
Agriculture, Forestry & Fishing	13.2	1.0	11.4	9.6	6.5	2.5	3.6	–13.7	–1.5	1.3	–10.9	5.2
Mining & Quarrying	22.8	5.7	–2.5	0.3	6.9	–6.8	7.5	3.3	3.3	–1.2	–1.6	3.7
Manufacturing	4.7	–6.9	1.2	–1.0	0.0	–0.9	–4.0	–2.5	–4.4	–0.7	0.9	0.6
Electricity & Water	6.9	1.9	3.8	3.3	–0.5	3.6	4.9	5.5	6.4	4.8	3.3	1.1
Construction & Installation	1.6	0.6	0.4	–0.5	–6.3	7.2	–5.4	–4.0	–5.8	–1.5	0.2	2.0
Distributive Trade	4.7	1.2	6.0	3.0	0.6	4.2	1.4	0.9	–1.6	–0.5	1.3	0.2
Transport, Storage & Communication	3.5	4.1	5.4	9.3	5.0	9.8	9.1	5.7	5.6	8.6	8.0	6.3
Financing & Insurance Services	10.5	18.6	7.9	–5.8	47.4	–1.5	–4.9	–18.7	–1.7	18.1	11.0	0.6
Real Estate & Business Services	8.7	5.9	6.1	4.1	6.4	4.5	1.8	–4.3	–1.2	–0.8	0.2	1.1
Producers of Government Services	–2.7	–0.8	–0.5	–0.3	–2.0	0.8	–0.2	1.1	0.5	0.2	–0.2	0.7
Miscellaneous Services	9.7	–1.5	1.9	5.7	0.0	2.9	2.1	2.5	1.9	2.2	4.8	–1.8
Household & Private Non-Profit Institutions	6.9	2.1	–12.7	–9.7	9.0	5.2	–4.5	–10.3	–6.3	–2.1	–1.6	0.3
LESS Imputed Bank Service Charge	13.8	12.7	27.6	2.7	53.6	9.8	11.5	–8.2	–0.3	21.3	10.0	1.5
Total GDP at Constant Prices	**6.3**	**0.8**	**1.7**	**2.0**	**0.9**	**1.0**	**–1.1**	**–1.7**	**–0.3**	**–0.4**	**0.7**	**1.7**

Source: Statistical Institute of Jamaica.

ANNEX TABLE A2.5: GROWTH ACCOUNTING ADJUSTING FOR HUMAN CAPITAL, 1961–2000

Variable of interest: Annual GDP growth rates and contributions from production inputs and TFP

Country	Growth Components	Period 1961–1970	1971–1980	1981–1990	1991–2000
Argentina	GDP	3.88	2.95	−1.50	4.57
	Labor	1.66	1.51	1.78	1.64
	Capital	2.00	1.91	0.03	0.44
	TFP2	0.21	−0.46	−3.31	2.49
Bolivia	GDP	2.68	4.15	0.10	3.83
	Labor	1.03	1.53	1.81	2.14
	Capital	1.63	1.93	−0.26	0.46
	TFP2	0.02	0.69	−1.45	1.23
Brazil	GDP	6.13	8.46	1.55	2.71
	Labor	2.46	1.77	2.39	2.08
	Capital	2.27	3.37	1.31	0.88
	TFP2	1.40	3.31	−2.15	−0.25
Chile	GDP	4.11	2.86	3.77	6.60
	Labor	1.65	1.58	1.26	1.32
	Capital	1.57	0.80	1.19	2.89
	TFP2	0.90	0.48	1.32	2.39
Colombia	GDP	5.26	5.51	3.38	2.68
	Labor	1.84	3.64	2.21	2.12
	Capital	1.42	1.73	1.53	1.43
	TFP2	2.00	0.14	−0.36	−0.87
Costa Rica	GDP	6.05	5.64	2.41	5.25
	Labor	3.25	4.53	2.91	2.41
	Capital	1.86	2.37	1.02	1.48
	TFP2	0.95	−1.26	−1.52	1.37
Dominican Republic	GDP	5.77	6.93	2.55	5.91
	Labor	3.23	2.82	2.86	2.02
	Capital	2.00	3.83	1.95	1.45
	TFP2	0.54	0.28	−2.26	2.44
Ecuador	GDP	4.29	8.90	2.09	1.76
	Labor	2.24	4.64	2.22	2.31
	Capital	1.69	2.57	1.07	0.75
	TFP2	0.36	1.69	−1.20	−1.31
El Salvador	GDP	5.64	2.27	−0.39	4.56
	Labor	2.88	1.82	1.90	2.27
	Capital	2.77	3.02	0.73	2.03
	TFP2	−0.01	−2.57	−3.01	0.25
Guatemala	GDP	5.50	5.65	0.87	4.06
	Labor	2.13	3.05	2.08	2.63
	Capital	1.90	2.22	0.70	1.32
	TFP2	1.47	0.39	−1.90	0.11

(continued)

ANNEX TABLE A2.5: GROWTH ACCOUNTING ADJUSTING FOR HUMAN CAPITAL, 1961–2000 (CONTINUED)
Variable of interest: Annual GDP growth rates and contributions from production inputs and TFP

Country	Growth Components	Period			
		1961–1970	1971–1980	1981–1990	1991–2000
Honduras	GDP	4.76	5.39	2.43	3.21
	Labor	2.29	2.93	3.91	2.86
	Capital	1.95	2.16	1.10	1.83
	TFP2	0.52	0.30	−2.59	−1.49
Jamaica	GDP	4.82	−0.79	2.46	0.31
	Labor	0.93	2.23	1.92	1.40
	Capital	2.05	0.89	0.10	1.90
	TFP2	1.84	−3.91	0.44	−3.00
Mexico	GDP	6.73	6.68	1.81	3.50
	Labor	2.72	3.06	3.50	1.87
	Capital	3.32	3.48	1.69	1.57
	TFP2	0.68	0.15	−3.39	0.06
Nicaragua	GDP	6.77	0.35	−1.36	3.28
	Labor	3.03	2.52	2.44	3.20
	Capital	2.85	1.77	0.84	0.69
	TFP2	0.90	−3.95	−4.64	−0.62
Panama	GDP	7.90	4.13	1.37	4.46
	Labor	2.34	4.15	3.39	2.04
	Capital	2.68	2.25	0.67	1.67
	TFP2	2.88	−2.26	−2.70	0.75
Paraguay	GDP	4.31	8.87	2.77	1.97
	Labor	2.01	2.93	2.91	1.88
	Capital	2.06	4.65	2.94	1.67
	TFP2	0.91	3.91	−2.17	−1.22
Peru	GDP	5.28	3.63	−0.80	4.10
	Labor	2.92	3.22	1.76	2.52
	Capital	1.95	1.74	0.96	1.09
	TFP2	0.41	−1.33	−3.52	0.48
Trinidad and Tobago	GDP	5.34	6.41	−0.04	3.08
	Labor	1.72	3.05	1.02	1.79
	Capital	1.40	2.60	1.13	1.51
	TFP2	2.23	0.76	−2.18	−0.21
Uruguay	GDP	1.38	3.01	−0.03	3.01
	Labor	0.70	0.57	1.05	0.83
	Capital	0.15	1.06	0.14	0.72
	TFP2	0.52	1.38	−1.22	1.45
Venezuela	GDP	5.05	2.70	0.82	2.02
	Labor	2.34	4.36	1.29	2.79
	Capital	1.18	2.93	0.76	0.69
	TFP2	1.54	−4.59	−1.24	−1.46

Source: Loayza et al., 2002.

ANNEX TABLE A2.6: JAMAICA—DETERMINANTS OF CHANGES IN GDP PER CAPITA

(A) Decades

Growth Determinants	1990s vs. 80s	1990s vs. 70s	1980s vs. 70s
Initial GDP per capita (in logs)	-0.30	0.15	0.45
Initial output gap (log [actual GDP/potential GDP])	-0.88	-0.45	0.22
Secondary enrollment (in logs)	0.21	0.40	0.18
Private domestic credit/GDP (in logs)	-0.07	0.02	0.09
Structure-adjusted trade volume/GDP (in logs)	0.16	0.34	0.18
Government consumption/GDP (in logs)	0.28	0.38	0.10
Main telephone lines per capita (in logs)	0.86	1.12	0.26
Inflation rate (in log [1 + inf. rate])	-0.05	-0.04	0.01
Std. Dev. of output gap	0.58	0.75	0.18
Index of real exchange rate overvaluation (in logs)	0.10	0.30	0.20
Frequency of years under banking crisis	-1.93	-1.93	0.00
Growth rate of terms of trade	-0.23	-0.03	0.19
Period shifts	-0.48	-1.72	-1.25
Projected Change	-1.73	-0.70	1.03
Actual Change	-1.86	1.50	3.36

(B) Five-Year Periods

Growth Determinants	1996–99 vs. 1991–95	1991–95 vs. 1986–90	1986–90 vs. 1981–85	1981–85 vs. 1976–80
Initial GDP per capita (in logs)	-0.03	-0.35	0.13	0.39
Initial output gap (log[actual GDP/potential GDP])	0.28	-1.86	0.10	1.16
Secondary enrollment (in logs)	0.30	0.05	0.05	0.04
Private domestic credit/GDP (in logs)	0.03	-0.12	0.07	0.12
Structure-adjusted trade volume/GDP (in logs)	0.03	0.01	0.27	0.07
Government consumption/GDP (in logs)	-0.48	0.31	0.37	0.11
Main telephone lines per capita (in logs)	0.41	0.59	0.19	0.10
Inflation rate (in log [1 + inf. rate])	0.11	-0.11	0.01	0.02
Std. Dev. of output gap	0.02	0.64	-0.14	-0.09
Index of real exchange rate overvaluation (in logs)	-0.20	0.11	0.17	0.13
Frequency of years under banking crisis	-1.73	-1.16	0.00	0.00
Growth rate of terms of trade	-0.53	0.01	0.01	0.37
Period shifts	-0.13	-0.64	0.44	-1.45
Projected Change	-1.93	-2.52	1.68	0.96
Actual Change	-2.26	-3.60	5.49	2.91

Source: Loayza et al., 2002.

ANNEX TABLE A2.7: JAMAICA—LABOR FORCE AND EMPLOYMENT BY INDUSTRY GROUP AND LABOR STATUS ('000), ANNUAL AVERAGE*

	1990	1991	1992	1993	1994	1995	1996	1997	1998	1999	2000	2001	2002
Labor Force	1058.5	1072.5	1074.9	1083.0	1140.2	1150.0	1142.7	1133.8	1128.6	1119.1	1105.3	1104.8	1124.5
Employed Labor Force	896.3	907.7	905.7	906.3	965.4	963.3	959.8	946.8	953.6	943.9	933.5	939.4	954.3
Agriculture, Forestry and Fishing	239.6	243.7	247.3	220.8	226.8	223.2	217.3	206.0	203.8	200.1	195.7	195.6	190.0
Mining	7.2	5.1	5.8	7.8	7.4	7.0	6.3	5.7	5.6	5.0	4.6	5.4	4.0
Manufacturing	108.2	99.0	101.9	97.8	97.7	104.7	100.4	88.9	84.1	79.0	69.6	66.8	66.9
Construction	56.9	58.2	59.1	62.1	69.7	76.0	81.2	79.5	79.7	77.9	81.5	80.2	87.6
Transport, Storage and Communication	34.2	35.8	36.3	40.1	42.5	44.5	48.3	53.3	54.9	56.3	59.4	59.9	65.2
Financing, Ins. Real Est. & Business Services	34.8	40.3	43.6	43.3	49.8	51.6	54.5	59.6	56.8	52.5	53.1	47.3	57.6
Community, Social and Personal Services	246.3	243.8	229.1	228.9	246.4	247.1	245.0	249.2	255.5	259.7	254.8	261.8	266.0
Electricity, Gas and Water	5.4	5.8	4.9	4.5	5.5	6.8	6.9	6.3	6.5	6.5	6.3	6.6	6.3
Wholesale and Retail trades, Hotels and Restaurant services	159.0	170.2	172.1	191.1	198.0	201.4	199.0	197.2	205.4	205.4	206.3	214.0	208.0
Industry not specified	4.8	5.8	5.8	9.9	21.9	1.1	0.8	0.9	1.3	1.6	2.3	2.0	3.0
Public Administration	98.1	96.2	85.6	91.0	91.4	90.5	91.5	101.3	99.9	102.2	106.0	102.9	119.8
Female Employment	383.2	389.6	389.7	397.1	415.5	412.4	406.5	397.9	400.7	393.6	381.1	384.7	401.6
Unemployed Labor Force	162.2	164.8	169.2	176.7	174.8	186.7	183.0	186.9	174.9	175.2	171.8	165.4	170.1
Unpaid water	—	—	—	20.1	22.1	27.2	23.5	21.7	21.1	21.3	18.2	18.5	13.6
Own account worker	—	—	—	339.2	356.8	331.7	337.8	325.1	340.9	337.4	332.1	336.6	321.6

*Average of January, April, July and October employments surveys.

Source: Economic and Social Survey of Jamaica, Planning Institute of Jamaica, various issues.

ANNEX TABLE A3.1: JAMAICA—NONFINANCIAL PUBLIC SECTOR DEBT
(J$ million)

	1990/91	1991/92	1992/93	1993/94	1994/95	1995/96	1996/97	1997/98	1998/99	1999/00	2000/01	2001/02	2002/03 prel.
Total debt	**45584**	**103989**	**98435**	**145553**	**171487**	**177379**	**189064**	**267876**	**322284**	**401997**	**443593**	**485458**	**588313**
Domestic debt 1/	12548	10039	18559	23661	50819	54537	84663	155229	203667	272471	281238	290794	355600
Central government domestic debt	11868	9359	17879	22981	50139	53857	79483	93639	126703	165600	200999	283491	346200
LRS	7448	5450	11144	15225	32986	36397	55889	67972	92621	118728	149472	199343	...
Treasury bills	3148	3644	6470	7491	11962	9655	11016	11650	10450	7467	6031	3807	...
Loans	565	5	5	5	2945	4958	4566	3089	5759	3253	3291	4690	...
Other	707	261	261	261	2246	2847	8012	10929	17873	36153	42205	75650	...
FINSAC/FIS securities	680	680	680	680	680	680	5180	61589	76964	105651	79297	...	...
Of which:													
Held by Bank of Jamaica	...	...	...	...	...	...	...	17715	20455	27473	15565	...	...
Government guaranteed debt	...	...	...	...	...	...	...	...	...	1220	942	7303	9400
External debt 2/	33036	93950	79876	121892	120668	122842	104401	112647	118617	129526	162355	194664	232713
External debt (in millions of US$) 2/	3942	3787	3598	3654	3612	3070	2977	3085	3099	3074	3554	4091	4150
Total debt	138.3	180.9	107.7	115.3	103.0	85.9	78.0	102.3	115.7	132.7	131.9	130.6	148.5
Domestic debt 1/	38.1	17.5	20.3	18.7	30.5	26.4	34.9	59.3	73.1	90.0	83.6	78.2	89.8
External debt 2/	100.2	163.4	87.4	96.5	72.5	59.5	43.0	43.0	42.6	42.8	48.3	52.4	58.8
Memo:													
GDP (J$ million)	32959	57491	91376	126257	166518	206586	242543	261877	278591	302850	336387	371803	396097
US$ linked domestic debt (in percent of total domestic stock)												15.4	19.9
Variable rate instrument (in percent of total domestic stock)												55.9	51.6

1/ Nonfinancial public sector domestic debt (excluding Bank of Jamaica), net of nonfinancial public enterprises holdings of FINSAC securities and government papers, and government guaranteed domestic debt.

2/ Nonfinancial public sector external debt (excluding Bank of Jamaica), including central government and government guaranteed debt, converted at end-period exchange rate.

Source: IMF.

ANNEX TABLE A3.2: JAMAICA—EXTERNAL PUBLIC DEBT OUTSTANDING
(US$ million, end of period) 1/

	1990/91	1991/92	1992/93	1993/94	1994/95	1995/96	1996/97	1997/98	1998/99	1999/00	2000/01	2001/02 est.
Total	3942	3787	3598	3654	3612	3403	3171	3223	3216	3166	3620	4015
Official creditors	3323	3238	3018	3136	3198	3014	2780	2590	2481	2348	2279	…
Bilateral	1992	1894	1770	1809	1900	1813	1714	1461	1420	1326	1176	…
OECD	—	—	—	—	—	—	1538	1316	1285	1159	…	…
Non-OECD	—	—	—	—	—	—	175	145	135	127	…	…
Multilateral	1331	1345	1248	1327	1298	1201	1066	1129	1061	1022	1103	…
IBRD	—	—	—	—	—	—	283	396	351	422	412	…
IMF	—	—	—	—	—	—	135	106	94	76	35	…
Other	—	—	—	—	—	—	648	627	616	524	656	…
Private creditors	**619**	**548**	**580**	**518**	**414**	**388**	**391**	**633**	**735**	**818**	**1341**	…
Commercial bank	360	342	330	394	308	297	281	283	155	137	…	…
Other	259	206	250	123	106	91	62	50	30	37	…	…
Bond issue	—	—	—	—	—	—	48	300	550	644	1016	…
Memo:												
Total debt (% of exports of GNFS)	166.2	169.6	154.4	147.9	131.2	99.1	94.2	94.8	95.9	92.5	100.6	105.1
Total external debt (% of GDP)	99.4	187.5	92.5	102.6	77.5	59.5	43.0	43.0	42.6	42.8	48.3	52.4

1/ Medium- and long-term outstanding external debt for the public sector, including Bank of Jamaica.
Data on private sector external debt are not available. As of end-December 2000, data from the Bank of International Settlements (BIS) showed that consolidated international claims of reporting banks on Jamaica amounted to US$1.2 billion, of which, US$0.8 billion represents claims on the private sector.

Source: IMF.

ANNEX TABLE A3.3: JAMAICA—CENTRAL GOVERNMENT REVENUES AND GRANTS, 1996/97–2002/03 (% of GDP)						
	1996/97	1997/98	1998/99	1999/00	2000/01	2001/02
Total Revenue & Grants	26.4	25.4	26.6	29.8	30.0	27.6
Tax Revenue	23.1	22.6	24.0	25.1	25.9	24.4
Income and profits	9.1	8.9	9.3	9.7	10.5	9.6
Bauxite/Alumina	0.0	0.1	0.2	0.0	0.1	0.2
Other companies	2.6	2.6	2.0	2.3	2.1	1.6
PAYE	5.0	5.0	5.4	4.7	4.9	5.1
Tax on dividends	0.2	0.1	0.3	0.3	0.3	0.2
Other individuals	0.3	0.3	0.3	0.4	0.3	0.2
Tax on interest	1.0	0.8	1.1	2.0	2.8	2.3
Production and consumption	7.2	7.0	7.5	7.6	7.9	7.7
SCT local	0.6	0.8	1.2	1.1	1.6	1.4
Motor vehicle licenses	0.2	0.1	0.3	0.2	0.2	0.2
Other licenses	0.0	0.0	0.0	0.0	0.0	0.0
Betting, gaming and lottery	0.1	0.1	0.1	0.2	0.1	0.2
Education tax	1.1	1.2	1.2	1.2	1.1	1.1
Contractors levy	0.1	0.1	0.1	0.1	0.1	0.1
GCT (local)	4.0	3.9	3.8	4.0	3.9	3.7
Stamp duty (local)	1.0	0.8	0.8	0.9	0.9	0.9
International trade	6.7	6.7	7.2	7.7	7.4	7.1
Custom duty	2.5	2.5	2.5	2.4	2.5	2.4
Stamp duty	0.2	0.3	0.3	0.2	0.2	0.2
Travel tax	0.4	0.4	0.5	0.6	0.6	0.5
GCT (imports)	3.6	3.5	3.2	2.7	2.8	2.5
SCT (imports)	—	—	0.7	1.8	1.2	1.4
Non-Tax Revenue	1.4	1.2	1.1	1.7	2.3	1.3
Bauxite Levy	1.2	1.1	1.0	1.8	0.8	0.6
Capital Revenue	0.3	0.2	0.2	0.9	0.5	0.8
Grants	0.4	0.3	0.2	0.3	0.5	0.5

Source: IMF.

ANNEX TABLE A6.1: CRIME RATE INDICES FOR JAMAICA, 1970–2001
(1990 = 100)

Year	Murder	Shooting	Rape and Carnal Abuse	Robbery	CRI*	Fraud Index	Real GDP Index
1970	36	63	70	53	53	56	89
1971	34	87	68	61	58	46	93
1972	39	48	70	60	51	73	101
1973	51	62	81	67	63	82	103
1974	43	55	55	53	50	100	98
1975	58	62	63	65	61	109	97
1976	79	83	78	63	78	177	91
1977	87	164	95	75	107	106	88
1978	80	71	80	84	78	89	89
1979	73	143	81	76	93	93	87
1980	182	315	85	98	182	94	82
1981	99	204	82	94	121	92	85
1982	81	75	96	73	82	115	86
1983	83	85	87	79	84	128	88
1984	93	100	93	96	95	115	87
1985	83	86	88	96	86	120	83
1986	85	78	92	90	86	126	84
1987	83	84	102	93	89	124	89
1988	78	74	113	84	86	121	91
1989	82	87	109	85	90	108	95
1990	**100**	**100**	**100**	**100**	**100**	**100**	**100**
1991	103	81	108	92	97	130	101
1992	114	77	108	90	101	133	102
1993	117	80	125	98	108	157	104
1994	123	88	102	98	106	140	105
1995	137	91	152	79	123	181	105
1996	161	119	168	79	144	169	103
1997	179	97	150	60	139	140	101
1998	162	82	130	51	123	178	100
1999	144	66	115	41	107	163	100
2000	151	68	119	40	112	82	101
2001	190	99	104	39	131	71	102

*Index is based on following weighting scheme: murder 40%, shooting 25%, robbery 10%, rape & carnal abuse 25%;
Source: Harriott et al., 2003.

ANNEX TABLE A6.2: JAMAICA AND NEW YORK—MURDER RATES PER 100,000, 1970–2000			
Year	Jamaica	New York	Ratio of Murder Rate Jamaica: Murder Rate New York
1970	8.2	7.9	1.0
1971	7.7	9.9	0.8
1972	8.9	11.0	0.8
1973	11.7	11.2	1.0
1974	9.9	10.6	0.9
1975	13.2	11.0	1.2
1976	18.0	10.9	1.7
1977	19.8	10.7	1.9
1978	18.3	10.3	1.8
1979	16.6	11.9	1.4
1980	41.7	12.7	3.3
1981	22.7	12.3	1.8
1982	18.4	11.4	1.6
1983	19.0	11.1	1.7
1984	21.3	10.1	2.1
1985	18.9	9.5	2.0
1986	19.4	10.7	1.8
1987	19.0	11.3	1.7
1988	17.8	12.5	1.4
1989	18.7	12.5	1.5
1990	22.9	14.5	1.6
1991	23.5	14.2	1.7
1992	26.1	13.2	2.0
1993	26.8	13.3	2.0
1994	28.1	11.1	2.5
1995	31.3	8.5	3.7
1996	36.8	7.4	5.0
1997	40.9	6.0	6.8
1998	37.0	5.1	7.3
1999	33.0	5.0	6.6
2000	33.7	5.0	6.7

Source: Harriott et al. 2003; Uniform Crime Reports, FBI (www.disastercenter.com).

ANNEX TABLE A6.3: MURDER RATES BY COUNTY AND PARISH, 1984–2001

(Per 100,000 of population)

COUNTY	PARISH	'84	'85	'86	'87	'88	'89	'90	'91	'92	'93	'94	'95	'96	'97	'98	'99	'00	'01	Avg. Rate
	KGN & St. Andrew	48	37	36	35	37	36	48	46	56	54	68	49	60	88	86	77	70	93	57
	Portland	11	8	12	7	3	12	11	21	18	13	10	10	15	19	20	11	10	21	13
	St. Thomas	25	10	15	12	19	11	19	24	20	9	17	17	10	15	32	23	23	21	18
SURREY		**41**	**31**	**32**	**30**	**32**	**31**	**42**	**42**	**50**	**46**	**57**	**42**	**51**	**74**	**75**	**65**	**59**	**79**	**49**
	St. Catherine	16	20	19	21	17	21	20	24	25	30	32	31	37	34	22	33	36	38	26
	Clarendon	13	18	12	10	11	10	9	8	11	10	12	12	12	12	9	13	17	24	12
	Manchester	11	8	11	3	6	8	8	11	8	8	6	6	14	10	8	8	11	15	9
	St. Ann	7	5	9	13	6	10	11	20	9	18	14	14	11	12	23	13	19	15	13
	St. Mary	14	14	15	15	14	9	7	7	11	15	16	16	12	15	9	6	13	23	13
MIDDLESEX		**13**	**15**	**14**	**14**	**13**	**14**	**14**	**17**	**17**	**19**	**19**	**19**	**21**	**20**	**16**	**19**	**23**	**26**	**17**
	St. James	20	14	21	21	19	14	21	18	21	20	31	30	18	21	22	16	34	42	22
	Westmoreland	14	18	15	14	8	15	17	12	13	18	15	14	17	12	23	12	13	29	15
	St. Elizabeth	8	8	6	11	9	8	9	8	9	10	10	12	9	7	7	5	11	12	9
	Trelawny	6	16	12	13	6	12	12	12	22	5	9	9	7	10	12	18	12	10	11
	Hanover	8	13	9	5	8	6	14	8	3	5	11	11	27	15	13	13	13	22	11
CORNWALL		**12**	**14**	**13**	**14**	**11**	**12**	**15**	**12**	**14**	**13**	**17**	**17**	**15**	**13**	**16**	**12**	**18**	**26**	**15**
NATIONAL AVERAGE		**21**	**19**	**19**	**19**	**18**	**18**	**23**	**23**	**26**	**26**	**28**	**31**	**37**	**41**	**37**	**33**	**34**	**44**	**28**

(% of total population)

COUNTY	PARISH	'84	'85	'86	'87	'88	'89	'90	'91	'92	'93	'94	'95	'96	'97	'98	'99	'00	'01	Avg. Rate
	KGN & St. Andrew	56.7	48.9	48.7	48.3	52.6	50.1	55.1	51.3	56.0	56.5	59.6	51.9	56.3	65.2	65.5	63.6	55.6	57.9	56.8
	Portland	1.6	1.4	2.0	1.1	0.5	2.1	1.5	2.9	2.2	1.5	1.0	1.2	1.6	1.6	1.8	1.1	0.9	1.5	1.5
	St. Thomas	4.1	1.8	2.7	2.3	3.8	2.1	3.0	3.6	2.7	1.2	1.9	2.3	1.2	1.4	3.2	2.5	2.4	1.7	2.3
SURREY		**62.4**	**52.0**	**53.3**	**51.7**	**56.8**	**54.2**	**59.5**	**57.7**	**60.8**	**59.3**	**62.6**	**55.4**	**59.1**	**68.2**	**70.5**	**67.1**	**58.9**	**61.0**	**60.6**
	St. Catherine	11.0	15.5	14.5	17.0	14.4	16.9	13.5	15.7	14.7	17.0	14.9	17.6	18.3	14.7	9.9	15.7	16.8	13.7	15.0
	Clarendon	5.5	8.8	6.3	5.4	6.8	6.2	5.0	4.8	6.1	3.2	3.5	4.1	3.4	2.9	2.3	3.4	4.4	4.8	4.5
	Manchester	3.3	2.5	3.6	1.1	2.1	3.0	2.4	3.0	2.0	2.0	1.4	1.7	3.3	1.9	1.6	1.7	2.3	2.4	2.2
	St. Ann	1.8	1.6	2.9	4.1	2.1	3.2	3.0	5.4	2.2	4.1	2.8	3.3	2.2	1.9	4.1	2.5	3.5	2.2	2.9
	St. Mary	3.0	3.4	3.6	3.6	3.5	2.3	1.5	1.4	1.9	2.6	2.3	2.7	1.9	1.8	1.1	0.8	1.7	2.3	2.1
MIDDLESEX		**24.6**	**31.8**	**30.8**	**31.3**	**29.0**	**31.4**	**25.3**	**30.4**	**27.0**	**28.9**	**24.9**	**29.4**	**29.1**	**23.4**	**19.0**	**24.1**	**28.6**	**25.4**	**26.8**
	St. James	5.5	4.5	6.7	6.8	6.6	4.8	5.7	4.8	5.0	4.9	6.4	7.6	4.0	3.8	4.1	3.3	6.7	6.6	5.4
	Westmoreland	3.5	5.0	4.0	3.9	2.4	4.3	3.9	2.7	2.5	3.5	2.4	2.7	3.0	1.7	3.4	1.9	2.0	3.5	3.0
	St. Elizabeth	2.2	2.5	2.0	3.6	3.1	2.5	2.4	2.1	2.0	2.3	1.9	2.7	1.7	1.1	1.1	0.9	1.8	1.6	1.9
	Trelawny	0.8	2.5	1.8	2.0	0.9	1.8	1.5	1.4	2.4	0.6	0.9	1.1	0.7	0.8	1.0	1.5	1.0	0.6	1.2
	Hanover	1.0	1.8	1.3	0.7	1.2	0.9	1.7	0.9	0.3	0.5	0.9	1.1	2.4	1.1	1.0	1.1	1.0	1.3	1.1
CORNWALL		**13.0**	**16.2**	**15.8**	**17.0**	**14.2**	**14.4**	**15.2**	**12.0**	**12.2**	**11.8**	**12.6**	**15.2**	**11.8**	**8.4**	**10.5**	**8.7**	**12.5**	**13.6**	**12.6**
TOTAL		**100**	**100**	**100**	**100**	**100**	**100**	**100**	**100**	**100**	**100**	**100**	**100**	**100**	**100**	**100**	**100**	**100**	**100**	**100**

Source: Harriott et al., 2003.

ANNEX TABLE A7.1a: JAMAICA's MAJOR EXPORTS AND IMPORTS
(US$ million)

	1980	1981	1982	1983	1984	1985	1986	1987	1988	1989	1990	1991	1992	1993	1994	1995	1996	1997	1998	1999	2000
Exports of Goods & Services	1368.6	1406.1	1253.2	1237.0	1282.7	1174.7	1345.5	1576.3	1712.6	1941.4	2246.6	2182.5	2226.1	2359.3	2548.2	2900.5	2988.7	3086.2	3060.7	3096.0	3242.6
Merchandise Exports*	962.7	974.0	767.4	685.7	702.0	569.0	590.0	708.0	884.0	1000.0	1157.0	1150.7	1053.6	1075.4	1219.5	1429.0	1386.9	1387.3	1290.3	1247.3	1293.1
Total Primary Commodities	905.7	905.5	689.0	600.9	649.1	528.4	547.6	662.4	824.9	931.5	1085.6	1087.6	993.6	1015.6	1161.5	1368.7	1331.6	1339.6	1244.6	1205.4	1244.4
Alumina	537.3	588.1	343.8	314.6	284.0	212.0	205.0	224.0	355.0	475.0	625.3	543.0	471.1	439.8	537.2	632.0	607.0	651.7	575.3	628.0	684.3
Bauxite	198.4	172.1	170.0	109.2	160.0	78.0	90.0	113.0	112.0	111.0	103.0	112.9	88.8	84.2	72.0	72.2	78.4	72.8	81.0	56.0	45.5
Sugar	54.4	46.5	49.0	57.3	66.0	50.0	62.0	74.0	92.0	68.0	85.8	87.4	82.5	97.5	68.6	96.0	109.2	101.9	94.5	95.3	83.3
Banana	10.5	4.3	4.7	6.8	1.5	4.0	9.0	19.0	16.0	19.0	37.6	45.1	39.6	35.6	46.1	48.2	45.2	45.7	33.2	29.8	22.9
Other Exports	105.1	94.5	121.5	113.0	137.6	184.4	181.6	232.4	249.9	258.5	233.9	299.2	311.6	358.5	437.6	520.3	491.8	467.5	460.5	396.3	408.4
Manufactures	133.8	118.1	95.5	84.0	91.0	106.3	112.2	166.6	183.1	206.6	174.7	239.1	231.1	267.7	340.0	410.3	363.4	319.7	313.2	253.5	192.2
Services	405.9	432.1	485.8	551.3	580.4	606.1	754.7	867.1	829.6	941.0	1089.1	1031.8	1172.5	1283.9	1328.7	1471.5	1601.8	1698.9	1770.4	1848.7	1949.5
Imports of Goods & Services	1367.9	1662.9	1602.4	1491.1	1421.9	1395.2	1233.7	1504.6	1779.2	2291.1	2339.8	2206.7	2192.9	2674.2	3059.7	3719.2	3864.4	4064.3	4037.4	3942.6	4415.2
Merchandise Imports	1170.0	1470.8	1379.5	1287.2	1183.0	1144.0	1042.3	1237.2	1452.4	1874.3	1850.0	1828.6	1775.3	2189.2	2177.2	2772.8	2933.9	3127.3	2961.0	2845.6	2988.0
Food	72.3	101.9	119.4	110.4	99.0	82.0	166.2	95.0	125.0	160.0	126.0	90.9	107.1	145.3	125.8	196.5	211.7	258.4	280.0	274.2	265.0
Other Consumer Goods	58.9	88.2	111.5	96.5	65.0	76.0	103.0	140.0	162.0	231.0	220.0	161.0	186.1	331.6	326.6	489.4	523.3	636.7	642.0	690.0	711.0
POL and Other Energy	446.5	488.8	406.8	397.3	349.0	368.0	199.1	237.2	195.4	274.3	403.7	325.2	315.5	343.2	328.4	351.4	451.8	410.7	294.0	321.2	382.0
Intermediate Goods	394.6	496.7	416.1	388.8	383.0	335.0	330.0	418.0	512.0	644.0	520.3	853.6	873.3	979.5	1035.4	1196.6	1198.9	1162.0	1194.0	1091.2	1119.0
Capital Goods	197.7	295.2	325.7	294.2	287.0	283.0	244.0	347.0	458.0	565.0	580.0	397.9	293.3	389.6	361.0	538.9	548.2	659.5	551.0	469.0	511.0
Services	208.3	205.5	235.7	223.3	250.8	391.0	396.3	443.5	538.9	684.7	660.2	531.7	663.7	794.1	1191.5	1093.8	1149.2	1231.7	1293.5	1308.2	1410.9

*excludes free-zone exports

Source: STATIN

Annex Table A7.1b: Jamaica's Major Exports and Imports
(% of exports of good and services)

	1980	1981	1982	1983	1984	1985	1986	1987	1988	1989	1990	1991	1992	1993	1994	1995	1996	1997	1998	1999	2000
Merchandise Exports	70.34	69.27	61.24	55.43	54.73	48.44	43.85	44.92	51.62	51.51	51.50	52.72	47.33	45.58	47.86	49.27	46.40	44.95	42.16	40.29	39.88
Total Primary Commodities	66.18	64.40	54.98	48.58	50.60	44.98	40.70	42.02	48.17	47.98	48.32	49.83	44.63	43.05	45.58	47.19	44.55	43.41	40.66	38.93	38.38
Alumina	39.26	41.82	27.43	25.43	22.14	18.05	15.24	14.21	20.73	24.47	27.83	24.88	21.16	18.64	21.08	21.79	20.31	21.12	18.80	20.28	21.10
Bauxite	14.50	12.24	13.57	8.83	12.47	6.64	6.69	7.17	6.54	5.72	4.58	5.17	3.99	3.57	2.83	2.49	2.62	2.36	2.65	1.81	1.40
Sugar	3.97	3.31	3.91	4.63	5.15	4.26	4.61	4.69	5.37	3.50	3.82	4.00	3.71	4.13	2.69	3.31	3.65	3.30	3.09	3.08	2.57
Banana	0.77	0.31	0.38	0.55	0.12	0.34	0.67	1.21	0.93	0.98	1.67	2.07	1.78	1.51	1.81	1.66	1.51	1.48	1.08	0.96	0.71
Other Exports	7.68	6.72	9.70	9.14	10.73	15.70	13.50	14.74	14.59	13.32	10.41	13.71	14.00	15.20	17.17	17.94	16.46	15.15	15.05	12.80	12.60
Manufactures	9.77	8.40	7.62	6.79	7.10	9.05	8.34	10.57	10.69	10.64	7.78	10.96	10.38	11.35	13.34	14.15	12.16	10.36	10.23	8.19	5.93
Services	29.66	30.73	38.76	44.57	45.25	51.60	58.09	55.01	48.44	48.47	48.48	47.28	52.67	54.42	52.14	50.73	53.60	55.05	57.84	59.71	60.12
Merchandise Imports	85.5	88.4	86.1	86.3	83.2	82.0	84.5	82.2	81.6	81.8	79.1	82.9	81.0	81.9	71.2	74.6	75.9	76.9	73.3	72.2	67.7
Food	5.3	6.1	7.5	7.4	7.0	5.9	13.5	6.3	7.0	7.0	5.4	4.1	4.9	5.4	4.1	5.3	5.5	6.4	6.9	7.0	6.0
Other Consumer Goods	4.3	5.3	7.0	6.5	4.6	5.4	8.3	9.3	9.1	10.1	9.4	7.3	8.5	12.4	10.7	13.2	13.5	15.7	15.9	17.5	16.1
POL and Other Energy	32.6	29.4	25.4	26.6	24.5	26.4	16.1	15.8	11.0	12.0	17.3	14.7	14.4	12.8	10.7	9.4	11.7	10.1	7.3	8.1	8.7
Intermediate Goods	28.8	29.9	26.0	26.1	26.9	24.0	26.7	27.5	28.8	28.1	22.2	38.7	39.8	36.6	33.8	32.2	31.0	28.6	29.6	27.7	25.3
Capital Goods	14.5	17.8	20.3	19.7	20.2	20.3	19.8	23.1	25.7	24.7	24.8	18.0	13.4	14.6	11.8	14.5	14.2	16.2	13.6	11.9	11.6
Services	15.2	12.4	14.7	15.0	17.6	28.0	32.1	29.5	30.3	29.9	28.2	28.6	30.3	29.7	38.9	29.4	29.7	30.3	32.0	33.2	32.0

Source: STATIN

ANNEX TABLE A7.2: JAMAICA: BALANCE OF PAYMENTS SUMMARY
(US$ million)

	1990	1995	1996	1997	1998	1999	2000	2001 1/
CURRENT ACCOUNT	−328.0	−98.9	−142.6	−332.2	−333.8	−216.3	−387	−788.4
GOODS BALANCE	−522.1	−829.3	−994.2	−1132.3	−1130.5	−1186.5	−1441.5	−1618.2
Exports (f.o.b.)	1157.5	1796.0	1721	1700.3	1613.4	1499.1	1562.8	1454.4
Imports (f.o.b.)	1679.6	2625.3	2715	2832.6	2743.9	2685.6	3004.3	3072.6
SERVICES BALANCE	450.2	494.1	452.6	467.2	476.8	655.4	583.6	381.5
Transportation	−130.8	−246.0	−270.3	−273.4	−278.4	−233.6	−256.6	−256.2
Travel	686.3	921.2	935.2	949.5	998.9	1052.4	1123.9	1026.2
Inflows	740	1068.8	1092.3	1130.8	1196.9	1279.6	1332.6	1232.2
Other Services	−105.3	−181.1	−212.3	−208.9	−243.7	−163.4	−283.7	−388.5
INCOME	−430	−370.7	−224.6	−291.9	−308.1	−332.5	−349.9	−437.8
Compensation of Employees	87.1	46.5	47.3	57.7	66.1	70.3	67.4	74.6
Investment Income	−517.1	−417.2	−271.9	−349.6	−374.2	−402.8	−417.3	−512.4
CURRENT TRANSFERS	271.4	607.0	623.6	624.8	628	647.3	820.8	886.1
Official	155.4	52.2	49.7	39.8	43.2	45.8	147.9	90.4
Private	116	554.8	573.9	585	584.8	601.5	672.9	795.7
CAPITAL & FINANCIAL A/C	340.9	99.1	142.6	332.2	333.8	216.3	387	788.4
CAPITAL ACCOUNT	−15.9	10.5	16.6	−11.6	−8.7	−10.9	2.2	−22.3
CAPITAL TRANSFERS								
Official	—	20.5	18.7	7	4.2	4.1	15.6	3.5
Private	—	−10.0	−2.1	−18.6	−12.9	−15	−13.4	−25.8
FINANCIAL ACCOUNT 2/	356.8	88.6	126.0	343.8	342.5	227.2	384.8	810.7
Direct Investment	93.8	81.1	90.4	146.7	287.1	428.8	394.1	524.9
Other Official Investment (Government loans)	101.2	−97.0	−144.7	43.1	−41.3	−331.4	383.6	653.4
Other Private Investments	220.9	124.2	549.3	139.4	423.1	425	524.2	1022.7
Change in Reserves (—denotes increase)	−59.1	−19.7	−287.6	161.3	−39.3	133.6	−523	−865.4
Memo:								
Current Account Deficit/GDP (%)	−7.1	−1.7	−2.2	−4.6	−4.5	−2.9	−5.0	−10.1
Gross International Reserves (minus gold)	168.2	681.3	880	682.1	709.5	554.5	1053.7	1900.9

1/ provisional

2/ includes errors and omissions

Source: Bank of Jamaica

ANNEX TABLE A7.3: FOREIGN DIRECT INVESTMENT IN JAMAICA (US$ MILLION), 1998–01				
Sector	**1998**	**1999**	**2000**	**2001**
Inflows	254.80	218.10	254.70	258.70
Manufacturing	53.2	18.3	14.7	22.5
Agricultural	0.7	0.1	0.0	0.0
Information Technology/communication	85.2	49.6	57.2	112.5
Minerals & Chemicals	3.1	29.5	9.6	15.7
Insurance	0.0	0.0	6.0	0.0
Tourism	2.7	52.8	69.4	24.3
Mining	109.9	67.8	97.8	83.7
Total Retained Earnings	101.1	87.3	116.1	115.9
Manufacturing	26.0	24.4	46.0	31.5
Agricultural	0.0	0	0	0
Information Technology/communication	45.5	39.1	36.4	16.4
Minerals & Chemicals	0.0	0.0	0	0
Insurance	0.0	0	1.5	2.8
Tourism	0.0	0.2	0	0
Mining	0.0	0	0	0
Banking	21.9	20.9	17.5	58.8
Other	7.7	2.7	14.7	6.4
Foreign Exchange record	13.2	41.1	56.7	5.3
Divestment	0.00	177.2	40.9	234.0
Insurance	0.00	38.0	1.3	39.5
Manufacturing	0.00	44.6	0.9	3.0
Tourism	0.00	20.5	38.7	0.0
Communication	0.00	0.00	0.00	0.1
Banking	0.00	7.7	0.0	0.0
Minerals	0.00	66.4	0.0	0.0
Electricity	0.00	0.0	0.0	191.4
Total Foreign Direct Investment	**369.10**	**523.70**	**468.40**	**613.90**

Source: Bank of Jamaica.

BIBLIOGRAPHY

Alesina A., R. Hausman, R. Hommes, and E. Stein. 1996. "Budget Institutions and Fiscal Performance in Latin America." Working Paper, Inter-American Development Bank.

Artana, D. and F. Navajas. 2002. "Fiscal Policy Issues in Jamaica: Budgetary Institutions, the Tax System and Public debt management." Paper presented at the conference "Toward Sustained Growth in Jamaica," December 10, 2002, Inter-American Development Bank, Washington, D.C.

Barro, R. 1991. "Economic Growth in a Cross Section of Countries," *Quarterly Journal of Economics* 106:407–43.

———. 2001. "Human Capital and Growth," *American Economic Review* 91(2):12–17.

Bartelsman, E. 2002. "Productivity Growth in Jamaica 1991–2000, An Exploratory Analysis." Processed background paper prepared for World Bank for this report. Economic and Social Institute, Free University Amsterdam.

Becker, G. S. 1968. "Crime and Punishment: An Economic Approach," *Journal of Political Economy* 76:169–217.

Benfield, W. 2002. "Identifying the Poor: How Robust are Poverty Profiles to Alternative Poverty Lines." Processed background paper prepared for World Bank for this report.

Bennett, K. 1995. "Economic Decline and the Growth of the Informal Sector: The Guyana and Jamaican Experience," *Journal of International Development* 7(2): 229–242.

Blank, L. and M. Monowa. 2000. "Youth-at-Risk in Jamaica." Processed. Policy Note. World Bank, Washington, D.C.

Boxill, I. and D. Alleyne. 2000. "Crime and Tourism in Jamaica." Paper presented at the 2nd Caribbean Conference on Crime and Criminal Justice, University of West Indies, Jamaica.

Bratsberg, B. and D. Terrell. 2002. "School Quality and Returns to Education of US Immigrants," *Economic Inquiry* 40(2):177–198.

Bruno, M. and W. Easterly. 1995. "Inflation Crises and Long-Run Growth." Policy Research Working Paper No. 1517, September 1995, World Bank, Washington, D.C.

Bulir, A. 1998. "Income Inequality: Does Inflation Matter?" IMF Working Paper WP/98/7, International Monetary Fund, Washington, D.C.

Buttrick, J. 1994. "Jamaicans Who Study Abroad," *Social and Economic Studies* 43(4):219–234.

Carrington, W. and E. Detragiache. 1998. "How Big Is the Brian Drain?" IMF Working Paper No. 102, International Monetary Fund, Washington, D.C.

Cerro, A. M. and O. Meloni. 2000. "Determinants of the Crime Rate in Argentina during the '90's'," *Estudios de Economia* 22(2):297–311.

Choudhri, E. and D. Hakura. 2001. "Exchange Rate Pass-through to Domestic Prices: Does the Inflationary Environment Matter?" IMF Working Paper No. 194, International Monetary Fund, Washington, D.C.

Dollar, D. and A. Kraay. 2001a. "Growth is Good for the Poor." Policy Research Working Paper No. 2587, World Bank, Washington, D.C.

———. 2001b. "Trade, Growth, and Poverty." Policy Research Working Paper No. 2615, World Bank. Washington, D.C.

Dornbusch, R. and L. T. Kuenzler. 1993. "Exchange Rate Policy: Options and Issues," in Dornbusch ed., *Policymaking in the Open Economy*. Washington, D.C.: Oxford University Press and the World Bank.

Ehrhardt, D., B. Sutherland, and W. Hay. 2003. "Jamaica Infrastructure Note." Processed background paper prepared for this report by Catalia Strategic Advisors.

Ellis, H. 1991. *Identifying Crime Correlates in a Developing Country*. New York: Peter Lang.

Ezemenari, K. and K. Subbarao. 1999. "Jamaica's Food Stamp Program: Impact on Poverty and Welfare." Policy Research Working Paper No. 2207, World Bank, Washington, D.C.

Fajnzylber, P., D. Lederman, and N. Loayza. 1998. "What causes violent crime?" Processed, World Bank, Washington, D.C.

———. 2000. "Criminal Victimization: An Economic Perspective," *Economia* (Fall 2000):219–278.

———. 2002. "Inequality and Violent Crime," *Journal of Law and Economics* XLV.

Feige, E. L. 1990. "Defining and Estimating Underground and Informal Activities: the New Institutional Economics Approach," *World Development* 18:989–1002.

Findlay, R., and S. Wellisz, eds. 1993. *Five Small Open Economies*. Oxford University Press, New York.

Francis, A. and K. T. Campbell. 2001. "A Supply Function for Violent Crime in Jamaica 1970–1999." Processed. University of West Indies, Kingston, Jamaica.

Francis, A., C. Kirton, L. Elvy, and T. Christie. 2001. "Crime in Jamaica: a Preliminary Analysis." University of West Indies, Kingston, Jamaica.

Government of Jamaica. 2002. Report of the National Committee on Crime and Violence.

Handa, S. 1996a. "The Determinants of Teenage Schooling in Jamaica: Rich vs. Poor, Females vs. Males," *Journal of Development Studies* 32(4):554–580.

———. 1996b. "Maternal Education and Child Attainment in Jamaica: Testing the Bargaining Power Hypothesis," *Oxford Bulletin of Economics and Statistics* 58(1):119–137.

Handa, S., E. Muhlstein, and Z. Dinsey Flores. 2001. "Jamaica: Social Sector Strategy." Paper presented at the conference "Toward Sustained Growth in Jamaica," December 10, 2002, Inter-American Development Bank, Washington, D.C.

Hanushek, E. and D. Kimko. 2000. "Schooling, Labor-Force Quality, and the Growth of Nations." *American Economic Review* 90(5):1184–1208.

Harriott, A. 2000. *Policy and Crime Control in Jamaica*. Kingston: University of the West Indies.

Harriott, A., A. Francis, C. Kirton, and G. Gibbison. 2003. "Crime and Development: The Jamaican experience." Background paper prepared for World Bank for this report. University of the West Indies, Kingston.

Harris, D. 1997. "Jamaica's Export Economy: Towards a Strategy of Export-led Growth," *Critical Issues in Caribbean Development* 5.

Havinga, I. 2002. "Jamaica—Study on Growth and Competitiveness during the 1990s: An Assessment of Macroeconomic Performance and Policy Environment and a Statistical Review of the Compilation Methodology and Exhaustiveness of GDP Estimates." Processed background paper prepared for World Bank for this report.

IADB. 1999. "Violencia en América Latina: epidemiología y costos." Inter-American Development Bank, Washington, D.C.

———. 2002. Informal Sector Study for Jamaica, November 2002. Processed. Inter-American Development Bank, Washington, D.C.

International Monetary Fund. *International Financial Statistics,* various issues, Washington, D.C.

Jamison, T. Dean, L. J. Lau, and J. Wang. "Technical Progress: How Much Does it Vary Across Countries, and Why?" Processed.

Jamison, E. 2002. "Heterogeneity in Education's Effect on GDP Levels and Growth Rates." Processed.

Kim, G. 2003. "Tertiary Education in Jamaica: Trends and Policy Issues for Development." Processed, World Bank, Washington, D.C.

King, D. 2001. "Globalization, Trade Policy and Sustainable Development in Jamaica." Processed, University of West Indies, Kingston.

King, D. and S. Handa. 2000. "Balance of Payment Liberalization, Poverty and Distribution in Jamaica." Processed, prepared for UNCTAD/UNDP program on "Globalisation, Liberalisation, and Sustainable Human Development."

KPMG. 1999. "Strategic Review of the Ministry of Finance and Planning." Processed.

Krueger, A. and M. Lindahl. 2001. "Education for Growth, Why and For Whom?" *Journal of Economic Literature* 39:1101–1136.

Kurt Salmon Associates. 1997. *Jamaica Competitive Study,* Vol. 1.

Lall, S. 2002. "Foreign Direct Investment and Competitiveness." In I. Nabi and M. Luthria (eds.), *Building Competitive Firms: Incentives and Capabilities 2002.* Washington, D.C.: World Bank.

Levine, R. and S. Levos. 1988. "Stock Markets, Banks, and Economic Growth," *American Economic Review* 88(3):537–88.

Loayza, N., P. Fajnzylber, and C. Calderon. 2002. "Economic Growth in Latin America and the Caribbean: Stylized Facts, Explanations, and Forecasts." Processed. World Bank, Washington, D.C.

Lucas, R. 1988. "On the Mechanics of Economic Development," *Journal of Monetary Economics* 22:3–42.

Meera, A. K. and M. D. Jayakumar. 1995. "Determinants of Crime in a Developing Country: A Regression Model," *Applied Economics* 27(5):455–460.

McCarthy, F. 2001. "Social Policy and Macroeconomics: The Irish Experience." Policy Research Working Paper No. 2736, World Bank, Washington, D.C.

McFarlane, L. 2002. "Consumer Price Inflation and Exchange Rate Pass-Through in Jamaica." Research Services Department, Research and Economic Programming Division, Bank of Jamaica, Kingston, Jamaica.

Naim, M. 2002. "The New Diaspora," *Foreign Policy* (July/August 2002):95–96.

Naranjo, N. and E. Osabela. 2002. "Jamaica Financial System: Diagnostic and Recommendations." Presented at the IDB conference, "Towards Sustained Growth in Jamaica," Inter-American Development Bank, Washington, D.C.

Nehru, V. and A. Dhareshwar. 1993. "A New Database on Physical Capital Stock: Sources, Methodology and Results," *Revista de Analisis Economico* 8(1):37–59.

PERF. 2001. *The Police Executive Research Forum Report.* Kingston, Jamaica: The American Chamber of Commerce of Jamaica.

Planning Institute of Jamaica. 1990. *Economic and Social Survey of Jamaica 1989.*

———. 1996. *Economic and Social Survey of Jamaica 1995.*

———. 2000. *Economic and Social Survey of Jamaica 1999.*

———. 2001. *Economic and Social Survey of Jamaica 2000.*

———. 2002. *Economic and Social Survey of Jamaica 2001.*

———. 2003. *Economic and Social Survey of Jamaica 2002.*

Planning Institute of Jamaica. *Jamaica Medium Term Strategy 2000–2002.*

Planning Institute of Jamaica and Statistical Institute of Jamaica. 1998. *Jamaica Survey of Living Conditions 1997.*

———. 2001. *Jamaica Survey of Living Conditions 2000.*

———. 2002. *Jamaica Survey of Living Conditions 2001.*

Polackova, H. et al. 1999. "Fiscal Adjustment and Contingent Government Liabilities: Case Studies of the Czech Republic and Macedonia." Policy Research Working Paper #2177, World Bank, Washington, D.C.

Poot, H. and W. van Riel. 2002. "Competitiveness in Jamaica." Processed background paper prepared for World Bank for this report, Netherlands Economic Institute.

Pritchett, L. 2000. "Where Has All the Education Gone?" *The World Bank Economic Review* 15(3):367–391.

Psacharopoulos, G., and A. Patrinos. 2002. "Returns to education: A further update." World Bank Policy Research Paper, No. 2881, World Bank, Washington, D.C.

Psacharopoulos, G. 1994. "Using evaluation indicators to track the performance of educational programs." In R. Picciotto and Ray C. Rist (eds.), "Evaluation and Development: Proceedings of the 1994 World Bank Conference." World Bank, Washington, D.C.

Pudney, S., D. Deadman, and D. Pyle. 2000. "The relationship between crime, punishment and economic conditions: is reliable inference possible when crimes are under recorded," *Journal of the Royal Statistical Society* 163(part 1):81–97.

Romer, C. and D. Romer. 1998. "Monetary Policy and the Well-Being of the Poor." NBER Working Paper 6793. National Bureau of Economic Research, Washington, D.C.

Sanchez-Paramo, C. and D. Steele. 2002. "The Effects on Poverty of Economic Growth and Income Distribution in Jamaica, 1991–2000." Processed background paper prepared for this report. World Bank, Washington, D.C.

Shatz, H. and D. Tarr. 2002. "Exchange Rate Overvaluation and Trade Protection." In B. Hoekman, A. Matoo, and P. English, (eds.) *Development, Trade, and the WTO: A Handbook.* Washington, D.C.: World Bank.

Solow, R. 1957. "Technical Change and the Aggregate Production Function," *Review of Economics and Statistics* 39:312–20.

Statistical Institute of Jamaica. *National Income and Product,* various issues. Kingston, Jamaica.

———. *Employment Earnings and Hours Worked in Large Establishments,* various issues. Kingston, Jamaica.

Stein, E., E. Talvi, and A. Grisanti. 1998. "Institutional Arrangements and Fiscal Performance: The Latin American Experience." Working Paper #367, RES, Inter-American Development Bank.

Subramanian, A. and D. Roy. 2001. "Who Can Explain The Mauritian Miracle: Meade, Romer, Sachs, or Rodrik?" Paper presented at the Conference on "Analytical Country Studies on Growth," http://ksghome.harvard.edu/~.drodrik.academic.ksg/growthprogram.html

Thomas, C. 1988. *The Poor and the Powerless.* New York: Monthly Review Press.

Topel, R. 1999. "Labor Markets and Economic Growth." In Ashenfelter, O. and D. Card (eds.), *Handbook of Labor Economics.* Amsterdam, North Holland.

UNDP. 2003. "Seventh United Nations Survey of Crime Trends and Operations of Criminal Justice Systems." Office of Drugs and Crime, Centre for International Crime Prevention.

UNICEF and PIOJ. 2000. "Jamaican Children and their Families: A Situation Assessment and Analysis 1999–2000."

Williamson, J. 2003. *The Washington Consensus and Beyond.* Washington, D.C.: Institute for International Economics.

Witter M. and C. Kirton. 1990. "The Informal Economy in Jamaica, Some Empirical Exercises." Institute of Social and Economic Research, UWI.

Wolfe, L. 1993. *Report of the National Task Force on Crime.* Kingston, Jamaica.

World Bank. 1994. "Jamaica: A Strategy for Growth and Poverty Reduction, Country Economic Memorandum." Report No. 12702-JM, World Bank, Washington, D.C.

———. 1997. "Jamaica: Violence and Urban Poverty in Jamaica: Breaking the Cycle." Washington, D.C.

———. 1999. "Jamaica Consultations with the Poor." Prepared for the Global Synthesis Workshop, September 22–23, 1999. Poverty Group, World Bank, Washington, D.C.

———. 2000a. "Report and Recommendation of the President on a Proposed Bank Restructuring & Debt Management Program Adjustment Loan." Report No. P 7397-JM, Washington, D.C.

———. 2000b. "Governance and Social Justice in Caribbean States." Paper presented to the 2000 Caribbean Group for Cooperation in Economic Development (CGCED). Washington, D.C.

———. 2001a. "Jamaica: Country Financial Accountability Assessment." Washington, D.C.

———. 2001b. "Youth and Violence in the Caribbean: A Literature Review." Processed. Washington, D.C.

———. 2001c. *Globalization, Growth, and Poverty: Building an Inclusive World Economy.* New York: Oxford University Press and the World Bank.

———. 2002a. "Youth Development in the Caribbean," Report No. 24163-LAC. Paper presented to the 2002 Caribbean Group for Cooperation in Economic Development, Washington, D.C.

———. 2002b. *World Development Indicators.* Washington, D.C.

———. 2002c. "Caribbean Economic Overview: Macroeconomic Volatility, Household Vulnerability, and Institutional and Policy Responses." Paper presented to the 2002 Caribbean Group for Cooperation in Economic Development (CGCED). Washington, D.C.

———. 2002d. "Monitoring Educational Performance in the Caribbean." Report No. 24337. World Bank, Washington, D.C.

———. 2002e. "Report and Recommendation of the President on a Proposed Second Bank Restructuring & Debt Management Program Adjustment Loan." Report No. P7527-JM, Washington, D.C.

———. 2003. *Closing the Gap in Education and Technology.* Latin American and Caribbean Studies. Washington, D.C.: World Bank.

———. forthcoming. "A Resource Guide for Municipalities: Community Based Crime and Violence Prevention In Urban Latin America." Processed. Washington, D.C.

World Economic Forum. 2002. *Global Competitiveness Report 2001/02.* New York: Oxford University Press and World Economic Forum.

———. 2003. *Global Competitiveness Report 2002/03.* New York: Oxford University Press and World Economic Forum.